Asian Americans in New England

Revisiting New England: The New Regionalism

SERIES EDITORS

Siobhan Senier
University of New Hampshire

Adam Sweeting
Boston University

Darren Ranco
Dartmouth College

David H. Watters
University of New Hampshire

This series presents fresh discussions of the distinctiveness of New England culture. The editors seek manuscripts examining the history of New England regionalism; the way its culture came to represent American national culture; the interaction between that "official" New England culture and the people who lived in the region; and local, subregional, or even biographical subjects as microcosms that explicitly open up and consider larger issues. The series welcomes new theoretical and historical perspectives and is designed to cross disciplinary boundaries and appeal to a wide audience.

For a complete list of books available in this series, please visit www.upne.com

Monica Chiu, editor, *Asian Americans in New England: Culture and Community*

Aife Murray, *Maid as Muse: How Servants Changed Emily Dickinson's Life and Language*

Scott Molloy, *Irish Titan, Irish Toilers: Joseph Banigan and Nineteenth-Century New England Labor*

Joseph A. Conforti, editor, *Creating Portland: History and Place in Northern New England*

Deborah Pickman Clifford and Nicholas R. Clifford, *"The Troubled Roar of the Waters": Vermont in Flood and Recovery, 1927-1931*

JerriAnne Boggis, Eve Allegra Raimon, and Barbara A. White, editors, *Harriet Wilson's New England: Race, Writing, and Region*

Kimberly A. Jarvis, *Franconia Notch and the Women Who Saved It*

Christopher Johnson, *This Grand and Magnificent Place: The Wilderness Heritage of the White Mountains*

William Brown and Joanne Pope Melish, editors, *The Life of William J. Brown of Providence, R.I.*

Denis R. Caron, *A Century in Captivity: The Life and Trials of Prince Mortimer, a Connecticut Slave*

David L. Richards, *Poland Spring: A Tale of the Gilded Age, 1860-1900*

Paul M. Searls, *Two Vermonts: Geography and Identity, 1865-1910*

Judith Bookbinder, *Boston Modern: Figurative Expressionism as Alternative Modernism*

Donna M. Cassidy, *Marsden Hartley: Race, Region, and Nation*

Maureen Elgersman Lee, *Black Bangor: African Americans in a Maine Community, 1880-1950*

Christopher J. Lenney, *Sightseeking: Clues to the Landscape History of New England*

T. A. Milford, *The Gardiners of Massachusetts: Provincial Ambition and British-American Career*

Donald W. Linebaugh, *The Man Who Found Thoreau: Roland W. Robbins and the Rise of Historical Archaeology in America*

Pauleena MacDougall, *The Penobscot Dance of Resistance: Tradition in the History of a People*

Jennifer C. Post, *Music in Rural New England Family and Community Life, 1870-1940*

Mark J. Sammons and Valerie Cunningham, *Black Portsmouth: Three Centuries of African-American Heritage*

Priscilla Paton, *Abandoned New England: Landscape in the Works of Homer, Frost, Hopper, Wyeth, and Bishop*

Adam Sweeting, *Beneath the Second Sun: A Cultural History of Indian Summer*

Asian Americans in New England

Culture and Community

Edited by Monica Chiu

University of New Hampshire Press
Durham, New Hampshire

PUBLISHED BY UNIVERSITY PRESS OF NEW ENGLAND
HANOVER AND LONDON

University of New Hampshire Press
Published by University Press of New England, One Court Street, Lebanon, NH 03766
www.upne.com

Sánchez-Eppler, Karen. "Copying and Conversion: An 1824 Friendship Album from a
Chinese Youth." *American Quarterly* 59:2 (207), 301–309. © The American Studies
Association. Reprinted with permission of The Johns Hopkins University Press.

An earlier version of Monica Chiu's "Performative Blackness and Lao Americans: Cool in a
New Hampshire School" originally appeared as "Americanization Against Academics: Racial
Contexts and Lao American Youths in a New Hampshire High School." In *Asian American
Education: Acculturation, Literacy Development, and Learning*, edited by Clara C. Clark,
Russell Endo, Stacy Lee, and Xue Lan Ron (Charlotte, N.C.: Information Age, 2007): 1–24.

Library of Congress Cataloging-in-Publication Data

Asian Americans in New England : culture and community / edited by Monica Chiu.
    p. cm. — (Revisiting New England : the new regionalism)
Includes bibliographical references and index.
ISBN 978-1-58465-794-1 (cloth : alk. paper)
1. Asian Americans—New England—History. 2. Asian Americans—New England—Ethnic
identity. 3. Asian Americans—Cultural assimilation—New England. 4. Asian Americans—
New England—Intellectual life. 5. New England—Ethnic relations. I. Chiu, Monica, 1965–
F15.A75A85   2009
974'.00495—dc22   2009006595

 University Press of New England is a member of the Green Press
Initiative. The paper used in this book meets their minimum
requirement for recycled paper.

To all Asian Americans in New England,

those arrived and those still arriving

Contents

Preface

The seed for this project was planted in 2003 when I discovered the resource-rich Institute for Asian American Studies, directed by Paul Watanabe, at the University of Massachusetts Boston. During discussions with the Institute's subgroup, members of the Asian Americans in New England Research Initiative (AANERI), and through an inaugural 2005 AANERI conference, I realized that I was sitting among a collection of impressive scholars whose important work deserved public circulation. I wanted to capture and disseminate this groundbreaking, regional research that certainly would impact the shape and scope of Asian American Studies nationally.

As contributors were writing their essays, an article appeared in my local New Hampshire newspaper in April 2007 that highlighted the impetus of this compilation (Alan B1, B7). The article emphasized the connections between New England and Asia through an exhibition of paintings and calligraphy at Boston's Museum of Fine Arts from the collection of Chinese immigrant Wan-go Weng. Weng, who moved in 1977 from his original post-immigrant location of New York to the Upper Valley Region of New Hampshire, stated that his collection of Chinese art has been passed down from generation to generation within his family, until it came into his possession. He likens himself to a link between generations and nations through art, a connection between past and present, between the United States and China, and between members of his extended family. Ultimately, he serves as a conduit to promote the practice of art and the appreciation and study of China.

A year later, another article about the relationship between these seemingly disparate regions of the Far East and New England appeared in the same local newspaper (Henry D1, D6). The article discussed how Chinese tourists, emerging from a national, economic boom, have been visiting

Newport mansions since 2007 in busloads, finding especially intriguing Alva Belmont's Chinese teahouse, constructed during America's Gilded Age. While Americans once recreated Chinese architecture for aesthetic reasons, Chinese visitors now tour such structures to gain an understanding of New England's penchant for things Chinese. In fact, marketing New England to Chinese tourists is good business: according to the article, such tourists visit the campuses of Harvard and the Massachusetts Institute of Technology, view Copley Square, and cruise the Boston harbor, learning of its history while watching for whales. Capitalizing on this eager clientele, states the journalist, Vermont's Chamber of Commerce now retains an office in Shanghai's commercial center, intends to make the state an attractive woodland getaway for weary Chinese urbanites, and will host a Chinese TV crew producing a documentary about Vermont for Chinese audiences. The region and its historical objects are attractions for Asian consumers.

This collection, the first to discuss Asians' and Asian Americans' contributions to New England, addresses community connections forged among places, ideas, history, and material culture. It recognizes and appreciates the importance of earlier regional studies, building on reports about the first Chinese and Japanese immigrants to New England, about the Vietnamese and Cambodian diasporas to Boston, and about Asian Americans' educational achievements, business successes, and community formations. Weng's intention to link people and aesthetics, the region's desire to capture reciprocal gazes exchanged between Asian nationals and New England citizens, and this collection's aim of naming Asian America as culturally, intellectually, and materially necessary to understanding New England all constitute exciting new directions in Asian American Studies. Locating Asian American Studies away from the focal point of the West Coast to highlight Asians' and Americans' intertwined histories on the East Coast, the collection rearticulates this place called New England as it introduces the actors who encouraged all manner of new images and invigorated our New England imaginations.

WORKS CITED

Alan, Ryan. "A Chinese Legacy Survives in the Granite State." *Foster's Sunday Citizen* (Laconia, N.H.), 15 April 2007, B1, B7.
Henry, Ray. "Chinese Tourists Courted." *Foster's Sunday Citizen* (Laconia, N.H.), 18 May 2008, D1, D6.

Acknowledgments

No collection comes into existence without a myriad of key supporters. The University of Massachusetts Boston's Institute for Asian American Studies was instrumental in introducing me to the lay of the Asian American land in New England and the scholars working within it. I especially am grateful to Paul Watanabe, who cheerfully and enthusiastically encouraged the book from the get-go, organized numerous meetings among regional scholars from whom I drew many of my contributors, and hosted a regional conference on Asian Americans in New England in November 2005. At that venue, I was fortunate to meet contributors Karen Sánchez-Eppler, Bandana Purkayastha, and Leakhena Nou. My term as a research fellow in the University of Massachusetts Boston's Institute for Asian American Studies (2003–4) provided me with an opportunity to begin the ethnographic work that grounds my own chapter in this collection. The Institute's able administrative assistants, Shauno Lo and Michael Liu, have been ever-helpful colleagues. When my home institution, the University of New Hampshire (UNH), hosted an Asian Americans in New England Research Initiative meeting in fall 2004, I appreciated the warm welcome and participation of Vice Provost and Chief Diversity Officer Wanda Mitchell and the former Vice Provost for Academic Affairs Alan Ray. UNH's Center for the Humanities, headed up by Burt Feintuch, generously supplied all seminar attendees with lunch, only one small gesture among its many larger and more academic ones that continue to support the humanities in rich and creative ways. The Office of the Provost generously provides subventions for University Press of New England authors, and I have benefitted from this provision. The Association for Asian American Studies has been a national, annual venue at which I have been presenting my work in progress (including a version of the chapter published here), and it introduced me to contributor Krystyn Moon, among numerous other supportive advocates, all of whom I cannot list here. I thank my writing group for their ongoing commentary and necessary support: Lisa Botshon, Melinda Plastas, Rebecca Herzig, Siobhan Senier, Robin Hackett, and Eve Raimon. I thank colleagues Siobhan and David Watters for encouraging me to discuss the emerging collection with Ellen Wicklum, editor at the University Press of New England (UPNE). In addition, David invited me to present a version of my essay included here at UNH's 2005 Conference on Community. Ellen's welcome nudging — in the form of regular e-mails inquiring about the book's progress and expressing UPNE's desire to be the first to review it — ushered the project along in timely fashion. Her superb guidance, especially during stretches when I thought I was at wit's end, steered me into calmer waters and final production. Special thanks, as always, to my mother, who consistently inquires into what I am reading and writing and whose ever-positive attitude would serve any academic well; she also spent countless hours playing with my children while I was finishing up this project. My husband, Brian, and my two children, Ellie and Roland, have survived the completion of yet another book. They are awesome contributors to my work in their own nonacademic ways.

Introduction

K. SCOTT WONG

I often begin many of my courses or teacher workshops with the claim "Asia has always been a part of American history. Well before the founding of the republic, Asia was a major factor in the development of American society and culture, and long before the Second World War, an important component of our foreign policy." This statement often elicits some raised eyebrows, furrowed brows, smirks, or looks of confusion. I then remind them that it was Asia, specifically China and India, that Christopher Columbus was seeking when he "discovered" what would come to be known as the New World. Once it was acknowledged that this land mass was, in fact, not Asia, many of the explorers who followed in Columbus's wake were seeking the Northeast Passage, a water route around North America to the Pacific that would lead them to Asia. After the British American colonies were established, there developed a brisk Asia trade from the East Coast, primarily in Boston, New York, and Philadelphia. It is well known that George and Martha Washington were fond of Chinese porcelains, including tea sets, and one of the most famous events leading up to the American Revolution was the Boston Tea Party, an event involving rebel colonists disguised as "Indians" throwing Indian (Ceylon) tea overboard in Boston Harbor. Hence Asian commercial goods were present at the founding of the American nation. And even after the republic was well established and the American territory greatly expanded through the Louisiana Purchase, Thomas Jefferson sent Lewis and Clark on their famous expedition, in large part to find a quick water passage running to the Pacific Ocean in order to facilitate trade with Asia. This drive west to "the East" would continue through the building of the Transcontinental Railroad. Called by some the "Iron Road to China," these rails would link the resource-rich West to the industrial East in the hopes that some of those manufactured goods could then be shipped to Asia. At the same time, New England sugar planters and missionaries were transforming the Hawaiian Islands into sugarcane plantations and native Hawaiians into Congregationalist Christians, finally resulting, by 1898, in the American annexation of the Philippine Islands, Hawaiʻi, and other Pacific possessions.

These East Coast—more specifically, New England—roots of Asian American history, however, are often forgotten amid more popular narratives, such as those of Chinese laborers during the Gold Rush, the building of the western half of the Transcontinental Railroad, and the incarceration of Japanese nationals and Japanese Americans in the western states during the Second World War. During the postwar era, especially after the passage of the Immigration Act of 1965 and following the influx of Southeast Asian immigrants after the war in Vietnam, the Asian American population became more national in scale; nonetheless, the West Coast has long remained the focus of both Asian American Studies and the location of most scholars in that field. Over the past two decades, these West Coast–based programs have produced a large number of scholars in Asian American Studies who have secured positions in colleges and universities all over the country. In 1991, a small group of Asian Americanists, mostly people with appointments in history, English, or American Studies departments or programs, was invited to Cornell University by Gary Okihiro to discuss common goals of promoting Asian American Studies on participants' respective campuses, all of which were in the Midwest or on the East Coast. This group eventually became known as "East of California" and began holding annual conferences, where mentoring relationships and friendships developed. The group discussed promoting research on Asian Americans in areas "east of California," though only a handful actually published anything dealing with this topic.

Fortunately, a decade later, in 2002, a new group of scholars came together, based in the Institute for Asian American Studies at the University of Massachusetts Boston, and created the Asian Americans in New England Research Initiative (AANERI), to document the experiences of Asian Americans in New England. The first major publication to come out of this project appeared in 2007, *Southeast Asian Refugees and Immigrants in the Mill City: Changing Families, Communities, Institutions — Thirty Years Afterward*, edited by Tuyet-Lan Pho, Jeffrey N. Gerson, and Sylvia R. Cowan (University of Vermont Press), a collection of essays about the Southeast Asian communities in Lowell, Massachusetts. The volume of essays you now hold in your hands follows in the footsteps of that first collection, but takes a broader chronological and geographical approach by addressing the presence of Asian Americans in New England from the early nineteenth century to the present.

Karen Sánchez-Eppler and Amy Bangerter offer two essays that place Chinese immigrants in the American educational system of New England as early as 1824 and the 1850s. Looking at the artistic expressions of Asians in New England, Krystyn Moon presents a lively account of troupes of Japanese acrobats that toured New England in the late 1860s while Constance Chen recounts the politics involved in the creation of the Department of Chinese and Japanese Art at the Boston Museum of Fine Arts in the late nineteenth and early twentieth centuries. Bandana Purkayastha and Anjana Narayan use the visit of Swami Vivekananda in the early twentieth century to trace some of the origins of the religio-racial constructions of our current society in terms of Asian American religious sensibilities.

Moving to more contemporary developments, Lucy Mae San Pablo Burns documents the politics of archive making through the history of the formation of the Roberta Uno Asian American Women Playwrights Scripts Collection at the University of Massachusetts Amherst. This collection, housed at the W. E. B. Du Bois Library, contains more than two hundred plays and other supplementary materials. Shirley Suet-ling Tang and James Điền Bùi trace the political consciousness and activism of the Vietnamese American community in Boston. Monica Chiu then offers an essay on how Lao American youths utilize hip-hop to negotiate their ethno-racial identity in a society dominated by a black-white paradigm. Finally, Leakhena Nou narrates the politically gendered experience of a Cambodian American woman conducting research on the psychosocial well-being of the Cambodian adult community in Massachusetts.

This groundbreaking collection of essays is a welcome addition to our understanding of the Asian American experience, especially in New England, a site where much of Asian American history can claim a "home base." Far from serving as a definitive history, it will inevitably invite more research on Asian Americans in New England, including histories of the Exclusion Era and essays on Korean Americans. These essays remind all of us that Asia and Asian Americans, from the very beginning, have helped to shape our nation. And we will continue to play important roles in American society well into the future.

K. Scott Wong is the James Phinney Baxter III Professor of History and American Studies and chair of the American Studies Program at Williams College. His recent book, *Americans First: Chinese Americans and the Second World War* (Harvard University Press, 2005), won an honorable mention (in the history category) from the Association for Asian American Studies in 2006. His research interests include looking at the meaning of citizenship in immigration history, the "Pro-Chinese Movement" in late nineteenth- and early twentieth-century America, and the study of history and historical memory.

Asian Americans in New England

1

Copying and Conversion

An 1824 Friendship Album "from a Chinese youth"

KAREN SÁNCHEZ-EPPLER

In 1824 a Chinese student at the Foreign Mission School in Cornwall, Connecticut, joined with his schoolmates to produce a friendship album. He used a cheap paper notebook for the purpose, with an etching of a rooster already printed on the cover and another of Oliver Hazard Perry's 1813 victory over the British at the Battle of Lake Erie printed on the back. Unopened, the copybook proclaims the yeoman patriotism characteristic of early nineteenth-century Yankee schooling. Inside, it devotes the bulk of its pages to a compendium of quite conventional Christian poetry copied by the hands of various students at the mission school in an apparently docile exercise in assimilation. Such albums are a type of cultural production that does not easily transfer into our national narratives. As a genre they seem to speak largely of compliance to pedagogical, national, and religious norms, and so tell us little that is new. Yet copying is not a neutral act: as I will demonstrate, the archival recovery of this friendship album powerfully alters our national narratives, providing us with nuanced and intimate access to one of the very earliest Chinese American interactions, and with it new ways of thinking about the processes of assimilation and conversion so central to ethnic and racial relations in the United States.

Blank books in which many different hands inscribe single pages as a token of remembrance, friendship albums capture a particular community, recording affectionate ties and the structure of relationships. As a form of manuscript book, friendship albums are poised between the long-standing tradition of the commonplace book, in which individuals preserved the gems of wisdom or eloquence they had found in their readings, and the later phenomenon of the autograph album, which collects signatures and brief messages from sundry acquaintances. Nineteenth-century friendship albums usually contain a mix of drawings, poems, and short prose compositions; these offerings could be original but were often copied from printed sources. Despite this derivativeness, each page is clearly intended as a gift from the specific friend who made it, and the design and decoration of pages is often quite elaborate, a testimony to care. Such attention to detail and lavishness of production in general distinguishes friendship albums from other more slapdash forms of manuscript books. The creation of such albums was a familiar and popular social practice in the early nineteenth century, though the evidence suggests that various social groups used the making of such books quite differently.[1] Friendship albums could be created gradually by informal networks of friends, the pages accruing over years; many, however, like the album discussed here, are occasional, prepared as a keepsake in anticipation of separations (a marriage or a move perhaps) or as a mode of celebration for a birthday or other accomplishment. Many have an institutional base: made at schools, clubs, churches, as a way of preserving the cords of membership even after the group itself physically disperses. Friendship albums thus offer a tangible record of relationships and a testament to the ways in which literary practices were used in this period to convey social and personal identities. The albums produced at the Cornwall Foreign Mission School provide a particularly poignant instance of how this medium expresses community, as the Foreign Mission School, an extremely unusual community for its time, contained an extraordinarily diverse group of students. In the album each student signs his nationality beside his name: "George Fox a native of Seneca," "Miles McKay a Choctaw," "Charles M. Arohekeah a native of Hawaii," "Wm A-lum a little boy of Chinese Youth your friend," "Done by your friend Chinese youth Henry Martyn."[2]

The album pictured in figure 1.1 was produced in the summer and fall of 1824 as a gift for Miss Cherry Stone by Henry Martyn A'lan, as he signs himself in English script, a name that honored the British missionary to India and Persia, or 胡蘭 as he writes in Chinese characters, a name pronounced Hu Lan in Mandarin, and Wu Lan in this young man's native Cantonese.[3] As is typical of the genre, pages by many other students are included in the album, but Wu Lan clearly takes charge of the production of this volume, and his writing both in English and in Chinese fills many of its pages, with most of the charming watercolor drawings apparently done by his hand. This album is quite possibly the earliest extant Chinese document produced in the United States. It was created a generation before the California protest writing with which Xiao-huang Yin begins his study *Chinese American Literature since the 1850s*. Chinese students studied at the Cornwall Foreign Mission School nearly thirty years before Wong Foon, Wong Shing, and Yung Wing were enrolled at the Monson Academy in Massachusetts.[4]

FIG. 1.1. Title Spread of 1824 Friendship Album for Miss Cherry Stone. *Collection of the Cornwall Historical Society, Cornwall, Connecticut.*

Thus this album constitutes a milestone in Chinese American history, demonstrating again, as many scholars have suspected, and this collection of essays affirms, that the Chinese presence in New England long preceded the far better documented and studied settlement on the West Coast.

Teaching literacy was central to Protestant mission work: how else could converts gain access to the Bible? Moreover, these literary behaviors were understood as necessary for the development of a properly civilized sensibility: to learn the pleasure of the book was to embrace the pleasures of the domestic scene and of the Anglo-Protestant civilization such homes were thought to embody.[5] A rare example of writing produced by missionary students, this album — while precisely the kind of indoctrinating literary pedagogy that characterized missionary work — nevertheless invites and enables us to see these systems of assimilation from a different vantage, one that emphasizes the individual desires and acts of agency within it. José Muñoz's concept of "disidentification" proves useful for approaching Wu Lan's album. This notion of reading "oneself and one's own life narrative in a moment, object, or subject that is not culturally coded to 'connect' with the disidentifying subject" suggests how Wu Lan could use the act of making this book, a school task freighted with goals of conversion and assimilation, as a site for self-expression (12).

But before I turn to Wu Lan's album, I need to describe the educational experiment that has left us this unusual document, particularly the evidence the school's records provide for the early history of U.S.-Chinese contacts. The Cornwall Foreign Mission School was founded in 1817 to educate "Heathen Youths, in such manner, as with subsequent professional instruction will qualify them to become useful Missionaries, Physicians, Surgeons, School Masters or Interpreters; and to communicate to the Heathen Nations such knowledge in agriculture and the arts, as may prove the means of promoting Christianity and civilization" ("Report of the Prudential Committee"). It was thought that gathering such students together in one establishment in a conventional and pious New England town would prove more efficient and effective than placing them in traditional missionary schools established within "heathen" settings; the young men enrolled at such a school thus would be severed from the alleged corrupting influences and "pagan customs" of their native communities (Joseph Harvey 23). It was hoped that, detached from their culture, these "heathen youths may be more completely civilized, more thoroughly Christianized, and their hearts more entirely won over to the missionary cause" ("Journey in New-England" 464). In its design, the school thus less resembled other mission schools than it presaged the development of new educational institutions within the United States, institutions that over the next two decades would offer to exchange education for colonization, teaching nonwhite students on the condition of their departure from the United States. This strategy promised the simultaneous benefits of exporting American beliefs and practices and thus Americanizing "Heathen Nations," while ridding America of these alien bodies. The founders of the African Education Society, for example, would quite explicitly claim for their 1829 initiative that "instead of creating disquiet in the country," their plan for the education of free blacks "may carry peace and joy to Africa." The ideology of colonization has a long history in the United States, but the educational institutions created to effect such a policy are peculiar to these years (*Report of the Proceedings at the Formation of the African Education Society* 9).[6]

The Cornwall Foreign Mission School remained unique, however, for the vast international diversity of its students. The impetus for the founding of the school came in response to some young men who had arrived in Connecticut and Massachusetts from Hawai'i, and the bulk of the student population would be Native Americans from a wide array of Indian nations; the school also included a scattering of students from Europe, Indonesia, Polynesian, and Asia (but not, it appears, Africa), with Chinese students considered for the school from the start. The 1816 announcement in the *Christian Herald* of the decision by the American Board of Commissioners of Foreign Missions (ABCFM) to establish such a school already mentions that "it has been proposed to the Board to take under their patronage a young Chinese, now in New York. It seems more probable, however, that he will be sent to England, where the London Missionary Society are paying particular attention to the education of Chinese youth" ("School for Heathen Youth" 39). By 1818 notices about the school list "two Chinese" among the seventeen students enrolled there (Rev. Chauncey Lee 264). These "two Chinese" appear in fact to have been one Chinese student, referred to as "Wong Arce," and one Malaysian man, "Joseph Botang Snow," who, as is explained in articles in the religious press, had been enslaved as a child in Canton: "His master then disposed of him to Mr. Samuel Snow, of Providence R.I. who was then a commercial agent of the U.S. at Canton, and who brought this Malay with him on returning to this country. Botang learnt the Chinese language while resident at Canton, and retains it still. He speaks English intelligibly" ("Foreign Mission School," *Christian Messenger* 200). Ultimately baptized in a Rhode Island church, and then enrolled at the Cornwall school, Botang's story epitomizes the incidental and arbitrary processes of cultural accretion. Hybridity is never stable, but rather garnered bit by bit through haphazard contacts — Malaysian, Chinese, American, commercial, religious, educational. Botang is thus "disposed of" in a historical trajectory that conveniently coincides with the ABCFM's sense of Providence.

Besides Wong Arce and Wu Lan, at least two other Chinese students would enroll at Cornwall, but there were others like Botang whose path to the Foreign Mission School ran through Canton.[7] Commerce creates and maintains the mechanisms of international contact, and both mission work and the choices of individual migrants move in those currents. Canton, the foreign entrepôt of the China trade, thus figures significantly in the peregrinations of many of the Cornwall students born outside the Americas, not just the Chinese. All of the Hawaiian students, for example, arrived in New England on trade ships that had first stopped there.[8] The popularity of Chinese goods in the U.S. market — not only the perennial silks and tea, but also a wide array of household finery from women's fans and haircombs to porcelain tableware and carved or painted furniture — prompted more and more American merchants to enter the Asian market. Yet it was even more difficult for the young republic than it was for European nations to produce articles for trade. As Emperor Chien-lung had asserted in 1793, "the productions of our Empire are manifold, and in great Abundance; nor do we stand in the least Need of the Produce of other Countries" (quoted in James R. Gibson 84). Wu Lan and the other young men who came to Cornwall from Canton were in fact traveling from one of the most wealthy and cosmopolitan of world cities to a small, isolated, and fairly rustic village. Such a trajectory in many ways reverses the usual missionary dictums that equate Christian conversion with civilization.

To trade for Chinese goods, American ships carried first Appalachian ginseng: by the early nineteenth century, as that market became saturated and the crop itself dwindled, the trade turned to sandalwood from Fiji and Hawai'i, sea otter pelts from Alaska, and sealskins collected all along this southern route. None of this produce could match the U.S. appetite for silk and tea, however, requiring most American merchants to purchase their Chinese goods with Spanish silver. Plagued by this market imbalance, Americans ultimately followed the British example and began to trade in opium as well. The first American ships carrying opium arrived in Canton in 1806, and by 1818 the size of the trade was significant enough to prompt Guangdong officials explicitly to prohibit U.S. sale of opium in China. In short, the China trade of the 1820s was marked by the strong desire for Chinese goods, the precarious but seductive potential for large profits, and the mounting tensions that would lead to the Opium Wars. The U.S. portion of the trade was not immune to any of these issues.[9]

The few studies of Chinese presence in the United States in the early nineteenth century confirm that the boats that brought tea, porcelain, and silk also sometimes brought people, but we know very little about the motivations or outcomes of these journeys. It was only with the initiation of the Opium Wars that significant numbers of Chinese men were transported to the Americas, mostly as laborers for Caribbean or South American plantations.[10] Of course, as Ronald Takaki notes, it was almost two decades later, with the California gold rush, that the number of Chinese in the United States burgeoned. Still, an 1855 census of lower Manhattan records thirty-nine Chinese residents, and John Tchen's insightful evaluation of this data locates one man who had been in New York as early as 1829 and another who had been a ship steward based in the city since 1825 (76–77).[11] The trajectories of the Chinese students at Cornwall, while in many ways highly unusual, do provide some individualized content to the more general profile of Chinese immigration, and especially to this earlier and less told story of the arrival of Chinese on the East Coast of the United States. In particular, the complex layering of the missionary and the mercantile evident in these cases resonates with other instances of early Chinese American contact. Studies of the foreign mission movement and of the China trade have tended to downplay such interconnections, but they are in fact ubiquitous.

The diverse and exotic origins of the Cornwall students fascinated visitors, and the Foreign Mission School was "reckoned with Yale College and the Deaf and Dumb Institution in Hartford as one of the three noteworthy things in the state to be visited by intelligent travelers" (Edward C. Starr 137). One such "intelligent traveler" from the southern states published impressions of the school in an 1822 essay titled "A Journey in New-England." The essay includes a poem the author identifies as "the production of one of the members of the school" and notes that although "there is certainly nothing very poetical" in these lines, they do "contain in as few words as possible an account of the institution" (465). This poem (fig. 1.2) also appears in Wu Lan's album in a slightly truncated form:

The Cornwall Seminary

Now in Connecticut there stands,
On Cornwall's low and pleasant lands,
A school composed of foreign youth,
For propagating gospel truth.
And on this consecrated ground
Are those from many nations round;
But mostly of the *Cherokees*,
The *Angloes*, and the *Owhyhees*.
The languages are now thirteen;
Twelve nations here likewise are seen,
And students thirty-two are found,
From regions of remotest bound.
But charity's propitious hand,
Which traverses o'er sea and land,
To seek for good, and lend her care,
Has brought these various nations here.[12]

Two years elapse between the publication of "A Journey in New-England" and the creation of Wu Lan's album. The album page that holds this poem is unsigned, although the handwriting appears similar to Wu Lan's, making it likely that he is the copyist. Interestingly, within this more autonomous, student-circulated version, the concluding lines have been lopped off, making the poem appear more flatly descriptive, less structured by religious teleology than in the earlier published version. The closing lines imagine that these foreign students have been sought abroad and brought to Cornwall by "charity's propitious hand," so that the school's remarkable diversity becomes a sign of missionary effort and concern. The imperfect rhyme of "here" and "care" in this final couplet makes this claim sound somehow not quite right, a moment of dissonance in an otherwise congratulatory account.

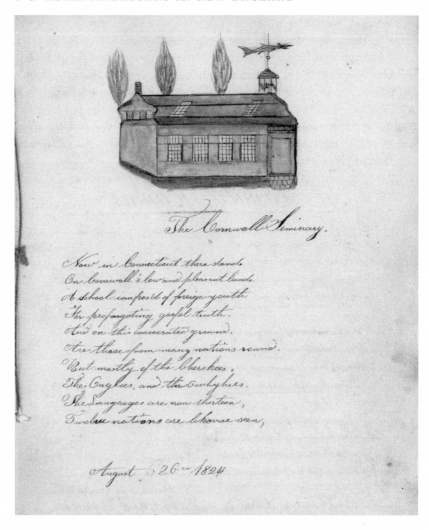

FIG. 1.2. "The Cornwall Seminary," 1824 Friendship Album for Miss Cherry Stone. *Collection of the Cornwall Historical Society, Cornwall, Connecticut.*

In fact, although some of the Native American students and the two young men from Greece were actively selected for the school in this way, it is clear that most of the students who arrived at Cornwall from other continents came, at least to the United States, through more various and haphazard means, and often by their own initiative. Going beyond mere dissonance, the hand that inscribed this poem in Wu Lan's album simply leaves out the philanthropic hand of missionary control.

Published reports from a September 1818 exhibition at the school similarly emphasize the multinational origins of the students in ways that invite questions about agency. The exhibition included recitations in which one Hawaiian student spoke in English, another in Hawaiian, and other pupils in Choctaw, Cherokee, and Tahitian, as well as English. One white American gave a declamation in Chinese; it seems, moreover, that the white New England lad had learned his Cantonese from the Malaysian Botang rather than from the Chinese student Wong, another instance of the complex forms that multiculturalism took at the Foreign Mission School. Such performances reveal the evangelical and assimilationist tension in the school's mission. While the school's goal was to convert its heathen pupils, their success as missionaries to their native communities depended on their preserving, and indeed expanding, linguistic skill and cultural knowledge. The school manifests an unusual cross between the goals of missionary training, which might include amassing linguistic and cultural information, and those of converting heathens, more usually linked to the eradication of "pagan" customs and skills. Thus aims generally consigned to quite different educational institutions, and elsewhere opposed in practice, were conjoined at Cornwall: "Many prayers are continually offered for the youths here assembled, that their souls might be saved, and they may carry salvation to multitudes of their brethren." Reports on the progress of individual students celebrate not only the student who "learns English well and is now hopefully pious" but also the one who "retains his native language in a high degree" ("Foreign Mission School," *Christian Messenger*).[13] Indeed the original constitution of the school includes the requirement that "exercises shall be instituted by the Principal, for the purpose of preserving to the students the knowledge of their respective languages" (*Panoplist and Missionary Magazine* 80).[14] What counts as civilizing knowledge is highly flexible, an elasticity based in pragmatism perhaps, but nevertheless one that cedes control, granting some space for native self-expression in what is otherwise a clearly required performance. After all, the declamations not done in English were "composed by the youths themselves," and it is doubtful that any in the audience could understand much, if anything, of what was said. The Chinese calligraphy in Wu Lan's album thus reflects a general tenet of the school; a Cornwall album created by a student from Greece similarly contains many pages written in Greek.[15]

As the reports of this exhibition reveal, there were a few white New England youth enrolled in the school, and observers were celebratory and explicit about the evangelical utility of such cultural exchange.

Future missionaries may in this way be educated in habits of daily intercourse with heathen youths. Young savages will learn a great deal of the arts, habits, manners and customs of civilized life from their fellow students, and christian young men may, in the course of their education, learn much of the language, habits and prejudices of the heathen to whom, hereafter, they may be sent as missionaries. And between young christians and heathens thus related there may grow up attachments of that peculiarly durable and powerful kind which are formed at college. ("Journey in New-England" 464–65)

The comparison to college friendships jars. Central to the founding legend of the Cornwall Foreign Mission School is the story of undergraduate Edwin Dwight finding the Hawaiian Opukahaia crying on the steps of Yale College, because he wished to learn (Starr 136). That is, the Cornwall school understood itself as necessary in part because "tawny and dusky youth" could not enroll as students in Connecticut colleges.[16] Opukahaia's experience reflects a far more complex process of literacy and conversion (and Dwight's *Memoir* would richly reward further study).[17] But that image of a heathen's tearful desire for the seat of learning, like this allusion to college friendships and the ideal of peer equality that religious education might produce, bespeaks the unusually reciprocal nature of this educational experiment. I don't wish to imply here that the Cornwall experiment was ultimately benign or egalitarian, but merely that the peculiar dynamics created by this multinational community, with its crossed goals of converting heathens and creating missionaries, produced a situation in which such equality and mutuality could be at least fleetingly imagined.

The Foreign Mission School has been of interest to historians precisely because it culminated in the imagining and enacting of just such mutual interracial attachments, the marriages of the Cherokee students John Ridge and Elias Boudinot to two white Cornwall girls from good families, Sarah Northrop and Harriett Gold. Controversy over these marriages ultimately precipitated the closing of the school in 1826. The marriages and the hostile response to them are particularly important because of the role Ridge and Boudinot would play in Cherokee history, as tribal leaders who, after initial advocacy for Cherokee rights, negotiated and signed the infamous New Echota treaty that ceded Cherokee land to the State of Georgia and precipitated the horrific relocations of the "Trail of Tears." Scholars vary widely in interpreting the influence of Ridge's and Boudinot's experiences at Cornwall on these notorious events.[18] I will not engage further with these questions of Cherokee history, but would note that the patterns of affiliation and exclusion so dramatically manifest in Ridge's and Boudinot's relations to the school say much about the fundamental tensions and contradictions in the way the Foreign Mission School treated all its students.

John Ridge and Sarah Northrop, the first of the couples, were married in January 1824. Following their marriage, editorials in local newspapers attacked the school for facilitating such connections:

> Have not the Agents, Principals, and Guardians of that Institution . . . treated these blacks and Indians with more marked attention and caresses, than the sons of our most worthy farmers, or common citizens? . . . Have not the females in that place been seen to ride and walk out with them arm in arm, by night and by day — spend evenings with them — invite them to tea parties — correspond with them by letters — suffer themselves to be complimented by them. . . ? ("Missionary School and Heathen Youths" 69).

Despite the school's impetus for interracial collegiality and exchange, there were implicit limits to integration: "blacks and Indians" could never ultimately be accounted "common citizens." As for social interactions with local women, however racist and inflammatory the editorial's tone, the charge that the school sought to enable such contacts is not wholly inaccurate; the first director of the school, Joseph Harvey, expressly argued that because "the situation and character of females in Christian society, is one important point of distinction between that and the society of heathen," Cornwall students "should be introduced into such society and educated in it" (Harvey 23–24). As Dwight explains in his memoir of Opukahaia, "in all heathen countries, females were degraded, and made the servants and drudges of men. The Gospel raises them from this servitude and makes them their equals and companions" (21). Wu Lan produced this album in the summer and fall of 1824 in the wake of this controversy, and the album itself is addressed to another elite, white Cornwall girl. Indeed, "Cherry Stone" may be the daughter of the Reverend Timothy Stone,[19] pastor of the Congregational Church in Cornwall and the man who persuaded the ABCFM to locate the Foreign Mission School there in part because in Cornwall "the youth of the society were then unusually sober and promising" (Stone).

What we know of Wu Lan's arrival in the United States and at the Cornwall Foreign Mission School comes mostly from the religious press. He and William A'lum arrived at the school together in the summer of 1823, a year before the making of this album:

> They are cousins; their ages are 19 and 21.
> The younger [William A'lum] left China about two years ago in a vessel for Amsterdam, from which place he arrived in this country in February.

The elder [Henry Martyn A'lan] arrived in this country direct from China, about two months ago.

Neither had any knowledge of the destination of the other to this country, until the arrival of the elder in Philadelphia, when they accidentally met in the streets.

They are cousins to the Chinese youth now in the school at Cornwall — had heard of his arrival in the Boston country, and that he was receiving an education there, and felt a great desire to be taught also. They arrived in this country friendless and pennyless. The younger lived with the supercargo of the ship in which he came from Amsterdam. The elder supported himself by making small toys, which he sold in the streets of Philadelphia, in which business he was engaged when he was accidentally met by a gentleman from the state of New-York, who was attending the meeting of the General Assembly of the Presbyterian Church. Upon being asked, principally by signs, whether he would like to be taught to read the English language, he immediately signified his desire, and appeared highly gratified with the idea, and informed the gentleman that he had a cousin in the city. The gentleman then took steps to bring their case before the Christian public. . . . Nearly $300 were immediately collected and more will doubtless be. . . .

On Thursday evening they were presented to the inhabitants of Hartford, in the brick meeting-house, dressed in their native costume. They read to the audience from the New Testament translated into the Chinese language by Dr. Morrison. A handsome collection was made for the school. They left this place for Cornwall ("Chinese Youth," *Christian Repository* 1823).

The enrollment of these young men in the Foreign Mission School was something of an event. Between May and August 1823, the religious and secular press published at least thirty new articles or reprints that reported on their arrival. Over the next two years a similar number of pieces appeared that recounted their progress, described their visits to various congregations, quoted from their letters, or announced donations made for their support. Despite this coverage, the specific ties between the general history of the China trade or the mission movement and the particular trajectory of these young men remain highly speculative. Why they left China on these trade ships is still a mystery, as is their decision to disembark in Philadelphia, as well as the decision of the third Chinese man, Lieaou A'See or William Botelho, to settle in Boston. The speed with which A'lum and A'lan found each other in this large, alien city bespeaks the tinyness of the Chinese presence there. The journalist's notion that these three men must all be cousins surely marks some moment of miscommunication; it also signals a depth of foreignness that would make all Chinese people seem related to a U.S. reporter, and would make a countryman feel like kin to young men so far from home. The network of merchants and sailors around Canton was tightly woven, as was that among the shipyards of Boston, New York, and Philadelphia, so these young men might well have been aware of each other's decision to try this new world. "I glad my countrymen Henry and William come here," Lieaou A'See writes in a letter from Cornwall that same July ("Foreign Mission School," *Religious Intelligencer* 445).

It seems clear, moreover, that these young men were not simply the "friendless and penniless" figures this article describes. Other articles on their arrival note that "they read, write and speak the Chinese language with facility" (*Connecticut Mirror* 3). Wu Lan's handwriting in English is remarkably elegant and colleagues assure me that his Chinese calligraphy has competence and style, a mark of an advanced education in China.[20] The supercargo of the ship is the man charged with the ship's economic transactions, the person who decides what cargo to unload where, what to take in its place; if William A'lum lodged with him, it is unlikely that he was merely a sailor lackey. It seems far more likely that both young men would have been the sons or close relatives of merchants. An article on these young men published a year later strengthens this sense of mercantile connections:

> A letter has been received from the father of one of these youths, in reply to an account given by his son of his present situation, prospects, &c. This letter exhibits a strong incredulity on the part of the parent. Accustomed to witness the operations of selfishness only in the human heart, he cannot conceive why expenses should be incurred and kindness be lavished, and he asks "Who will pay the debt?" May the future multiplicity of similar deeds of benevolence leave on the Pagan heart impressions favorable to the reception of the Gospel of Christ. ("Chinese Youth," *Religious Intelligencer* 94).[21]

Reading through the missionary prejudice and zeal, this evidence of the young man's continued contact with his father further attests to his social status; it suggests parental interest in this venture as well as family access to international communication networks. Even the worries about debt correspond well to the economic situation of Chinese merchants during this period.[22] Later experiences of an illustrious Chinese theater troupe, stranded in New York in the 1850s and reduced to street trades and begging, demonstrate how difficult it would be for even skilled Chinese to find other sorts of employment in American cities (Tchen 86–90). Like Wu Lan making and selling toys on the streets of Philadelphia, Lieaou A'See "supported himself for some time in Boston, by making various trifles, which he sold as curiosities" ("Foreign Mission School: Letter of A'See" 379). What we know of the histories of other students at the school—the Cherokee leaders Ridge and Boudinot, the Hawaiian Opukahaia raised by a priest, or Tamoree son of the "King of Atooi"—suggests that most of the young men educated in Cornwall came from elite and ambitious families in their own communities.

The earliest article on the appearance of these young men in Philadelphia reports that Wu Lan had "arrived here on a ship belonging to Edward Thompson Esq" ("Heathen Youth" 164). Referred to in the press as "an opulent merchant of Philadelphia," Edward Thompson epitomizes many of the complex interrelations between the missionary and mercantile worlds ("Miscellany Paragraphs" 83). Coincidentally, in the report on the annual board meeting of the ABCFM in which "the petition respecting the establishment of a school for the education of heathen youth" was accepted, the board also recorded thanks to "Mr. Edward Thompson, of Philadelphia, for his generous offer of a gratuitous passage to such missionaries, as the board may soon wish to send into India" ("American Board of Commissioners" 445). The following year the ABCFM rewarded his generosity in transporting missionaries by electing him an honorary member of the convention. In traveling to Philadelphia on one of Thompson's ships, Wu Lan may thus have experienced missionary influences during his journey, arriving in the United States already somewhat prepared for the "accidental" meeting that led to his enrollment at Cornwall. Merchant ships should be understood as potential sites for evangelical work. Opukahaia had first learned of Christianity and the English alphabet from a sailor (Dwight 16). Thompson's ties to the ABCFM point, moreover, to the possibility of more mercenary connections between commercial profits and missionary work. In 1825, just two years after Wu Lan sailed on one of his ships, Thompson was successfully charged with having evaded customs payments on imported tea totaling an astounding nine hundred thousand dollars. On a smaller scale, such maneuvers were a common feature of the China trade. Still, Thompson's generosity to missionaries may well have provided some evangelical credibility to what was essentially a voluminous and prestigious smuggling operation. If it seems possible that Wu Lan may have traveled from China in the company of missionaries, it seems probable that the ship that carried him also carried contraband tea.[23]

The high profile of these young men from China in the religious press was matched by their success in raising funds for the school, particularly, it appears, among the ladies. After their performance at the Presbyterian Assembly in Philadelphia "a number of ladies immediately formed a Society for the purpose of educating them" ("Chinese Youth," *Boston Recorder*), while "the attention of several ladies" in New York City was similarly "directed more particularly to this institution by the arrival on our shores of two Chinese youths" ("Foreign Mission School," *Religious Intelligencer*). Such individual patronage obviously benefited the school as a whole, but it did produce problematic inequities. Two years later amid the criticisms of the school prompted by the Cherokee marriages, such favoritism is included among "subjects of complaint," prompting Timothy Stone to explain that "while most of the scholars are very plainly clad some by particular patrons are furnished with better and richer clothing. This we wish to remedy as far as possible." Similarly, he notes that it is "inexpedient that scholars be allowed pocket money, by friends" ("The Foreign Mission School" pamphlet 6–7). Such justifications suggest that prior to all this censure, school procedure had been more lax, and certainly both of these Chinese students received at least some pocket money from their benefactors, and spent it on small personal luxuries. The 1824 ledger for Kellogg's general store in Cornwall records that on January 30 "William Allum" spent forty-four cents on a "hair comb" and "shell bonnet paper" (112), and on March 10 "Henry Martyn (Chinese)" spent a dollar on a "silk Flagg Handkerchief" (131).

Like the exhibitions at the school, the fund-raising stops A'lum and A'lan made during their journey to Cornwall blend the exotic with the civilized. "Dressed in their native costume," they are spectacles of foreignness, living versions of the Chinese dioramas with their life-size wax figures that were put on display in Peale's Philadelphia Museum in 1805, and religious precursors of such carnival attractions as the "Chinese Lady" (A'fong Moy, who sat in her silks and bound feet to be ogled by visitors to Barnum's American Museum in the 1830s), or even the famous "Siamese Twins" Eng and Chang Bunker, who were first displayed in Boston in 1829 (Lee, *Orientals* 28–30; Tchen 101–13, 134–45). Yet central to this spectacle of otherness is a vision of sameness, a missionary faith in a shared salvation.

Robert Morrison was the first Protestant missionary to China. Although trained by the London Missionary Society, he arrived in China and began his work there under American auspices because the British East India Company was afraid that transporting a missionary might be detrimental to trade relations. Outlawed from open evangelizing, he instead invested his energies into literary labors, founding the already mentioned Anglo Chinese College, and translating the Bible into Chinese. Indeed it was in 1823, the very year that these young men arrived in Philadelphia, that Morrison completed publication of both the Chinese Bible and the first English-

Chinese dictionary. The New Testament William A'lum and Henry Martyn A'lan read from in Hartford had come earlier, first published in 1814. Still, the sense of providential conjunction runs deep. During a quarter century of missionary work in China, Morrison baptized only ten Chinese.[24] An 1823 report from the London Missionary Society notes that "Dr. Morrison continues to view with deep concern the small effect produced by his labors among the few Chinese, to whom, from time to time, he has been enabled to impart religious instruction" ("China Canton"). Who would have guessed that his translations would find some of their first readers in Connecticut?

"Of the Christian religion," another article notes, "they had never heard or read until they were shown this translation in their own language" (*Middlesex Gazette*). Yet by the fall of 1823, Henry Martyn A'lan and William A'lum would already be charged with evangelical efforts:

> There is a Chinese in Philadelphia, who has a wife and children. He has resided in this country 15 years, but still believes in the polytheism of China, and cannot conceive how one God could make so many and so great things as sun, moon, stars, &c. in six days. He was lately visited by the two Chinese youth who are at the Foreign Mission in Cornwall, who endeavored to convince him that there is but one God and that he is invisible. These youths, it is said, have confused ideas of Jesus Christ, but are fully persuaded that there is but one God, and that he is a Spirit. (*Farmer's Cabinet*)

Set against fifteen years of recalcitrant polytheism, the six-month miracle of teaching these young men to believe in one God modestly imitates Genesis itself. In its missionary calling, Cornwall yearns to do "so many and so great things." Yet if William A'lum and Henry Martyn A'lan can be presented as a success story, the limits of missionary accomplishment still remain clear: nothing in this notice suggest that the "Chinese" was much swayed by this visit, while the unfinished nature of their own conversion is faithfully recorded. In such accounts the intricacies of these young men's responses to the missionary education offered them at Cornwall remains "confused" and "invisible" too, buried within all that is scripted and scornful in how the school and the press describe them. John Tchen writes poignantly of how little we actually know about even such celebrated figures as Eng and Chang Bunker; while the Siamese twins were popular topics for press coverage, reporters rarely asked them even the most basic questions about their past histories or present feelings. Such silences heighten the remarkableness of this friendship album, made by Wu Lan, even though it offers a most limited representation of him. In fact we know his Chinese as well as his English names only because he signed this book in Chinese characters. We lack similar proper Chinese names for the famous Bunker twins, or for the "Chinese Lady" A'fong Moy—a name whose A' prefix, like that of A'lan, A'lum, and A'See, marks it as informal. Moreover, the religious experiment of the Foreign Mission School, with its stress on individual academic and spiritual progress, meant that the religious press, unlike the popular press, was interested in what these young men might wish to say about themselves, at least on these topics, and printed many letters by Cornwall students, including a few by the young men from China.

In a letter dated 20 December 1823, Henry Martyn A'lan writes, "I feel now contented and wish to learn as fast as I can. I can now read some in the New Testament; I read in my Chinese Testament most every day. I hope I shall learn to be good and have that new heart which the Bible and my Christian friends tell me" ("Chinese Youth," *Christian Repository* 1824). While clearly the ABCFM had plans for them—immediately in raising funds for the school and ultimately in conversion and a missionary future— these young men also saw ways in which the Cornwall Foreign Mission school could be useful to them. For the mission movement, English literacy may have been primarily valued as a means of conversion, but it was also an increasingly desirable skill for anyone involved in international trade. Yung Wing would use such economic speculations to explain his parents' decision to send him to the mission school at Macao in 1835: "on the theory that as foreign intercourse with China was just beginning to grow, my parents . . . thought it worthwhile to take time by the forelock and put one of their sons to learning English that he might become one of the advanced interpreters and have a more advantageous position from which to make his way into the business and diplomatic world" (2–3). The Presbyterian gentleman had stressed language and literacy instruction in urging that these young men join the school, and their letters confirm their interest in learning English. "I learn to read and write a little. I find many good friends here," writes Henry Martyn A'lan. "It come hard for me to learn English: but I try and it grows easier. I like the school very much," writes William A'lum ("Foreign Mission School," *Religious Intelligencer*).

The album itself begins with what seems to be practice writing (see fig. 1.1). The ideograms on the opening page start as a short poem but quickly degenerate into random words, so that the page shows off Wu Lan's calligraphy to an audience he knows cannot read it anyhow.[25] The title identifies the picture in his not quite grammatical English as "These Chinese Lady" and in Chinese as "The noble Lady Liu Jin Hua." Jin Hua is a figure from

Chao Opera; she refuses a wealthy suitor, and accepts hard work in the mountains, out of love for a poor student, Liu Yong (Chao Opera). The legend of this noble lady and her student lover provides a fairly pointed introduction to the album, offered as a gift to a young woman who may well have been a minister's daughter and given only months after the scandalous marriage of a Cherokee student to the daughter of the school's Steward. Of course the implications of this figure would remain invisible to American viewers, who would see in her only a graceful Chinese lady, a charming image to place across from the iconographically American inscription of Cherry Stone's name carried by an eagle. Thus in his cunning arrangement of this opening page, Wu Lan hides his possible meanings in plain view — a tactic that will prove characteristic of the album as a whole.

The next page has more missionary utility (fig. 1.3). Here the Lord's Prayer is beautifully copied in English and Chinese "Written by Henry Martyn Alan." The translation, of course, is based on Morrison's. As in the school exhibitions, what is being performed on this page beneath a theatrical curtain is the translatability of faith. But the performance rests on a different kind of transfer, that of copying. There is a certain irony here in that Jesus Christ offered this prayer, which would become the most routinely intoned of Christian texts, as an unadorned, authentic display of faith, in contrast to the mere copying of forms: "when ye pray, use not vain repetitions, as the heathen do," Jesus enjoined before voicing this model prayer (Mathew 6:7). In his elegant English transcription, Wu Lan capitalizes each word, setting them carefully so that each line is perfectly justified, creating a solid block of text whose horizontal lines would make a perfect grid with the vertical lines of Chinese characters inscribed below. The English is spotted with small errors ("As In It In Heaven Give Us This Days Our Daily Bread," "Lead Us Not Into Temption") that record the gap between Wu Lan's graceful copying of English letters and, barely a year after arriving in Philadelphia, his imperfect command of the language. Thus the page appears essentially visual and decorative, iconic text on display, highlighting both the symmetry between English and Chinese and their radical difference, literally running along different axes.

The stakes of copying suffuse the album as a whole. Most of the English poetry in it is quite conventionally Christian, and it seems extremely likely that the young men copied these pieces from various published sources. This copying is a usual practice for all sorts of friendship albums, in which the value of each page comes not from the originality of the words written, but from the act of personal connection and care entailed in choosing particular poems and inscribing them. By copying poems in their own hands,

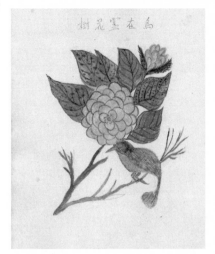 

FIG. 1.3. Lord's Prayer, 1824 Friendship Album for Miss Cherry Stone. *Collection of the Cornwall Historical Society, Cornwall, Connecticut.*

friends turn generic sentiments into acts of relation and remembrance. Moreover, the virtues of copying were central to literacy training at all American schools in this period. Copying was also a mainstay of Chinese education, so that the practices that put these poems in this book mark a rare shared emphasis in these very different pedagogical traditions. Copying certainly developed penmanship skills, but the idea behind American primers was that the tracing of letters was tied to the tracing of ideas, and the prefaces to schoolbooks of this period advertise the high moral content of their sample phrases.[26] The same is true of the *San Tzu Ching*, the "three-character classic" that had been the elementary guide for Chinese literacy since the thirteenth century; its 356 rhyming three-character lines insist on the importance of thorough learning and provide a scaffold of injunctions for right living and a summary of Chinese history.[27] In both traditions, memorization and imitation are understood to have simultaneous pedagogical and moral force. The poems copied into this album are by and large so conventional that it is difficult to discern their particular relevance for the young men who so carefully wrote them on these pages. But surely the act of writing sanctioned English words in precise English script is in itself the major point and message of this endeavor. Such obedient good manners are the best gifts these young men can give to Miss Stone. The making of this album stands as an achievement in assimilation to Christian and domestic pieties—and yet its methods may have felt quite familiar to Wu Lan.

Nonetheless, as Homi Bhabha notes, the role of imitation in colonial practice is far more ambivalent than the discourse of assimilation would suggest. The "almost the same but not quite" of colonial "mimic men" retains an edge of difference, a mark of the alien, that can also serve as a mechanism of critique (85–92). Moreover, the dynamics of imitation may be more complexly multidirectional than even Bhabha's account acknowledges. The Lord's Prayer might appear below a stylized Western curtain, but the image on the facing page reflects a Chinese aesthetic, the birds and flowers also evident in nineteenth-century Qing albums. Other paintings have the decorative clarity associated with those designs painted on porce-

FIG. 1.4. Chinese Gold Fish, 1824 Friendship Album for Miss Cherry Stone. *Collection of the Cornwall Historical Society, Cornwall, Connecticut.*

lain or silk that were such mainstays of the China trade (fig. 1.4). In the late eighteenth and early nineteenth centuries, objects made in China occupied a place of distinction in the American domestic scene, connoting not savagery, but elegance, civility, and refinement. Domesticity has material as well as spiritual dimensions, the "cult of domesticity" manifesting itself both in piety and in tea sets. And while Wu Lan copied the Lord's Prayer, in English and Chinese, many Chinese domestic practices and accouterments were being imitated and adapted to American households. By the early nineteenth century, virtually every urban middle-class American home contained at least a few pieces of chinoiserie, Americans of all classes drank tea, and even period recipes for apple pie call for cinnamon, another staple of the China trade.[28] Thus the relation between missionary goals and domestic practices proves rather circular, as in so many ways it was China that secured the gentility of the American home.

The Chinese aesthetics evident in many of these drawings thus both express Wu Lan's past and accommodate an American audience known to appreciate Chinese things. American influences are clearly visible in many of these images. Indeed the very layout of the pages with titles at the top, running horizontal despite the Chinese characters, echoes the textual practices of American books. Some drawings seem highly botanical. The Chinese titling above a drawing of a sunflower translates as "the sunflower has three circles of petals" — the sort of information one was likely to learn in botany classes of the time. Other images of flowers in the book have even more of this herbarium precision, although they may be drawn from memory rather than specimens, like the graceful "Chinese sugarcane" (fig. 1.5). The "Flowers By the Southern Window," as Wu Lan titles another drawing, is pure New England, a Yankee still life (fig. 1.6). The angel can be readily found on the headstones of New England graveyards (fig. 1.7).

Such dislocation of colliding aesthetic traditions can even occur within a single drawing — crossing styles and perspectives to fracture all proportion (fig. 1.8). The lines below this image celebrate unity:

> In the morning and the evening, before
> The day brake, and just the sun set, we
> Hear the little Birds sing sweetly among the
> Trees, and we who are better shan [*sic*] the Birds must
> Unite our voices together in offering our prayers
> And praises to God.
>   Done by
>   August 25th 1824   your friend Chinese Alan

FIG. 1.5. Chinese Sugarcane, 1824 Friendship Album for Miss Cherry Stone. *Collection of the Cornwall Historical Society, Cornwall, Connecticut.*

They are set like a poem, capitalized at the beginning of each line, but the lines break in the wrong places. Clearly the poem was not copied from an English source. Is it something Wu Lan had been taught to recite with the other students, their voices united together, so that he is writing here what he has learned to say, but has not seen on the page? Or are these lines an original composition in English? Or an effort to translate into English a poem Wu Lan had known in Cantonese? It is, in any event, the only piece in the album with such strange lineation, just as this picture is the only one with so disproportionate a sense of scale. Wu Lan's bird embodies the issues of focus at stake in these acts of inscription. The birds of the poem are plu-

(a)   (b)

FIG. 1.6. Spread of (a) "A Family Hymn" written by James Terrsell and (b) Flowers by the Southern Window, 1824 Friendship Album for Miss Cherry Stone. *Collection of the Cornwall Historical Society, Cornwall, Connecticut.*

ral, tokens of an indiscriminate and natural faith. The poem urges birdsong as a model for prayer, something we humans should copy, and yet insists that we "are better [t]han the Birds." If human prayer and praises imitate, they also assert their superiority. But the relations between imitation and hierarchy are not simple, and it is a single, individual, enormous bird that dominates this picture. Out of place, out of scale, foreignness perches, hardly fitting in this rural landscape.

"The Tang Dynasty Emperor Lishi Min" (fig. 1.9) is a Han hero cherished by the Cantonese in defiance of the Manchurian Qing dynasty — one mark in this album of the ways in which Wu Lan might have found his native Guangdong itself uncomfortably occupied territory. On the facing page, his friend William A'lum has made a scriptural acrostic of Cherry Stone's name, a conventional and highly pious way to honor her. He squeezed a small poem at the bottom of the page, apparently as an afterthought. It translates: "A poem written clumsily, offered as a memento to [your] charming person." Paola Zamperini, the colleague who translated the album for me, notes that the word she had rendered as "charming" is a bit more sensual than that — more like "foxy."

Interestingly, while William A'lum created this page in the album, and there are pages signed by eleven other students at the school, there is no

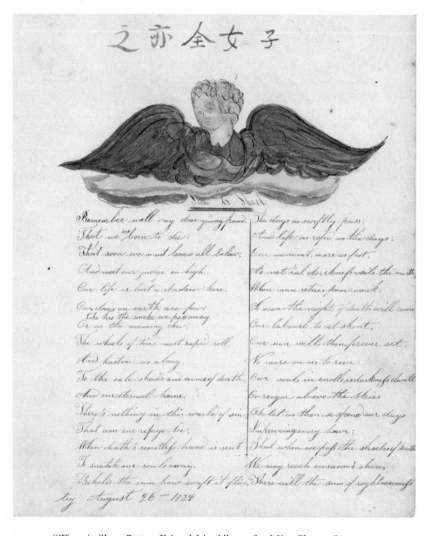

FIG. 1.7. "Time is Short," 1824 Friendship Album for Miss Cherry Stone.
Collection of the Cornwall Historical Society, Cornwall, Connecticut.

page from the third Chinese student: Lieaou A'See, William Botelho. He was still at the school in December 1824, his name appears in the school enrollment lists for that month, and a letter from him bearing that date was published in the religious press. In it he expresses a missionary zeal that must have been greatly pleasing to the school, which in the year following John Ridge's marriage was eager for positive reports to counterbalance those attacks. "I long to finish my education," he writes, "wish to go back,

FIG. 1.8. "In the morning and the evening," 1824 Friendship Album for Miss Cherry Stone. *Collection of the Cornwall Historical Society, Cornwall, Connecticut.*

tell my countrymen how Christ have done so much for my heart, and tell them the great salvation to their immortal souls." Two years later he would write again "a farewell letter": "Now I expect to be going to my native home, I shall remember you all at the throne of grace in my prayers to God" ("Chinese Youth," *American Sunday School Magazine*). Such an evangelical call is, of course, precisely the outcome the school desired. In a another farewell letter, William Botelho reaffirms the school's missionary aims and

FIG. 1.9. Chinese King, 1824 Friendship Album for Miss Cherry Stone. *Collection of the Cornwall Historical Society, Cornwall, Connecticut.*

compares the experiences of Cornwall students brought "from distant lands" to the immigration of Christ himself "who left *his* bright throne and came into this lower world." Even so, he also notes how the school's enrollment had dwindled over the past year and clearly mourned this fall from its earlier expansive ambitions: "the school is now very small; no more than 14 scholars at present. And these 14, we hope, will bear the glad tidings of the gospel to their respective nations" ("Letter from a Native Chinese"). It appears that by the time he wrote this letter, William A'lum and Henry Martyn A'lan had already left the school, but on rather different terms than those Botelho hoped for: A'lum was "dismissed for misconduct" and A'lan "deserted the school through A'lum's influence, [and has] been dismissed" (Starr 145). In August 1825, after her sister Harriett's marriage to Elias Boudinot, Catharine Gold wrote a letter describing the gradual disbanding of the school, in which she notes: "Alun left Cornwall immediately after the affair was settled, he did not wait to see the agents, for fear of being expelled He has gone to England" (Gaul 126). Over the years, school reports reveal many instances of students who had been dismissed "after longer or shorter trial" ("Report of the Prudential Committee" 3); it had been similarly reported, for example, that Wong Arce was "taken into the school for a season; but was dismissed for misconduct" ("Foreign Mission School," *Christian Messenger* 199), but it is also clear that the sense of crises after the Boudinot-Gold marriage produced an unusually severe spate of expulsions and departures.[29] Given William A'lum's cheeky secret poem in this album, it is not hard to imagine him proving a troublesome student in this increasingly anxious atmosphere. The poem may help explain as well why Wu Lan should exclude from this album the one far more pious student at the school capable of reading such inscriptions.

Near the end of the album, Wu Lan created a page he may have found even more important to keep from Lieaou A'See. Here he uses Chinese calligraphy not just to flirt and joke but secretly to court Miss Stone (fig. 1.10). In its efforts at simple realism, the portraiture on these facing pages is highly unusual for the album. The letter above the portrait of Cherry Stone speaks with clear if stumbling affection, but remains structured by the school's goals of Christian conversion: "Dear friend, I write in this Book for you to remember me by. Take my pen to write these few lines for you to open the eyes see that kingdom of the high place. I hope you will remember the me say these few words. I acquainted you few weeks, I can say to so much for you, you much give the new spirit to self. I hope you never forget me." When writing in Chinese, Wu Lan is more eloquent, and less concerned with "spirit" and "that kingdom of the high place": "My constant heart tolerates suffering. I will never forget in my heart of hearts your beautiful face. Today I leave with this image [of you]. One should not hold on to the passage of time, but once the image of the flower is gone [I] will come to you again." He signs here both as "Wu Lan" from "Whampoa Village, Guangdong Province" and with the name of a British missionary that the school had given him. Paola Zamperini tells me that the "you" in the last line of this poem is informal, the pronoun used for an intimate, and that the word she has translated as "flower" is traditionally employed in Chinese poetry to refer to a young beautiful woman. What are we to make of these love verses in Chinese? Did Henry Martyn tell Cherry Stone what they said and yet inscribe them in a form few in Connecticut could decipher? Or are these sentiments kept secret from her as well, words he could record only because he believed they would remain unread? We can tell, in any case, that after finishing this page he closed the book with unusual swiftness. The album contains nineteen pages of watercolor paintings and Wu Lan was careful to allow each of the others to fully dry before closing the book, so that although the shadow of the painting on the verso is often visible through the thin paper, none leave any mark on the facing page. But here the outlines of Wu Lan's head and jacket impress a clear stain that encircles the figure of Miss Stone. The mark testifies both to Wu Lan's reluctance to leave this page lying open for long, and to the fact that when he closed the book, the drawings kiss. Decorously enough, his own

FIG. 1.10. Portraits of Miss Cherry Stone (above) and Henry Martyn (facing page), 1824 Friendship Album for Miss Cherry Stone. *Collection of the Cornwall Historical Society, Cornwall, Connecticut.*

portrait stops at the waist; if he had drawn himself in full length, more than their faces would touch.

The experiences and desires discernible in this manuscript book don't quite fit the more familiar versions of Chinese American history. Nor do they suggest the docility of a domesticating literary history, in which the making of such books serves merely as a tool of institutionally controlled

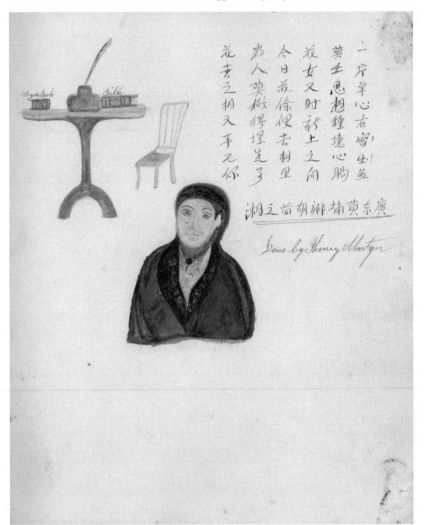

FIG. I.IO (continued).

assimilation. Domestic literary practices do mediate national and race relations, but not in simple or predictable ways. Instead, in Wu Lan's hands the
making of this album, a task that may well have been imposed upon him as
a means of teaching language and faith, offers to other possibilities of expression and gestures toward other possible relations. Inside the back cover
of this book he has written one line in Chinese: "Fate rules human life,

Heaven bestows riches and fortune." Again running oddly horizontal, the character furthest to the left, the Mandarin "tien" or Cantonese "tin" (and here, the first character encountered by an English reader) means sky or heaven. It was the character used by Morrison to name God, the "Heavenly King." So Wu Lan closes his book by provocatively linking this aura of Christian faith with the embrace of a Chinese proverbial fatalism.

This is a stance of wary and complex hybridity, a canny balancing of the claims of two cultures and disparate faiths that Wu Lan retains even after his return to China. A decade later, in 1834, the ABCFM published the following letter from Mr. Williams, a missionary to Canton charged with setting up a mission-press in the city:

> Among the class of natives, called outside shop-men, that is those who are not connected with hong merchants, we have met with one who was formerly a Chinese pupil in the Cornwall school, in Connecticut. He can talk English with considerable freedom, and is employed to some extent in teaching English to the servants in the factories, and has three scholars in our hong. He has been in business here a length of time, how long I do not know, and was found in the capital by a man at Whampoa. We have had some conversation with him on religion, but he appears desirous to avoid the imputation of singularity, and yet to keep his conscience quiet by abstaining from prostration to idols. He is, however, averse to direct conversation, and endeavors to go away as soon as he is questioned closely. He has a verse of the hymn, "When I can read my title clear," etc., written on his fan, and is often showing it; but when asked if he can read his title clear, he replies that his title is different from ours. He supplies us with printing paper, and his case is interesting. May the Lord turn his heart to a knowledge of the truth. His name is Henry Martyn Alan. ("China: Letter from Mr. Williams" 413)

Profiting from his English skills and skittish about his engagement with missionaries, Wu Lan had turned his Cornwall years more to economic than to Christian gains. "Outside shop-men," although legally confined to trade in small items, often arranged a highly profitable underground market in even the central staples of silk and tea. More precariously situated than the established hong merchants, they were also less hedged in by government regulations and taxes—their greater risks often accompanied by higher profits both for them and for their Western trading partners. There is much evidence, in fact, that American merchants, thwarted by the larger-scale and longer-standing relations the British East India Company held with the hong merchants, preferred to deal with outside shop men, and I suspect that Wu Lan, with his breadth of American experience and "considerable freedom" in English, was well positioned to make the most of such preferences.[30] This evidence that Wu Lan was able to turn his U.S. sojourn to his own mercantile advantage suggests the ultimate flexibility of the evangelical tools of copying and conversion.

Mr. Williams's missionary disappointment is palpable in this letter, as is Wu Lan's distrust of such connections and his insistence on reserve. Clearly, if his experiences with American missionaries had given him useful skills, they also carried associations and demands that he had no desire to renew. Here in Canton, Wu Lan refuses even to talk with missionaries, much less fulfill their evangelical hopes; he remains, however, quite willing to sell them paper for their new bookmaking venture. With elegant and ironic symmetry, the young man who may have been the first Chinese person to create a book in the United States later procures the paper for these early Protestant publishing ventures in China. So, too, the delight Wu Lan takes in showing Canton acquaintances the English words of a hymn inscribed on his Chinese fan echoes against the evident pleasure he took in filling his Cornwall album with Chinese characters. In both cases the alien script garnered for Wu Lan an exotic celebrity status, while the precise messages he recorded remain cunningly enigmatic. The full verse of the hymn affirms: "When I can read my title clear to mansions in the skies, / I bid farewell to every fear, and wipe my weeping eyes" (Watts 65).[31] Separation, fear, and tears were surely part of Wu Lan's journey, as was the sense of promise and ownership that suffuses these lines. He learned to read English at Cornwall and he undoubtedly learned to sing Watts's familiar hymn there too. He had informed Mr. Williams "that his title is different from ours." Evidently, Wu Lan also had learned how to write and live in the gap made by that difference.

ACKNOWLEDGMENTS

The album and many of the other materials drawn upon for this essay are part of the Foreign Mission School Collection of the Cornwall Historical Society. My thanks to the society and especially to its curator, Ann Schillinger, for use of these materials and support and assistance of all kinds; to Hilary Wyss for first informing me of the existence of this album; to Paola Zamperini and Weijia Li for their help in translating the Chinese text; to Ginni Chen and Katie Baker for research assistance; and to Marni Sandweiss, Hilary Moss, Tony Lee, Robert G. Lee, and K. Scott Wong for their willingness to discuss this document with me. I also thank audiences at the Asian Americans in New England Conference at the University of Massachusetts

Boston, November 2005, and at the Race and Domesticity Conference at the University of Florida, Gainesville, February 2006, for perceptive comments on earlier versions of this essay, and to the editors of *American Quarterly* who so generously supported the initial publication of this essay.

NOTES

1. This essay is part of a larger project on manuscript books tentatively titled "The Unpublished Republic: Manuscript Cultures of the Mid-Nineteenth-Century United States." Although simultaneously unique and highly conventional texts (both suspicious grounds in historiography), manuscript books can provide a valuable vantage on national life, in all its individual and quotidian variety. Earle Havens provides the best general overview of that genre. Mary Louise Kete's analysis of "Harriet Gould's Book" provides a model of using an idiosyncratic manuscript volume to explore a wide range of far more generalized cultural practices. In "Recasting the Culture of Ephemera," Todd Gernes makes a similar argument for the value of paying attention to such literary ephemera as commonplace books, scrapbooks, and autograph albums as repositories of women's culture. Ellen Gruber Garvey's essays on scrapbooks sketch out a methodology for understanding the literary practice of making one's own book through the cutting and pasting of already printed work, a strategy that has much in common with the construction of friendship albums. As yet, there has not been much scholarship on friendship albums as a genre. Catherine Kelly discusses the ways in which rural New England girls made friendship albums to memorialize school while Erica Armstrong describes how friendship albums served as a tool for the long-term maintenance of social networks among a group of free black women in antebellum Philadelphia. The differences in the attitudes and practices of these two groups of women begin to suggest the range of possibilities enabled by this form of communal bookmaking.

2. The Foreign Mission School Collection of the Cornwall Historical Society contains not only this album made by Henry Martyn A'lan, but also a commonplace book produced by the Hawaiian student Charles Arohekeah from 1822 to 1823, a facsimile of a friendship album made by the Portuguese student John Joseph Loy that includes poems inscribed by both Henry Martyn A'lan and William A'lum, the partial remains of an album for the Greek students Anastasius Karabelles and Photius Kavasales, as well as a more finely bound commonplace book begun by Kavasales in 1825, a year or so after leaving the Foreign Mission School, when he had come to use the last name of his patron and so had become Photius Fisk. The portions of Henry Martyn A'lan's friendship album written in Chinese characters have been translated into English by my colleague Paola Zamperini of the Department of Asian Languages and Civilization, Amherst College.

3. Henry Martyn served as a chaplain under the British East India Company and

as an Anglican missionary to India from 1806; he then moved to Persia in 1811. He died at Tocat, Turkey, the next year. Martyn was a gifted linguist, and during his six short years of missionary service, he translated the New Testament into both Hindi and Farsi. Many of the students at the Cornwall School took on English names that honored either their individual patrons or famous Protestant missionaries.

4. These three Chinese students enrolled in the Monson Academy in 1847, and Yung Wing went on to become the first Chinese student to be educated in an American college, graduating from Yale in 1854. In the 1870s Yung Wing organized the Chinese Educational Mission, which eventually brought 120 Chinese students to schools and colleges in Massachusetts and Connecticut. Amy Nelson Bangerter's Ph.D. dissertation traces the experiences of these late nineteenth-century students, with a focus on their utility in propagating American ideology in a pattern that often echoes the ABCFM's "civilizing" and Christianizing aims for their students. Yung Wing published his own account of these experiences in an autobiography perceptively analyzed by K. Scott Wong and Floyd Cheung (in Cheung and Laurence, eds., *Recovered Legacies*).

5. See my *Dependent States: The Child's Part in Nineteenth-Century American Culture* (210–13).

6. I discuss this more general dynamic in *Dependent States* (202). The African Mission School founded in nearby Hartford, Connecticut, in 1828 is another school of this type. Vincent P. Franklin gives a good overview of these educational initiatives and institutions, as does *History of Schools for the Colored Population*, and especially the work of Hilary J. Moss.

7. A number of sources on the Cornwall School refer to five Chinese students. In my research I have been able to uncover information on four specific students: Wong Arce, Wu Lan (Henry Martyn A'lan), William A'lum, and Lieaou A'See (William Botelho). It is possible that the idea of there being a fifth refers to Joseph Botang Snow. The names John Tredwell and Chop A'See also appear in a variety of Cornwall School lists for 1824–25 in reference to a Chinese student, but it is not entirely clear whether these names refer to the same person, or indeed whether they might be alternative names for William A'lum or Henry Martyn A'lan, who were also enrolled in the school at this time.

8. The Rev. E. W. Dwight's *Memoir of Henry Obookiah* notes that the ship that took Opukahaia from Hawai'i stopped for six months in Canton to sell seal skins and load up with tea, cinnamon, nankeens, and silk (16–18). See also *A Narrative of Five Youth from the Sandwich Islands.*

9. For discussions of the China trade during this period, see James R. Gibson, Valery M. Garrett, Yen Ping Hao, Charles Clarkson Stelle, and Jacques M. Downs. Ernest R. May and John K. Fairbank's *America's China Trade in Historical Perspective* covers a far longer period and emphasizes the relative unimportance of this trade to either economy. Michael Lazich details American Protestant missionaries' opposition to the opium trade from the early 1830s.

10. Walton Look Lai provides an insightful account of this quite different history. As we will see, the class background of the Cornwall students appears to be much higher than that of this later mass migration.

11. Tchen notes the "first documented visit of a Chinese person to New York" as that of "Mr. Winchong," a merchant who came to the city in 1808 in an effort to collect on a bad debt from an American trader (42).

12. In addition to being truncated, the album version of the poem contains a slight variant: its final line is "Twelve nations are likewise seen," which, copying the similar line in the printed version, ends with a comma.

13. These accounts of student fluency describe two Hawaiian students, "William Kummo-oo-tah" and "Honooree." This Cornwall exhibition is also summarized by Starr, who mistakenly believes that the white student learned his Chinese "from a Chinese pupil" (140).

14. Though highly unusual in missionary conduct generally, the sort of literary exchange manifested here also was evoked during precisely these years among British missionaries to China. An 1819 report in a New Haven paper describes the purpose of the Anglo Chinese College that Dr. Morrison hoped to found in Malacca as "the reciprocal cultivation of Chinese and European literature" and notes that Morrison planned to enroll not only American or European students with missionary or mercantile motivations for such study, but also Native youths "who will not be required to profess the Christian religion" ("Anglo Chinese College" 337).

15. See both the album remnants and the commonplace book of Photius (Kavasales) Fisk in the Foreign Mission School Collection of the Cornwall Historical Society. A loose album page in this group also contains a poem written "in Mohawk."

16. Indeed, for the African American community, educational and citizenship rights markedly decreased over the next two decades. Free blacks, who previously had enjoyed the same voting rights as whites, were formally disenfranchised in Connecticut in 1818. In the late 1820s, attempts of a black minister in New Haven to enroll two academically talented black parishioners proved fruitless as "the colleges were all closed against them." In 1831, proposals advanced by New Haven abolitionists to found the first black college in the country were swiftly squelched (see Hillary J. Moss). It is important to remember, of course, that at this time a college education was rarely available to white youth either.

17. In a passage quoted from Opukahaia's own narrative of his life, Dwight's *Memoir of Henry Obookiah* does not describe the young man as crying; instead, he presents Dwight as initiating Opukahaia's religious education: "He [Dwight] then asked me [Opukahaia] if I wished to learn to read and write. I told him that I was. He wished me to come to his room that night and begin to learn" (22). Here all the asking and wishing is on Dwight's side, although Dwight's own narrative voice on the following page describes how Opukahaia's whole being was transformed by his question.

18. Karen Woods Weierman begins her study of interracial marriage with the story of the Foreign Mission School marriages, which she views as a lesson in white racism that demonstrated the limits of missionary inclusion and taught Boudinot and Ridge that "the Cherokee's best chance of survival was separation from white society" (11). Theda Perdue provides a more nuanced account of Boudinot's experience, stressing how his investment in missionary education separated him from the Cherokee people, so that while she recognizes the sincerity of his commitment to preserving the Cherokee Nation, she is skeptical about his ability to recognize Cherokee priorities and desires. Similarly James W. Parins's account of John Ridge's story that introduces his biography of his son stresses Ridge's continuing commitment to the ABCFM and the founding of mission schools even after the removal to New Echota. Theresa Strouth Gaul's collection of letters concerning the Boudinot-Gold marriage and her wonderful introduction emphasize the enormous differences in attitudes toward interracial marriage even within the Gold family, and suggest both the idealism and the realism in Boudinot's actions.

19. The nickname "Cherry" is difficult to match to existing records. Timothy Stone's daughter Eunice was born in 1814 (so she was just ten in 1824); his daughter, Mary, was married in 1834 to Ezekial Birdseye, and, although I have not found a record of Mary's birth, the 1850 census, which lists the names of all household members, marks her as living in her parents' house at age forty-three, so she would have been in her mid-teens at this time. The 1820 census, which only gives the name of the head of household, shows one female from ten to sixteen and another from sixteen to twenty-six living in the Reverend Stone's household. Given her father's close connection to the school, Mary Stone appears to be a good candidate for "Cherry." According to the 1830 census, an Eli Stone was also living in Cornwall during these years; one female under five, one female between ten and fifteen, and two females between fifteen and twenty all lived in his household. His daughter Chrissy was baptized on 22 September 1810, and given the closeness of her name is another good candidate for "Cherry Stone," as is his daughter Lucy Ann, born in 1804. His daughter Jerusha was born on 21 April 1817, and so would have been only seven when this album was made.

20. David Johnson notes the regional dispersion but class specificity of high-level literacy skills. He estimates that in the early nineteenth century only about 5 percent of the adult male population could write fluently (59). See also Ping-Chen Hsuing's account of the range of literacy skills required by different vocational paths in late imperial China (211).

21. The ABCFM prized student letters to their families and often had them published as powerful testimony to the differences between heathen and Christian values. See, for example, Tamoree's letter to his father ("Foreign Mission School," *Panoplist and Missionary Herald*).

22. See Kuo-Tung Anthony Ch'en's *The Insolvency of the Chinese Hong Merchants,*

Garrett's detailed account of the factory system, and Gibson's discussion of the economic pressures on both hong merchants and "outside merchants." Yung Wing, it is interesting to note, gives much attention in his biography to the difficulties of financing his travel and study, explaining how his initial patrons, a combination of American and Scottish merchants, not only arranged passage to the United States and paid for his education at the Monson Academy, but also provided two years of support to his family in Nam Ping to compensate for the loss of his earnings (19–20).

23. In 2005 dollars this unpaid customs duty would amount to almost $18 million in comparable purchasing power (or an even more astronomical $14 billion if calculated in terms of portions of the gross domestic product); these figures are derived using the calculators provided by the Economic History Association at http://eh.net/hmit/compare (accessed June 2006). Thompson was of course bankrupted by the discovery. For articles recounting this scandal, see the *Niles Weekly Register*. Often referred to as "The Tea Case," the scandal spiraled to involve both the Philadelphia Customs House and eventually the secretary of the treasury, who was ultimately sued by other merchants for his extreme measures in commandeering ships and cargo in an effort to recoup some of this lost government revenue ("The Tea Case"). Hao and Gibson both detail the fall in the profitability of the tea trade during the second half of the 1820s. Gibson points out that during this period American tea duties could run as high as 40 percent (100). While Stelle focuses on the smuggling required by the illicit trade in opium, he does emphasize that even in the most general terms, during this period "smuggling was an accepted method of American commercial enterprise" (7).

24. The primary source on Robert Morrison is Mary Morrison's *Memoirs of the Life and Labours of Robert Morrison*. See also Marshall Broomhall, John K. Fairbank, and Suzanne W. Barnett.

25. There is an interesting parallel to this celebration of random words in the reverence shown to even incomplete scraps of writing by the "societies for cherishing writing" formed in eighteenth-century China (Alexander Des Forges 143).

26. See Sánchez-Eppler, 3–40.

27. *San Tzu Ching* begins: "Men at their birth are naturally good. Their natures are much the same; their habits become widely different. If foolishly there is no teaching, the nature will deteriorate. The right way in teaching is to attach the utmost importance to thoroughness" (1–5). See also Limin Bai for a rich discussion of how traditional Chinese education sought to integrate literacy skills, good manners, and moral instruction.

28. Ellen Paul Denker, Rodris Roth, Jean Gordon Lee, and John Kuo Wei Tchen provide rich accounts of the influence of the China trade on American taste.

29. Catharine Gold's letter clearly implies that the present spate of expulsions was unprecedented and unjust; she writes, "I have no doubt that they meant to do what they thought best, but they have dismissed some of the best scholars" (Gaul 126).

30. See Garrett's *Heaven is High* (73–96) and Gibson's *Otter Skins, Boston Ships, and China Goods* (88–98).
31. Interestingly this hymn would develop a powerful place in the African American community and the antislavery movement; it is, for example, what Simon Legree hears Uncle Tom sing after he is beaten.

WORKS CITED

A'lan, Henry Martyn (Wu Lan). Friendship album for Miss Cherry Stone. 1824. Foreign Mission School Collection of the Cornwall Historical Society, Cornwall, Connecticut.

"American Board of Commissioners for Foreign Missions." *Panoplist and Missionary Magazine*, October 1816, 444–46.

"Anglo Chinese College." *Religious Intelligencer*, 30 October 1819, 337.

Armstrong, Erica. "A Mental and Moral Feast: Reading, Writing, and Sentimentality in Black Philadelphia," *Journal of Women's History* 16 (Winter 2004): 78–201.

Bai, Limin. *Shaping the Ideal Child: Children and Their Primers in Late Imperial China*. Hong Kong: Chinese University Press, 2005.

Bangerter, Amy Nelson. "Chinese Youth and American Educational Institutions, 1850–1881." Ph.D. diss., George Washington University, 2005.

Barnett, Suzanne W. "Silent Evangelism: Presbyterians and the Mission Press in China, 1807–1860." *Journal of Presbyterian History* 49 (Winter 1971): 287–302.

Bhabha, Homi K. "Of Mimicry and Man: The Ambivalence of Colonial Discourse." In *The Location of Culture*. New York: Routledge, 1994.

Broomhall, Marshall. *Robert Morrison: A Master-Builder*. New York: Student Christian Movement, 1924.

Chao Opera. "A Girl Named Jin Hua (*Jin Hua Nu*)." July 2006. http://www.shme .com/culture/opera/chao.htm.

Ch'en, Kuo-Tung Anthony. *The Insolvency of the Chinese Hong Merchants, 1760–1843*. Taipei: Institute of Economics, Academia Sinica, 1990.

Cheung, Floyd. "Early Chinese American Autobiography: Reconsidering the Works of Yan Phou Lee and Yung Wing." In *Recovered Legacies: Authority and Identity in Early Asian American Literature*, edited by Floyd Cheung and Keith Laurence, 24–41. Philadelphia: Temple University Press, 2005.

"China Canton." *Christian Repository*, 30 May 1823, 238.

"China: Letter from Mr. Williams, Dated December 20, 1834." *Missionary Herald*, November 1835, 412-13.

"Chinese Youth." *Boston Recorder*, 21 June 1823, 99.

"Chinese Youth." *Christian Repository*, 4 July 1823, 259. Reprinted in *The Guardian, or Youth's Religious Instructor*, July 1823, 145–46, and *The Religious Miscellany*, 11 July 1823, 389–90.

"Chinese Youth." *Christian Repository*, 6 February 1824, 383.

"Chinese Youth." *Religious Intelligencer*, 10 July 1824, 94.

"Chinese Youth." *American Sunday School Magazine*, December 1826, 382–83.

Connecticut Mirror. Untitled article, 9 June 1823, 3.

Denker, Ellen Paul. *After the Chinese Taste: China's Influence in America, 1730–1930.* Salem, Mass.: Peabody Museum, 1985.

Des Forges, Alexander. "Burning with Reverence: The Economics and Aesthetics of Words in Qing (1644–1911) China." *PMLA* 121 (January 2006): 139–55.

Downs, Jacques M. "American Merchants and the China Opium Trade, 1800–1840." *Business History Review* 17 (Winter 1968): 418–42.

Dwight, Rev. E. W. *Memoir of Henry Obookiah: A Native of the Sandwich Islands who Died at Cornwall, Connecticut, February 17, 1818, Aged 26.* New York: American Tract Society, n.d.

Fairbank, John K., ed. *The Missionary Enterprise in China and America.* Cambridge, Mass.: Harvard University Press, 1974.

Farmers' Cabinet. Untitled article, 29 November 1823, 1.

"Foreign Mission School." *Christian Messenger*, 30 January 1819, 198–201.

"Foreign Mission School." *Panoplist and Missionary Herald*, December 1818, 562–65.

"Foreign Mission School." *Religious Intelligencer*, 13 December 1823, 445.

"The Foreign Mission School." June 1825. A pamphlet in the Foreign Mission School Collection of the Cornwall Historical Society.

"Foreign Mission School: Letter of A'See, a Chinese Youth." *Missionary Herald*, December 1824, 378–90. Reprinted in the *Religious Intelligencer*, 18 December 1824, 461–62, and as "A'See, a Chinese Youth." *Latter Day Luminary*, February 1825, 57–59.

Franklin, Vincent P. "Education for Colonization: Attempts to Educate Free Blacks in the United States for Emigration to Africa, 1823–1833." *Journal of Negro Education* 43 (Winter 1974): 91–103.

Garrett, Valery M. *Heaven Is High, the Emperor Far Away: Merchants and Mandarins in Old Canton.* New York: Oxford University Press, 2002.

Garvey, Ellen Gruber. "Anonymity, Authorship, and Recirculation: A Civil War Episode." *Book History* 9 (2006): 159–78.

———. "Scissoring and Scrapbooks: Nineteenth-Century Reading, Remaking, and Recirculating." In *New Media: 1740–1915*, edited by Lisa Gitelman and Geoff Pingree, 206–27. Cambridge, Mass.: MIT Press, 2003.

Gaul, Theresa Strouth. *To Marry an Indian: The Marriage of Harriett Gold and Elias Boudinot in Letters, 1823–1839.* Chapel Hill: University of North Carolina Press, 2005.

Gernes, Todd. "Recasting the Culture of Ephemera." In *Popular Literacy: Studies in Cultural Practices and Poetics*, edited by John Trimbur, 107–27. Pittsburgh, Pa.: University of Pittsburgh Press, 2001.

Gibson, James R. *Otter Skins, Boston Ships, and China Goods: The Maritime Fur Trade of the Northwest Coast, 1785–1841.* Seattle: University of Washington Press, 1992.

Hao, Yen Ping. *The Commercial Revolution in Nineteenth-Century China: The Rise of*

Sino-Western Mercantile Capitalism. Berkeley and Los Angeles: University of California Press, 1986.

Harvey, Joseph. *The Banner of Christ Set Up*. New Haven, Conn.: Nathan Whiting, 1819.

Havens, Earle. *Commonplace Books: A History of Manuscripts and Printed Books from Antiquity to the Twentieth Century*. New Haven, Conn.: Beinecke Rare Book and Manuscript Library, 2001.

"Heathen Youth." *Religious Remembrancer*, 31 May 1823, 164.

History of Schools for the Colored Population. 1871. New York: Arno Press, 1969.

Hsuing, Ping-Chen. *A Tender Voyage: Children and Childhood in Late Imperial China*. Stanford, Calif.: Stanford University Press, 2005.

Johnson, David. "Communication, Class, and Consciousness in Late Imperial China." In *Popular Culture in Late Imperial China*, edited by David Johnson, Andrew J. Nathan, and Evelyn S. Rawski, 34–72. Berkeley and Los Angeles: University of California Press, 1985.

"A Journey in New-England." *Evangelical and Literary Magazine*, September 1822, 463–74.

Kellogg, L. and F. Account book for Cornwall General Store. 1823. Cornwall Historical Society.

Kelly, Catherine. *In the New England Fashion: Reshaping Women's Lives in the Nineteenth Century*. Ithaca, N.Y.: Cornell University Press, 1999.

Kete, Mary Louise. *Sentimental Collaborations: Mourning and Middle-Class Identity in Nineteenth-Century America*. Durham, N.C.: Duke University Press, 2000.

Lai, Walton Look. *Indentured Labor, Caribbean Sugar: Chinese and Indian Migrants to the British West Indies, 1838–1918*. Baltimore: Johns Hopkins University Press, 1993.

Lazich, Michael. "American Missionaries and the Opium Trade in Nineteenth-Century China." *Journal of World History* 17 (Spring 2006): 197–223.

Lee, Rev. Chauncey. "Foreign Mission School." *Evangelical Recorder*, 11 July 1818, 264.

Lee, Jean Gordon. *Philadelphians and the China Trade, 1784–1844*. Philadelphia: Philadelphia Museum of Art, 1984.

Lee, Robert G. *Orientals: Asian Americans in Popular Culture*. Philadelphia: Temple University Press, 1999.

"Letter from a Native Chinese." *Religious Intelligencer*, 14 January 1826, 521. Reprinted in *Connecticut Courant*, 17 January 1826, 1.

Martyn, Henry. *Journal and Letters of the Rev. Henry Martyn*. Edited by the Rev. S. Wilberforce. New York: M. W. Dodd, 1851.

May, Ernest R. and John K. Fairbank, eds. *America's China Trade in Historical Perspective: The Chinese and American Performance*. Cambridge, Mass.: Harvard University Press, 1986.

Middlesex Gazette. Untitled article, 26 June 1823, 3.

"Miscellany Paragraphs." *Port-Folio*, January 1873, 83.

"Missionary School and Heathen Youths." *Reformer*, 1 March 1824, 69–71.

Morrison, Mary. *Memoirs of the Life and Labours of Robert Morrison*. London: n.p., 1839.

Moss, Hilary J. "Opportunity and Opposition: The African American Struggle for Education in New Haven, Baltimore and Boston, 1825–1855." Ph.D. diss. Brandeis University, 2004.

Muñoz, José. *Disidentifications: Queers of Color and the Performance of Politics*. Minneapolis: University of Minnesota Press, 1999.

A Narrative of Five Youth from the Sandwich Islands; viz. Obookiah, Hopoo, Tennooe, Honoore, and Prince Tamoree, Now Receiving an Education in this Country. New York: J. Seymour, 1816.

Niles Weekly Register. 23 December 1826, 260, and 24 December 1825, 258.

Panoplist and Missionary Magazine. Untitled article, February 1817, 77–81.

Parins, James W. *John Rollin Ridge: His Life and Works*. Lincoln: University of Nebraska Press, 1991.

Perdue, Theda. *Cherokee Editor: The Writings of Elias Boudinot*. Athens: University of Georgia Press, 1996.

Report of the Proceedings at the Formation of the African Education Society: Instituted at Washington, December 28, 1829. Washington, D.C.: James C. Dunn, Georgetown, D.C., 1830.

"Report of the Prudential Committee." *Missionary Herald*, January 1821, 2–13.

Roth, Rodris. "Tea Drinking in Eighteenth-Century America: Its Etiquette and Equipage." In *Material Life in America, 1600–1800*, edited by Robert Blair St. George, 439–63. Boston: Northeastern University Press, 1988.

San Tzu Ching: Elementary Chinese. Translated by Herbert A. Giles. New York: Frederick Ungar, 1963.

Sánchez-Eppler, Karen. *Dependent States: The Child's Part in Nineteenth-Century American Culture*. Chicago: University of Chicago Press, 2005.

"School for Heathen Youth." *Christian Herald*, 12 October 1816, 38–39.

Starr, Edward C. *A History of Cornwall, Connecticut: A Typical New England Town*. 1926. Torrington, Conn.: Rainbow Press, 1982.

Stelle, Charles Clarkson. *Americans and the China Opium Trade in the Nineteenth Century*. New York: Arno Press, 1981.

Stone, Rev. Timothy. *Ecclesiastical History of the Church of Cornwall*. Connecticut: n.p., 1840.

Takaki, Ronald. *A Different Mirror: A History of Multicultural America*. Boston: Little, Brown, 1993.

Tchen, John Kuo Wei. *New York Before Chinatown: Orientalism and the Shaping of American Culture, 1776–1882*. Baltimore: Johns Hopkins University Press, 1999.

"The Tea Case." *New York Telescope*, 29 March 1828, 176.

Watts, Isaac. *Hymns and Spiritual Songs: In Three Books*. Book 2. Boston: Lincoln and Edmunds, 1816.

Weierman, Karen Woods. *One Nation, One Blood: Interracial Marriage in American*

Fiction, Scandal, and Law, 1820–1870. Amherst: University of Massachusetts Press, 2005.

Wing, Yung. *My Life in China and America*. New York: Holt, 1909.

Wong, Kevin Scott. "The Transformation of Culture: Three Chinese Views of America." *American Quarterly* 48, no. 2 (Spring 1996): 201–32.

Yin, Xiao-huang. *Chinese American Literature since the 1850s*. Urbana: University of Illinois Press, 2000.

2

The New Englandization of Yung Wing

Family, Nation, Region

AMY BANGERTER

The story of Yung Wing is, in many ways, a story of New England.[1] Although Yung was not born in New England, while still a youth in China he began studying in a well-known mission school under the tutelage of a New England minister, the Reverend Samuel Robbins Brown. Yung returned with Brown to the United States in 1847; the half-a-lifetime that he resided in America, including his most formative years, was spent exclusively in New England. He graduated from Yale College in 1854, and while at Yale he became a naturalized American citizen. In 1872, Yung commenced work on a lifelong dream he had envisioned while still a student at Yale: the creation of the Chinese Educational Mission. This mission was a revolutionary visiting scholars program in which 120 Chinese youth were to receive "American" educations, under Yung's supervision, in schools located throughout the New England Connecticut valley area. In 1875, Yung married Mary Kellogg, a New Englander from a well-established family. She bore two sons who were both born and raised in New England. Yung eventually died in Hartford, Connecticut, in the fall of 1912.

Owing to his geographical and ideological connections to New England, Yung's experience as a Chinese pioneer in America must be examined through the lens of regionalism. Such a focus on region is also important because of the unique persistence of New Englanders in creating and maintaining their sense of regional identity, as argued persuasively by scholar Joseph Conforti. By focusing on regionality, Conforti questions traditional observations of "Americanization" as a linear movement toward a cohesive identity; however, his connection between regionality and the Asian American experience remains elusive. Substantive reference to an Asian/Asian American presence in New England is noticeably absent, especially during discussions of labor strikes in shoe factories and the demographics of larger

New England towns. Even in his treatment of New Englanders — such as Harriet Wilson and others — who worked to disrupt the "grand narrative" of New England's history, Conforti does not acknowledge a voice like Yung's whose work and writings to abolish the Chinese coolie trade as an American continental practice are equally significant. In another recent publication focusing on New England — Dane Morrison and Nancy Schultz's collection *Salem: Place, Myth, and Memory* — Morrison's essay "Salem as Citizen of the World" focuses on how the architecture of Salem was affected by the town's early trading relationship with China. While this revisionist essay questions the traditionally accepted directional flow of influence (from America to China), there is no focused discussion in the collection on the life of the Chinese in Salem, an absence that limits the perception of the Chinese sphere of influence to historical curiosities or antiquated artifacts.

Yung's life and writings have received more notice from scholars of Asian American studies than from New England regional specialists. Yung has been the subject of a number of articles and a few dissertations and theses, many of which have presented much needed information and analysis about Yung's life.[2] Much of the critical analysis of Yung's writings, particularly of his autobiography *My Life in China and America*, has been situated within a larger discourse about political resistance to white hegemony. Most notable are essays by Floyd Cheung, Frank Chin, Amy Ling, and K. Scott Wong. Wong reads Yung as a kind of "cultural broker" who, while resistant to white hegemony, was also busy defending his presence in America. Cheung's work is, is in part, a critique of works by Amy Ling and Frank Chin whose influential perspectives, as Cheung writes, fault Yung for "not being masculine enough" to resist and conversely for "being too masculine" to resist (78).[3] Cheung himself reads Yung's work as a more nuanced strategy of another kind of resistance.

Even with as nuanced a reading as Cheung's, these works remain fixed within a dichotomy. The danger of such a dichotomy between resistance on the one hand and immigrant naïveté or passivity on the other is that it tends to oversimplify conflicting loyalties and complicated identity markers. An examination of regional institutions and attitudes that influenced Yung reveals more clearly that his complicated choices were usually related to balancing personal responsibilities, difficult allegiances, and social ambitions, and less about political resistance. For example, Yung spent the greater part of his life engrossed in the development of the Chinese Educational Mission, a project aimed at promoting China's ability and right to protect itself from Western imperialists through the "Americanization" of a number of Chinese youth.[4] The project's seemingly contradictory facets and its conception at Yale are examples of the complex relationship among Yung's education in New England, his own "Americanization," and his desire to serve China.

While Asian American scholars have been cognizant of Yung's conflicting loyalties, a few, such as Edmund Worthy, have even suggested that such conflicts began at Yale. Nonetheless, a thorough discussion of how Yale as a New England institution may have affected, exacerbated, or even created these conflicts has not yet materialized. This chapter is just such a discussion. I argue that Yung's conflicts of loyalty arose in part because of his substantial ties to New England (while at Yale and throughout his life) and also because of the unique persistence of New Englanders in creating and maintaining their sense of regional identity. New England's own brand of colonialism (including the heritage bequeathed to it from imperialists such as Elihu Yale), its need to quell the derogatory images of "commercial shrewdness" and "restless mobility" that came to characterize the Yankee during this time, and the new reliance upon "physical distinctiveness" that began to develop while Yung was at Yale—all had a powerful effect on Yung's personal life (Conforti 151, 114). Such regional factors negatively affected Yung's ties to his family in China, nourished his claim to American citizenship while simultaneously rejecting his claim to a New England ethnicity, and more broadly informed his concept of what an acceptable American was.

Conflicts of Family

Prior to Yung's studies at Yale, the Western education he received both in China and America had a positive effect on his relationship with his family through the financial sustenance it provided them. In his autobiography, Yung surmises that his unusual enrollment at age seven in Mrs. Gutzlaff's School, a German Protestant mission school in Macao, was financially motivated. His father recognized that foreign trade with China was "just beginning to grow" (2–3) and likely hoped that Yung's knowledge of English would secure his own fortune in the business world as well as improve the financial security and social status of his entire family. Unfortunately, the breakup of the mission school and the death of Yung's father in the fall of 1840 forced Yung to give up his language studies in order to hawk candy and glean rice to help support the family. Despite this blow to his formal education, Yung's knowledge of English still came to his financial rescue on one occasion when he exchanged it for several sheaves of rice (9–10).

Shortly after this incident, Yung was hired by a priest in Macao for his ability to read numerals in English. Later, he was discovered by Dr. Benjamin Hobson, a medical missionary who placed him in the Morrison Education Society School (a British mission school in Canton) under the charge of the Reverend Samuel Brown.

Yung's mother consented to his enrollment despite some reluctance (most likely because of the family's reliance on Yung's income). Yung's placement in the Morrison School, however, was to become a financial blessing for his family. At the Reverend Brown's invitation, Yung traveled with him to the United States in 1847 to study for two years at Monson Academy in Massachusetts. Yung records that thanks to Brown's influence, the Hong Kong benefactors of this educational project "bore a conspicuous part in defraying our expenses while in America, besides providing for the support of our aged parents" (20).[5] Such an opportunity for Yung exemplifies the complicated ways in which even his earliest Western education simultaneously heightened his sense of responsibility for providing for his family, particularly his widowed mother, while diminishing his physical and emotional attachment to them.

With Yung's decision to attend Yale College after completing two years at Monson, however, the pursuance of his Western education became a great financial burden and a source of conflict between himself and his family. Yung was unable to finance his Yale education independently or provide for his family, and his absence at the time of his older brother's death and mother's concurrent illness further exacerbated familial tension. The expectations Yung's mother placed upon his education at Yale were another source of conflict. Upon Yung's return to China shortly after his graduation, he tried to explain the importance of his Yale degree to his mother by comparing it to a Chinese title of similar status. When she inquired how much money his American education had conferred on him, as in the Chinese manner, Yung gave the following reply:

> I said it did not confer any money at once, but it enabled one to make money quicker and easier than one can who has not been educated; that it gave one greater influence and power among men and if he built on his college education, he would be more likely to become the leader of men. . . . I told her my college education was worth more to me than money, and that I was confident of making plenty of money. (50)

It is unclear whether Yung's statement convinced his mother of the worth of his education. What seems clear, however, is the dichotomy in Yung's own mind between the Chinese system of titles and monetary rewards that were directly tied to education and his view of education as a means to a more virtuous end — a view he would have become familiar with while studying at Yale College. The New Haven Scholars, a group of influential educators at Yale, advocated the philosophy that the primary responsibility of Yale's educated elite was to become a positive moral influence upon their communities.[6] As such, their thoughts and ambitions should focus on more lofty goals than mere financial gain. Indeed, in formal statements such as "The Yale Report of 1828,"[7] the college constructs a dichotomy between the marketable skill-set developed through professional studies and the foundation of such studies, a foundation steeped in the principles of virtue and order. Furthermore, the report clearly states that it has no interest in training its graduates in such professional studies.

It is no coincidence that Yale's espousal of this philosophy paralleled the rise of the "commercial shrewdness" that began to define the Yankee character of antebellum America.

The Yankee, typically, was on the move and on the make. The Yankee signaled a real and imagined decline in classical republicanism whose emphasis on order, restraint, deference, and the public good was increasingly supplanted by the ethos of a dynamic market economy that redefined virtue in more individualistic and opportunistic terms as the commoner's natural ability (a natural shrewdness) to seize the main chance, get ahead, and outdo one's competitors and social superiors. (Conforti 151)

While New Englanders were anxious to distance themselves from the stereotypical "sharpers" and peddlers that tainted their regional reputation, the dependence of New England's idyllic, orderly, central village on a successful, dynamic market economy complicated Yale's attitudes toward such "commercial shrewdness" (Conforti 157). New Englanders would have welcomed economic progress as long as it did not "erode civic virtue" (Conforti 187). In other words, as New England's leading cultural institution, Yale would have been less interested in quelling ideas of "commercial shrewdness" in its students and more interested in redefining such shrewdness as virtuous, industrious enterprise.

Yung's dream that his Western education could bring about political change or rejuvenation for China illustrates his conviction that his education is "worth more than money." In trying to reconcile the utilitarianism of his American education with what he described as China's "lamentable condition," Yung comes to the following conclusion:

Before the close of my last year in college I had already sketched out what I should do.[8] I was determined that the rising generation of China should enjoy the same educational advantages that I had enjoyed; that through western education China might be regenerated, become enlightened and powerful. . . . Towards such a goal, I directed all my mental resources and energy. Through thick and thin, and the vicissitudes of a checkered life from 1854 to 1872, I labored and waited for its consummation. (41)

Yung's need to illustrate that his education is worth more than money leads him to the discovery of a truly noble goal: the regeneration of China. In other places in his autobiography, Yung portrays some seemingly unrelated life experiences (various business ventures and a post in the Chinese government) as methodical choices that would ultimately lead to the consummation of his goal. During his first return trip to China after graduating from Yale, Yung mastered the Chinese language, an act he later couched in his autobiography as a preliminary step toward achieving his life's ambition of establishing an educational mission to the United States (57). He then records that he "at once set to work to find a position in which [he] could not only support [himself] and [his] mother, but also form a plan for working out [his] ideas of reform in China" (58). Yung's need to justify the provision of his own family within the framework of a larger, more noble goal and his insistence that he find a professional position that would be vital to the carrying out of China's reformation are other evidences of his need to imbue his life's experiences with a purpose that seems befitting a Yale graduate.

While Yung felt the need to justify his successful business ventures, there were some jobs that he refused to accept. When Yung was offered a position in a firm as comprador on his first trip to China, he immediately refused the position because, as he writes, "I could not think of bringing discredit to my Alma Mater. . . . What would the college and my class-mates think of me, if they should hear that I was a comprador — the head servant of servants in an English establishment?" (77). Yung's revulsion to such servitude did not merely stem from the concept of virtuous enterprise that he had learned at Yale, however. Indeed, such revulsion also may have stemmed from Yung's status as a member of the Yale collegiate family and as a metaphorical son of imperialist Elihu Yale.

After his father's death, Yung's need for a father figure was filled by the Reverend Brown at the Morrison School and then by Principal Hammond at Monson Academy. Even though Yung was discouraged by both men from pursuing education after his graduation from Monson Academy, it was no coincidence that Yung chose to attend Yale College, the alma mater of the two men who had played such a fatherly role in his life. The sense of family that Yale bestowed upon its sons held deep roots at Yale and in New England society at large. "The Yale Report of 1828" makes it clear that the relationship between the faculty and the students was akin to a parent-son relationship.[9] The report suggests that a "substitute be provided for *parental superintendence*," and that such substitution "should approach as near to the character of parental control as the circumstances of the case will admit" (quoted in Hofstadter and Smith 280). Because the structure and government of college life at Yale was viewed as a substitution for the students' own families, on some level Yung became part of a new family. Yale students theoretically became more than a surrogate family of their own: as Gauri Viswanathan suggests, they also belonged to another surrogate family, as symbolic sons to the childless Elihu Yale. This relationship, a form of affiliation that began with the naming of the college after Yale, attempts to re-create a filial relationship through culture rather than through nature (89–90).[10] It is an example, Viswanathan explains, of material capital accumulated (often illegally) in a global market and then reinvested in another market, the market of cultural capital (90). Instead of Elihu Yale leaving his wealth to his biological heirs, he leaves it to a cultural institution through the bonds of affiliation; inasmuch as these institutions came to "[replicate] the functions of the family in disseminating values, principle, and dogma," the substitution of culture for nature was made logical and seamless (90).

But such a substitution was not so seamless for Yung as it might have been for others of his peers. Although as a Yalie Yung stood to benefit tremendously from Elihu Yale's colonial wealth, as a person of Chinese descent, he represented those who were thus abused so that such wealth could be made and bestowed upon an institution.[11] Through the connection between imperialist material capital and the foundation of Western institutions such as Yale College, even if Yung desired to become Elihu Yale's heir through affiliation, his claim to such an identity would be paradoxical at best. How could he simultaneously be both colonized as a person of Chinese descent and be the heir to a Western colonizer?

It was not only Elihu Yale's own history of imperialism, but also the imperialistic attitudes embraced by the earliest New Englanders that exacerbated such an impossible identity for Yung. By viewing themselves less as pioneers trying to claim an American heritage and more as British imperialists who would win the New World for the British Empire, New Englanders had been vested in imperialistic attitudes from the very beginning.[12] In the century that followed, these attitudes continued to play a vital role in the development of New England's regional identity. For example, just a few short decades before Yung arrived at Yale, former Yale president Timothy Dwight penned the following paean to New England imperialism:

> Soon shall thy sons across the mainland roam;
> And claim, on far Pacific shores, their home;
> Their rule, religion, manners, arts convey,
> And spread their freedom to the Asian sea."
> (quoted in Conforti 96)

Just as the early Puritans had acted more as British colonialists than emerging American citizens, their progeny dreamed of extending New England beyond the Western boundaries of the United States and on to China. Thus, Yung's Chinese ancestry and his status as a Chinese national made his identity as a Western imperialist impossible. Yung's acceptance of an identity as one of Yale's descendants actually furthered his own colonization and therefore increased the inequity between himself and his peers at Yale. While becoming a Yalie estranged him from his family in China, his race and nationality estranged him from his adoptive family at Yale.

Conflicts of Nation

One way Yung could have constructed himself as an heir and not a servant would have been by becoming a national citizen of a Western power. By becoming an heir to the American family, he could justify his identity as an heir to the Yale family. Yung became a naturalized American citizen in New Haven on 30 October 1852, while still a student at Yale. Wong posits that Yung's naturalization "spoke strongly of his changing self-perception: he was no longer simply a Chinese student in America; he was formally staking his claim as a Chinese American" (22). However, even as early as the mid-eighteenth century, persons of Asian descent, especially Chinese descent, had already been racialized in American common knowledge as "non-white" and therefore considered by many to be ineligible for citizenship. Although such ideas were not legally codified until 1882 with the passage of the Chinese Exclusion Act, Yung's application for citizenship would have been tenuous at best. It was his status as a student at Yale College and his presence in New England that complicated his racial categorization as "non-white," thus facilitating his naturalization.

Ian Lopez argues that racial categorizations become imbued with meaning only in relation to other aspects of a person's identity: "Whether one is

White therefore depends in part on other elements of identity — for example, on whether one is wealthy or poor, Protestant or Muslim, male or female — just as these aspects of identity are given shape and significance by whether or not one is White" (xiii). In Yung's case, his status as a student at an American college made him appear more white than other persons of Chinese descent — mainly laborers and merchants — who may have simultaneously been denied naturalization. In particular, his status as a student at Yale, a national institution that was, at the time, the largest college in the country, lent him even greater respectability. Paul Harris notes that at the time of Yung's matriculation, Yale students were viewed as an "educated elite" and the "cream of American civilization" (95). To deny citizenship to one of the "cream of American civilization" would have been absurd. Yung's application for naturalization in a more liberal-minded state and more racially sympathetic Northern city — one experiencing a stimulating economic upturn at midcentury — and his attendance at an institution so closely linked to the State of Connecticut may have also facilitated his bid for citizenship.[13]

The classical education Yung received at Yale also seemed to provide him with cultural parity as an American. Greek and Latin dominated the curriculum of higher learning around the country almost from the founding of American colleges until the late nineteenth century. As Caroline Winterer suggests, even though the first twenty-five colleges established in America before 1800 were "geographically and religiously diverse, they were remarkably uniform in their classical curriculum and their classically based admission requirements" (12). "The Yale Report of 1828" vehemently defended the classical curriculum; even when new courses were added, there were no reductions in the traditional subjects such as Latin and Greek.[14] Indeed, during Yung's years at Yale, the curriculum was slightly revised so that less emphasis was placed on the languages of ancient Greece and Rome and more emphasis placed on their respective cultures. Winterer suggests that such a move from "words to worlds" was "a process of becoming Greek, literally of self-transformation through a historicized encounter with the classical past. 'We are all Greeks,' Percy Bysshe Shelley (1792–1822) had declared in 1821, a manifesto that echoed in American classrooms for the remainder of the nineteenth century" (78). Such an ideological shift would have allowed Yung, regardless of his personal background, to lay legitimate claim to a cultural heritage that constructed its roots within classical Greek and Roman civilizations.

The collegiate classical system reached beyond the walls of the college campus and permeated numerous areas of American life. By so doing, the study of these classical cultures provided a way in which American life itself could take on a more homogenized identity. Consequently, those students who studied and embraced classicism also became part of an imagined culturally homogenous American society. Because of his status as a college student, Yung would have become connected to other college students regardless of race and background by adoption into the Greek civilization through study and knowledge of that civilization, thereby connecting himself to American society writ large. This connection becomes apparent in Yung's autobiography, where he uses his classical education as a marker of his insider status as a member of American society. In one instance, Yung compares his trip to buy some yellow silk in the Ho-Yung district to Jason's search for the Golden Fleece (89). Through references such as this, Yung illustrates the connection between himself and his white American readership via his knowledge of Greek and Roman culture. Yung's education at Yale facilitated his bid for citizenship and offered him inclusion within a shared "Western" cultural heritage, thus building within Yung a loyalty to this shared past and a heightened expectation for future privileges.

Conflicts at Yale

While Yung's attendance at Yale College seemed to ensure his place in an imagined cohesive American society, his untraditional preparation and class status, combined with Yale's attempts to maintain its own ideals, kept him aloof on campus. In his history of Yale University, Brooks Mather Kelley points out that by the late 1700s, Yale's dedication to more democratic ideals on campus became apparent with the alphabetical ordering of students replacing the "special order based in varying degrees at different times on appraisals of family position, intellectual promise, and parental relationship to the college" (75).[15] By the mid-1800s, according to Kelley, Yale also prided itself on its democratic nature by claiming students were admitted to the institution regardless of their financial means or their parentage; proposals to raise student tuition were often rejected. During Yung's matriculation, however, student tuition was raised and it would be soon again. Because of the recurrence of such tuition raises, Yale's democracy was brought into question, and the institution was "increasingly criticized as a rich man's college, a place where it was becoming difficult for the poor man to work his way through" (309). In order to combat this and other criticisms from the start, states Kelley, Yale President Theodore Woolsey — inaugurated only four years before Yung's entrance — made "sound scholarship" the central theme of his presidency: "He promoted competitive scholarships, even funding some himself. He published the names of winners of prizes and scholarships in the college catalogue. He began, in 1848, to list the academic rank of graduating seniors in the commencement program" (174). In 1851, Woolsey also instituted a much more rigorous system of testing that included oral examinations and two written biennial examinations (Kelley 174).

Woolsey's emphasis on academic achievement rather than personal connections had both positive and negative effects on Yung's educational and social life at Yale. While such an emphasis allowed him, as one of the poorer and less connected students, more chances for social parity based on his own achievement, higher academic standards also made that achievement much more difficult due to the many obstacles unique to Yung's educational experience: studying in a second language, attending school in a foreign country, receiving untraditional preparatory schooling, suffering extended separation from family, and making ends meet without significant financial support. Test scores and grades indicate that Yung's academic performance was mediocre, even poor on occasion. In a letter to Samuel Wells Williams dated 25 December 1850, Yung attributes his poor marks to the "disparity in scholarship" and the "unequal grounds of contest" stemming from a lack of preparation in his unusual precollegiate schooling (quoted in Worthy 269). In his autobiography, Yung also admits that his recitations in class proved to himself as well as to his classmates that his preparation had been deficient (37). His fellow students could not have helped noticing such a discrepancy in classroom performance, and some may have consequently classed Yung as an unequal scholar.[16]

While his scholarship often placed him on "unequal grounds of contest" with his schoolmates, his financial struggles also limited the amount of free time Yung could spend with classmates, either intimately or as part of organized extracurricular activities. Unfortunately, Yung's lack of time for college life outside the classroom corresponded to a rise in its general importance. As Helen Horowitz argues, during much of the 1800s college life became an important aspect of the educational experience. Those students who, for whatever reason, chose not to participate in extracurricular activities ran the risk of being seen as selfish. Yung did find time to participate in at least one extracurricular club: he was a member of the Brothers of Unity literary society. Such male youth groups helped students develop personal bonds with each other, and Yung reports that his status as librarian for the Brothers allowed him to be known by more of the students on campus.[17] While membership in literary or debating societies was evidence of embracing college life, it wasn't necessarily a sign of elite social distinction inasmuch as "all undergraduates were members of either Linonia or Brothers," the two literary clubs on campus at midcentury (Kelley 107). Indeed, the age of the literary society was already waning by the time Yung reached Yale, partly due to the growth of the college and partly due to the rise of the fraternity.

In almost direct contrast to the aims of the literary club, the emergence of the fraternal system actually highlighted disparities among students.[18] The rise of the fraternity highlighted the disparity between Yung and most of his fellow Yalies in both economic and psychological ways. The cost of fraternal membership at Yale made it impossible for Yung to join, and because of his desperate financial situation, he found himself in the employ of at least one fraternity on campus, buying groceries and waiting tables for their parties.[19] Yung's employment at the college — often doing work traditionally reserved for women — and his reliance upon a benevolent ladies' society in Georgia for monetary assistance were two factors that would have led to a greater scrutiny of his masculinity and therefore a greater struggle to maintain his sense of brotherhood with his fellow students.[20] An examination of Yung's boyhood experiences and the culture of masculinity at Yale reveals the ways in which he was forced to battle stereotypes of Chinese men as emasculated coolies.

Early in his Western education, Yung was one of only two boys who attended Mrs. Gutzlaff's School for Girls until a small boys' class was temporarily incorporated into her school. During this time, Yung was kept cloistered from the outside world along with the rest of his female schoolmates. During his early years in America while enrolled in Monson Academy, Yung and other Chinese students lived with Brown's mother, Phoebe Hinsdale Brown, where the pattern of Yung's experiences in China was repeated. Brown reports the boys' comportment in America to the Morrison Society in the following terms: "Of course they have been great objects of curiosity, and it has been annoying to them to be gazed at; but their aversion to it is a security against any evil consequences, while I have taken every pain to keep them out of sight, and unexposed to temptation. . . . Hitherto there is not the slightest symptom of injury to the boys. On the contrary they are noted for their modesty" (quoted in Worthy 267). While Brown aimed to secure the boys from temptation, his isolation of the boys can also be read as a "strategy for defusing unwanted attention from peers who often mistook them for girls" (Harris 92). By cloistering Yung and his fellow students from other boys who "mistook them for girls," Brown makes the students appear even less like young boys and more like girls. The shielding of the boys from evil and temptation and the concern over the development of their modesty also suggests the boys were viewed more like girls living in

Victorian America than like young boys. Such a view was especially significant considering the contemporary differentiation between the world of boys and everyone else. As Anthony Rotundo points out, the world of boys was "a distinct cultural world with its own rituals and its own symbols and values. As a social sphere, it was separate both from the domestic world of women, girls, and small children, and from the public world of men and commerce" (29). Although Brown reports that the boys had "adapted readily to their schoolwork and the American way of life," he fails to make a distinction between gendered ways of American life (quoted in Worthy 267).

The Yale College that Yung entered in 1850 was decidedly a male institution, both demographically and metaphorically. The college was often personified as a man or a man-child by students, teachers, and administrators alike, according to Kelley. And according to Louise L. Stevenson, the New Haven Scholars "saw men as the central actors in history, developed an educational system designed to nurture men who could play this role in desirable ways, conceived of politics as an arena in which men could influence public life, and wrote for an audience of educated men" (13). The conflation of masculinity and leadership — and conversely femininity and servitude — at Yale was an idea that Yung himself came to embrace. Yung writes in his autobiography that while seeking employment in China after he graduated from Yale, he determined not to "sacrifice [his] manhood for the sake of making money in a position which is commonly held to be servile" (78). That Yung equates servility with femininity is due in part to the ways in which his poverty feminized him at Yale. Even though Yung's status as a Yalie seems to differentiate him in terms of race and class from the majority of Chinese men in America in the 1800s, it appears that "women's work" was the kind readily available to them both.

Conflict of Regional/Ethnic Identity

Yung's inability to fully immerse himself in the culture at Yale, in part due to his poverty and its attendant consequences, foreshadows his alienation from the greater New England society. Indeed, the external circumstances responsible for Yung's poverty are in themselves a rejection of his claims to a New England regional identity. Not only was Yung's enrollment at Yale against the wishes of his family in China, it was, as the Reverend Joseph Twitchell noted, "against the views and hopes of most of those who were around him" (quoted in Yung 254). Indeed, many of the most ardent supporters of Yung's earlier educational endeavors were strikingly opposed to his desire to remain in America and pursue higher education at Yale. Yung's inability to find someone to continue financially sponsoring his education indicates his changing status from foreigner to alien. In his book *Orientals,* Robert Lee posits that not all foreign objects are aliens, "only objects or persons whose presence disrupts the narrative structure of the community" (3). Upon his arrival in New England, Yung's presence does not disrupt the community, but rather fulfills one of its needs. Like the students he later recruits for the Chinese Educational Mission, Yung's presence provides his host family and their community with the chance to be part of the great missionary effort already under way in China and consequently raises their own status as Christians and Americans.[21] The boys were viewed by their host families as innocent and savage, children in need of Christian upbringing whose souls could still be salvaged. As one of their guardians later wrote, "They seemed like innocent, helpless wild animals of the woods that ought to be sent immediately back to their mothers" (Eugene C. Gardener quoted in McCunn 19). Instead, however, surrogate Christian mothers were provided for the boys. The boys' presence in New England, therefore, fulfilled their communities' need to provide temporal and spiritual guidance to China's future generations. Such generous acts of maternalism provided New Englanders who could not be missionaries in China similar domestic opportunities for missionary work and Christian service.

Lee posits that the difference between a foreigner and an alien also hinges on intentionality. A foreigner is defined by his temporary presence, whereas an alien is defined by his intention to stay. The consequences of these two different identities are considerably different, Lee argues, and "only when aliens exit or are 'naturalized' (cleansed of their foreignness and remade) can they shed their status as pollutants" (3). Inasmuch as the length of Yung's stay in America was delineated before his arrival, he would have been viewed as a foreigner: innocuous, perhaps even desirable. However, Yung's aspiration to continue his education first at Yale and then to pursue professional studies at the Sheffield School of Engineering could have been interpreted as an intention to remain in America indefinitely. According to Lee's definition, such an intention could change an outsider's status to that of alien and therefore necessitate either his exit or his naturalization. Yung became a naturalized citizen just two years after entering Yale; this naturalization, however, only served to complicate matters. Even though Yung's status as visiting student — and therefore innocuous foreigner — facilitated his bid for naturalization, the act of his naturalization cast doubt upon his intention to leave. Indeed, it could be argued that Yung was allowed to naturalize *because* he had demonstrated intent to leave. Yung's inability to find employment in New England after his graduation from Yale, attributable in large part to discrimination against Asians, is evidence that Yung was viewed more as an undesirable alien than an innocuous foreigner.[22]

One of Yung's only recourses to financial aid at this time was a contingent fund at Monson Academy for indigent students who pledged to study for the ministry and become missionaries. Most interestingly, in Yung's case, the fund's trustees added the stipulation that he go back to China and proselytize. While Yung attributes their desire for him to return to China as benevolence of character, scholar Pei-de Wan rightly suggests that their purpose was clear from the beginning: "Their goal was the Christianization of millions of Chinese, not the Americanization of one individual. They were eager to see him return to China and not to further extend his stay in America" (49). The great concern shown by Yung's friends, associates, and superiors over the length of his stay in New England can be read as an indication that Yung's role in the New England community already has been fulfilled. After his graduation from Yale, Yung writes that he again was "induced to return" to China by his friends, stemming in part from fears that "a longer stay in this country might keep me here for good, and China would lose me altogether" (42).

The express fear that China might lose Yung actually reveals complex and localized attitudes of New Englanders toward place and status. The fact that Yung's friends and colleagues encouraged him to return to China, not just leave the United States, is a salient example of the theory of divinely ordained community espoused at Yale and by New Englanders writ large. The New Haven Scholars believed that not only was a member of the educated elite responsible for becoming a positive moral influence, he was responsible for influencing the "divinely ordained community" of which he was part (Stevenson 119). After his graduation from Yale, the uses toward which Yung's professors, associates, and friends thought his education should be put were similar to those of other Yalies with one important distinction: while Yung's classmates were being trained to influence American society, Yung was being trained to influence Chinese society.

This belief in the concept of divinely ordained community can be directly tied to New Englanders' efforts to quell the kind of "restless mobility" that came to define the Yankee character in antebellum America. Not only was the Yankee peddler's geographic mobility a threat to New England's image of order and constancy, but also the livelihood itself was often temporary in nature, "pursued on the journey toward another occupation" (Conforti 157). With the redefinition of a segment of the population as restless and in some ways even aimless, it can be argued that New England cultural institutions, such as Yale College, would have ensured that its students understood the dangers of condoning this type of lifestyle. In Yung's case, because of the construction of the Chinese laborer as a greedy sojourner in American popular culture,[23] the dangers of restlessness dealt even harsher consequences. While Yung was not a laborer, his status as student implied his stay was temporary and that he was therefore restlessly mobile. Even though Yung's temporary status may have facilitated his entrance into Yale and his naturalization as an American, it ironically inhibited his inclusion in New England's regional identity, an identity at midcentury that was based in large part on permanence, stability, and history.

Yung's express desire to remain in the United States and pursue his professional education after graduating from Yale is evidence of his desire for this permanence and stability. Such an attitude makes his sudden return to China shortly after his graduation very problematic. In a speech delivered at Yale Law School on 10 April 1878, the Reverend Joseph Twitchell, one of Yung's closest friends in New England, explains the outcome by constructing Yung as a selfless Christian soldier whose return to China was not only completely voluntary, but also divinely ordained.[24] Twitchell remarks that upon Yung's earlier conversion, Yung "heard and at once accepted his Divine call to devote his life to the Christian service of his nation" (quoted in Yung 254). Twitchell emphasizes Yung's selfless acceptance of his "Divine call" by highlighting that not only was Yung thoroughly naturalized, with at least one job offer awaiting him if he decided to stay in America, but that China lay before him "a cheerless, forbidding prospect. . . . The thought of going back was the thought of exile" (quoted in Yung 257).[25] Nevertheless, a verse in the Bible was enough to convince Yung to return and face the "prejudice, suspicion, [and] hostility" Twitchell was certain the Chinese would exhibit (quoted in Yung 257). Through this characterization, Twitchell is able to justify Yung's almost forced return to China by suggesting that China was not only where Yung should be, but also where Yung should want to be. He explains Yung's departure in terms befitting the way Yung's fellows at Yale saw his utility: as a selfless Christian soldier determined to use Christianity to save his country. Twitchell's construction of Yung as the ultimate agent, a man capable of self-conscious sacrifice for the benefit of others, reaffirms Yale's — indeed New England's — cultural acceptance of Yung even as it ensures his return to China.

One of the reasons Yung was unable to become rooted in a New England regional identity was the transformation of this identity to one based more firmly upon markers of ethnicity. In fact, Yung possessed many of the traits upon which earlier definitions of regional identity had been based: he had spent some of his most formative years in New England; he had formulated plans to continue living, working, and studying in New England; and, as a Yalie, he held a place of special distinction within the "literate" New England region.[26] Yung's racial categorization as Chinese, however, precluded his acceptance into a nascent New England ethnic identity that was based, for the first time, on physical distinctiveness. Indeed, the impetus behind this transformation was the threat to New England's homogenous "racial" identity posed by immigrants and strangers to the region, people like Yung himself. Because Yung had already been granted U.S. citizenship, connecting the ideas of physical distinctiveness to divinely ordained communities was vital for other New Englanders to establish Yung's place outside of New England. Because of his naturalization, it appeared possible that Yung's divinely ordained community could be located outside the country of his birth. The fact that racial ideology, not national identity, was the linchpin for determining community, however, helped New Englanders maintain their racially homogenous identity, while the ideology of divinely ordained communities helped justify these definitions and ensure the image of a racially sympathetic New England.

Conclusion: Revocation of Yung's Citizenship

Yung's youth was remarkable due to the privileges he enjoyed as a Chinese living in America. Yung's arrival in America at midcentury, prior to the rise of intense anti-Chinese sentiment, his naturalization, his identity as a graduate of Yale, and his life in New England—all seemed to grant him more cultural parity and civic privileges than any Chinese had enjoyed or would enjoy for many years. However, the expectations such favorable circumstances and events surely created in Yung's mind were rarely realized as the century and Yung's own life progressed, a situation perhaps best exemplified by the revocation of Yung's citizenship in 1898.[27] This revocation alienated Yung from his American-born children, his brothers at Yale, and his fellow New Englanders.

In 1898, the Supreme Court's ruling in the case *U.S. v. Wong Kim Ark* allowed that native-born children were birthright citizens of the United States regardless of the status of their parents (Lopez 40–41). Due to this decision (reached the same year Yung was stripped of his naturalized citizenship), his sons became eligible for birthright citizenship; thus Yung became separated from his sons by nationality. The situation was doubly unfortunate: not only did Yung and his sons possess different nationalities, but Yung was not considered fit to share their national heritage. In early court cases defining racial identity, justices first tried to define what whiteness was and then established that to be white meant one was fit for naturalization, and to be *nonwhite* meant one was unfit for such a designation. The division between the terms white and *nonwhite*, however, also carried with it a multitude of positive and negative connotations: "[t]o be unfit for naturalization — that is, to be non-White — implied a certain degeneracy of intellect, morals, self-restraint, and political values; to be suited for citizenship — to be White — suggested moral maturity, self-assurance, personal independence, and political sophistication" (Lopez 16). These connotations also alienated Yung from his classmates at Yale by implying that they, and not he, possessed intellect, self-restraint, and moral values.

Yung's eventual status as noncitizen would have alienated him from his former brothers at Yale in another way. Just as Yung's admittance to Yale seemed to designate both his whiteness and his masculinity, the revocation of Yung's citizenship questioned both. If, as Lisa Lowe suggests, citizenship has always been tied not only to whiteness but also to maleness, particularly in the case of Asian immigrants, the prohibition of their naturalization has left their "racial formation" a "gendered formation" (11).[28] So while the revocation of Yung's citizenship defined him as *nonwhite*, it also questioned his formal designation as male. Inasmuch as his becoming a citizen suggested maleness (as females were not allowed to vote), the revocation of that citizenship was a theoretical refutation of his status as male.

Yung's citizenship was revoked not only because he was deemed non-White, but also because he had been racialized as Chinese, an identity that was viewed as the equivalent of inassimilable. Such a designation was unfortunate for Yung, particularly in New England where colonial revivals that celebrated the heritage of Anglo-Puritan descendants also aimed to help Americanize new immigrants by inculcating in them a respect for New England's (read America's) history. Yung's best chance to become, on some level, part of the New England that he loved became impossible with the revocation of his citizenship. The fear that he was not capable of becoming the right kind of American actually precluded him from becoming any kind of American at all.

Yung's life is awash with conflicts and connections among his families, his nations, and his ethnicities. Experiences like the revocation of his citizenship may have led him to the kind of ambivalence that is discernible in his autobiography. In particular, some of the obvious omissions from his autobiography can be read as Yung's ambivalence toward his familial, national, and ethnic identity. Most notably absent are an account of his first marriage to a Chinese woman in China after his graduation from Yale, an account of his application for and the revocation of his U.S. citizenship, and an account of his somewhat clandestine return to New England after having been denied readmission into the country. These last two events in particular appear problematic when contrasted with his autobiography's fierce defense of American ideals. Even if, as some critics may argue, the omission of these events are Yung's conscious pandering to his white audience in an attempt to sell more copies of his autobiography, such a move is still evidence of his ambivalence toward where his loyalties should lie.

Yung's ambivalence is also our own. While it is true that Yung's "social and vocational integration in America was very limited," we cannot know with certainty the extent to which Yung chose to limit that integration or how much of this limitation was unique to the circumstances of Yung's life and time (Wan 6).[29] What can be argued, however, is that Yung's experiences at Yale influenced his place of residency, his choice of vocation, his bid for U.S. citizenship, his relationship with his family in China, the formation of his own family in America, his ability to integrate into New England society, and the responsibility he felt toward China and the United States. Through a proffered sense of inclusion, his education instilled in him the belief that he could assimilate into American culture through the acceptance of privileges offered by that culture and the fulfillment of responsibilities to it. Nevertheless, that education also developed in him a cognizance of the responsibilities he had to his family in China and to the Chinese nation. Yung's education empowered him while simultaneously imbuing his choices with complexity. His education in New England both afforded him a greater sense of agency and ultimately affected the ways in which he was able to use that agency.

NOTES

1. Yung Wing is perhaps best well known as the first Chinese student to graduate from an American institution of higher learning. His autobiography, *My Life in China and America*, also holds special historical import as one of the first autobiographies by a Chinese author to be published in English in America. Yan Phou Lee's *When I Was a Boy in China* is considered the first.
2. Most notably, see Floyd Cheung's biographical essay "Yung Wing (1828–1912)"; Paul Harris's "A Checkered Life: Yung Wing's American Education"; Pei-de Wan's dissertation, "Yung Wing, 1828–1912: A Critical Portrait"; and Edmund Worthy's "Yung Wing in America."

3. See Frank Chin's "Come All Ye Asian American Writers of the Real and the Fake," and Amy Ling's "Reading Her/stories against His/stories in Early Chinese American Literature."

4. For a more in-depth study of the mission, see Thomas LaFargue's *China's First Hundred: Educational Mission Students in the United States, 1872–1881*; and "The Chinese Educational Mission," a chapter from the author's dissertation: "Chinese Youth and American Educational Institutions, 1850–1881."

5. Yung lists the names of these benefactors in his autobiography as Andrew Shortrede, A. A. Ritchie, A. A. Campbell, David Talbot, and Robert Olyphant. He describes the benefactors as merchants and businessmen who were motivated by pure "Christian philanthropy" to help him obtain an education (20).

6. See Louise L. Stevenson's *Scholarly Means to Evangelical Ends: The New Haven Scholars and the Transformation of Higher Learning in America, 1830–1890*.

7. A copy of this report is included in the edited collection by Richard Hofstadter and Wilson Smith, *American Higher Education: A Documentary History*.

8. Yung's plan for the regeneration of China came to be known as the Chinese Educational Mission. Yung's vision included sending about 120 Chinese youths, between ages twelve and fourteen on average, to American schools and colleges for a number of years in order to gain a thoroughly American education. After their graduation from institutions of higher learning (which included military academies), the students were to return and spend their lives in public service to their country (Yung 173). The Mission was disbanded after only a few students had reached the collegiate levels owing in part to the refusal of U.S. officials to allow the students to enter military academies as promised.

9. That the "affectionate guardian" would be male, and that the absence of a mother figure is seemingly negligible, is evidence of the American Victorian philosophy that within institutions belonging to the public sphere, such as colleges, the molding of character still was considered the task of fathers. For a more in-depth study of male gender roles in the late 1800s, see Anthony E. Rotundo's *American Manhood: Transformation in Masculinity from the Revolution to the Modern Era*.

10. Viswanathan references Edward Said's theories on affiliation here.

11. Although the colonial wealth Elihu Yale bestowed upon Yale College was amassed in India, not China, Viswanathan's observations about British imperialism in India can readily be applied to British (and American) imperialism in China. For a detailed account, see Michael H. Hunt's *The Making of a Special Relationship: The United States and China to 1914*.

12. Conforti references this revisionist argument in his book.

13. See Brooks Mather Kelley's *Yale: A History* for more on Yale's link to the State of Connecticut and the federal government.

14. See Burton J. Bledstein's *The Culture of Professionalism: The Middle Class and the Development of Higher Education in America*.

15. The responses to President Daggett's move by both students and faculty alike

were generally positive. Most seemed to welcome a system of gradation that was not based upon, as one Yalie put it, "possession of the finest coat or largest ruffles" (David Avery qtd. in Kelley 78).

16. Yung describes the two awards in English composition he received as being "the only redeeming features that saved me as a student in the class of 1854" (38). While Yung is rather modest about these awards, prizes for literary composition were of the few that actually had great merit. For further detail, see Helen Lefkowitz Horowitz's *Campus Life: Undergraduate Cultures from the End of the Eighteenth Century to the Present*.

17. See Rotundo for more on collegiate male youth groups during this era.

18. See Horowitz for more on the development of fraternities.

19. Yung writes that this job provided him with significant income, enough to pay for his board "through the latter half of my college course" (38).

20. Financing Yung's college education required some creative thinking, both on his part and on the part of Samuel Brown. Yung reports that "during the summer of 1850, it seems that Brown who had been making a visit in the South to see his sister, while there had occasion to call on some of the members of 'The Ladies' Association' in Savannah, Ga., to whom he mentioned my case. . . . He said that the members of the association agreed to help me in college" (36). This help came in the form of financial remittances and was "supplemented with donations of shirts and stockings from ladies who took an interest in my education" (39).

21. In the case of the Educational Mission students, Yung's queries to secure homes in which the boys could reside were met with an overwhelming response. Educational Mission scholar Thomas La Fargue points out that "[t]hese families were amply paid for their services by the Educational Mission, but the immediate response to the calls for homes and the quality of the families who opened their homes to the boys demonstrated that there was a genuine desire on the part of the people of Connecticut to share in an experiment which held such promise for the future of China" (34–35). The future of China hoped for by the people of Connecticut was one in which American education would first civilize and then democratize the Chinese nation in order to bring about a greater acceptance of Christianity. Indeed, for missionaries like the Reverend Brown, this proselytizing ideology provided the rationale behind the establishment of mission schools in China, schools like the one that Yung attended.

22. Pei-de Wan rightly reports that "[i]n mid-nineteenth century America discrimination against Asian employment was strong. Despite his conversion to Christianity and his acquisition of US citizenship [Yung] was still seen as a foreigner, and as such he was quite unlikely to find appropriate employment on his own strength" (50). For more, see Pei-de Wan's "Yung Wing, 1828–1912: A Critical Portrait." The fact that all Chinese, whether laborers or Yale graduates, were grouped together as undesirable aliens illustrates how the stigma of national identity crossed class boundaries.

23. Lee reports that "critics of the Chinese often charged Chinese immigrants with stripping the United States of its resources and Americans of their hard-earned cash while having no intention of settling in the United States" (72).

24. The speech in its entirety is included in Yung's autobiography as an appendix.

25. My research does not indicate such an offer awaited Yung, nor does Yung mention anything of the kind.

26. Conforti reports: "From the seventeenth to the nineteenth century . . . Puritan commitment to literacy placed New England in the forefront of American education, newspaper publishing, and lyceum founding. . . . Puritanism propagated a New England sense of moral and intellectual superiority that often irritated outsiders" (4).

27. The revocation was "a result of the enforcement of the 1878 *In re Ah Yup* decision, which declared Chinese immigrants ineligible for American citizenship" owing to their legal classification as non-whites (Lopez 30). Lopez notes that the *In re Ah Yup* decision in 1878 later affected the passage of the broader Chinese Exclusion Law of 1882, a law that not only provided for the exclusion of Chinese immigration, but also resulted in "an explicit disqualification of Chinese persons from naturalization" (44). Lopez goes on to state that "while Blacks were permitted to naturalize beginning in 1870, the Chinese and most 'other non-Whites' would have to wait until the 1940s for the right to naturalize" (44).

28. Even some critics like Edmund Worthy cite examples of "masculine" endeavors such as an ability to play football as evidence of Yung's Americanization. Also see David L. Eng's *Racial Castration: Managing Masculinity in Asian America*.

29. Wan points out that notwithstanding Yung's "long residence in America [two-thirds of his adult life], his desire for assimilation, and his biculturalism, his social and vocational integration in America was very limited. His careers as businessman, educator, government official, and political activist were all essentially based in China. The financial means that sustained his life in America was income he acquired from Chinese sources" (6).

WORKS CITED

Bangerter, Amy. "Chinese Youth and American Educational Institutions, 1850–1881." Ph.D. diss., George Washington University, 2005.

Bledstein, Burton J. *The Culture of Professionalism: The Middle Class and the Development of Higher Education in America*. New York: Norton, 1976.

Cheung, Floyd. "Political Resistance, Cultural Appropriation, and the Performance of Manhood in Yung Wing's *My Life in China and America (1909)*." In *Form and Transformation in Asian American Literature*, edited by Zhou Xiaojing and Samina Najmi, 77–100. Seattle: University of Washington Press, 2005.

———. "Yung Wing (1828–1912)." *Asian American Autobiographers: A Bio-Biblio-*

graphical Sourcebook, edited by Guiyou Huang, 413–17. Westport, Conn.: Greenwood Press, 2001.

Chin, Frank. "Come All Ye Asian American Writers of the Real and the Fake." In *The Big Aiiieeeee! An Anthology of Chinese American and Japanese American Literature*, edited by Jeffrey Paul Chan, Frank Chin, Lawson Fusao Inada, and Shawn Wong, 1–92. New York: Meridian, 1991.

Conforti, Joseph A. *Imagining New England: Explorations of Regional Identity from the Pilgrims to the Mid-Twentieth Century*. Chapel Hill: University of North Carolina Press, 2001.

Eng, David L. *Racial Castration: Managing Masculinity in Asian America*. Duke University Press, 2000.

Harris, Paul W. "A Checkered Life: Yung Wing's American Education." *American Journal of Chinese Studies* 2, no. 1 (April 1994): 87–107.

Hofstadter, Richard, and Wilson Smith, eds. *American Higher Education: A Documentary History*. 2 vols. Chicago: University of Chicago Press, 1961.

Horowitz, Helen Lefkowitz. *Campus Life: Undergraduate Cultures from the End of the Eighteenth Century to the Present*. New York: Knopf, 1987.

Hunt, Michael H. *The Making of a Special Relationship: The United States and China to 1914*. New York: Columbia University Press, 1983.

Kelley, Brooks Mather. *Yale: A History*. New Haven: Yale University Press, 1974.

La Fargue, Thomas. *China's First Hundred: Educational Mission Students in the United States, 1872–1881*. 1942. Pullman: Washington State University Press, 1987.

Lee, Robert G. *Orientals: Asian Americans in Popular Culture*. Philadelphia: Temple University Press, 1999.

Lee, Yan Phou. *When I Was a Boy in China*. Boston: Lothrop, 1887.

Ling, Amy. "Reading Her/stories against His/stories in Early Chinese American Literature. In *American Realism and the Canon*, edited by Tom Quirk and Gary Scharnhorst, 69–86. Newark: University of Delaware Press, 1994.

Lopez, Ian F. Haney. *White by Law: The Legal Construction of Race*. New York: New York University Press, 1996.

Lowe, Lisa. *Immigrant Acts: On Asian American Cultural Politics*. Durham: Duke University Press, 1996.

McCunn, Ruthanne Lum. *Chinese American Portraits: Personal Histories 1828–1988*. San Francisco: Chronicle Books, 1988.

Morrison, Dane Anthony. "Salem as Citizen of the World." In *Salem: Place, Myth, and Memory*, edited by Dane Anthony Morrison and Nancy Lusignan Schultz, 107–127. Boston: Northeastern University Press, 2004.

Rotundo, Anthony E. *American Manhood: Transformation in Masculinity from the Revolution to the Modern Era*. New York: Basic Books, 1993.

Stevenson, Louise L. *Scholarly Means to Evangelical Ends: The New Haven Scholars and the Transformation of Higher Learning in America, 1830–1890*. Baltimore: Johns Hopkins University Press, 1986.

Viswanathan, Gauri. "The Naming of Yale College: British Imperialism and American Higher Education." In *Cultures of United States Imperialism*, edited by Amy Kaplan and Donald E. Pease, 85–108. Durham: Duke University Press, 1993.

Wan, Pei-de. "Yung Wing, 1828-1912: A Critical Portrait." Ph.D. diss., Harvard University, 1997.

Winterer, Caroline. *The Culture of Classicism: Ancient Greece and Rome in American Intellectual Life, 1780–1910*. Baltimore: Johns Hopkins University Press, 2002.

Wong, K Scott. "Cultural Defenders and Brokers: Chinese Responses to the Anti-Chinese Movement." In *Claiming America: Constructing Chinese American Identities during the Exclusion Era*, edited by K. Scott Wong and Sucheng Chan, 3–4. Philadelphia: Temple University Press, 1998.

Worthy, Edmund H., Jr. "Yung Wing in America." *Pacific Historical Review* 34 (August 1965): 265–87.

Yung Wing. *My Life in China and America*. 1909. New York: Arno Press, 1978.

❧ 3

Paper Butterflies

Japanese Acrobats in Mid-Nineteenth-Century New England

KRYSTYN R. MOON

In April 1867, the residents of Worcester, Massachusetts, witnessed one of the major sensations to hit the American stage that year — Maguire's Imperial Troupe of Japanese Acrobats. Its act was a series of acrobatic, juggling, and magic routines, many of which had never been seen outside of Japan. The program opened with foot juggling followed by sleight-of-hand tricks, more juggling, and aerial routines, all of which were accompanied by music and narrated by the stage manager. Several tricks were quite notable, but perhaps the most unique was what known as the butterfly trick. Developed in Osaka at the beginning of the nineteenth century, the butterfly trick consisted of making origami butterflies fly across the stage with the use of fans. At the end of the act, real butterflies — if available — were released into the audience. The two-night engagement at Mechanic's Hall in Worcester brought full houses, and the local newspaper described the acrobats as "absolutely astonishing" and "perform[ing] with ease many things which seem to border on the impossible" ("Japanese Acrobats" 2).

Hired by San Francisco impresario Thomas Maguire, Maguire's Imperial Troupe of Japanese Acrobats was one of several companies of Japanese performers to tour the United States starting in December 1866. Very few Japanese had visited the United States by the late 1860s, and for the majority of Americans the appearance of these performers was the first time that they were able to observe people of Japanese descent. Worcester, a bustling, industrial town about forty-five miles west of Boston, had no major connections to Japan, but residents had most likely read about the newly opened nation in local newspapers or travel narratives, purchased Japanese trade goods, or seen the handful of Japanese students and sailors who had lived in the state. Maguire's troupe, however, was one of the largest assemblies of Japanese to come to the United States and to visit smaller cities and towns such as Worcester. As the anonymous writer from the above-mentioned article stated, "[t]he performers themselves may be considered quite an attraction, as so large a delegation of this strange people have been seldom seen together in this western world of ours ("Japanese Acrobats" 2). Worcester's residents went to see these visitors, not just because they were great performers, but also because they were Japanese.

The arrival of Japanese acrobats in New England was the result of enormous changes in the late 1860s stemming from American expansion across the Pacific and the push to exploit Asian markets. Like ceramics and lacquerware, these performers were imported to the United States as objects for display with the stage functioning as a curios cabinet for audiences. Americans, however, saw their performances as more than examples of Japanese entertainment; they were also expressions of what it meant to be Japanese. Ideas about Japanese identity were relatively fluid in the 1860s, ranging from biologically based forms of racism to associating Japanese culture with that from Europe. This openness allowed American audiences to praise the skills of Japanese acrobats, all the while supporting conceptions of Japanese difference and inferiority in other venues. While their impact is difficult to quantify, Japanese acrobats left a deep cultural imprint on American audiences and helped to formulate the race-based vocabulary that would be used in discussions of Japan throughout the late nineteenth and twentieth centuries.

In order to explore the link between the United States and Japan through acrobatics in the late 1860s, I will focus on the movement of and responses to Japanese acrobats in one region of the United States—New England. Both before and after the signing of the Treaty of Kanagawa in 1854, New England was connected to Japan through its seafaring, missionary, and educational traditions. Yet most historians who have written on the presence of Japanese in the United States prior to World War II have focused on the recruitment of Japanese laborers for sugar plantations in Hawai'i, agricultural communities in the Far West, and the establishment of Nihonmachis (Little Tokyos) in cities such as Los Angeles, San Francisco, and Seattle. Focusing on New England moves us away from thinking about Japanese migration as primarily a West Coast or Hawaiian phenomenon to considering the movement of Japanese men and women within a larger context. Furthermore, although acrobats toured other parts of the country in the late 1860s, they spent an extensive amount of time performing in New England. When Japanese performers first arrived in the United States in December 1866, the West was still sparsely populated and the South was recovering from the ravages of the Civil War. In comparison, New England was relatively untouched by war, had a large number of cities and towns that were close together, and had an expansive transportation network of trains and waterways that easily could be used for moving intraregionally. More than anything else, New Englanders were willing to accommodate Japanese acrobats and their theatrical agents, who were looking for places where they could entertain as many people as possible and bring in large profits.

Early New England Contact with Japan

When Japanese acrobats first arrived in New England in the spring of 1867, contact between New England (and the United States generally) and Japan was limited, but not nonexistent. Information about the islands had been available through Dutch and other European sources since the sixteenth and seventeenth centuries. A spate of travel narratives was written in response to the opening of Japan to formal diplomatic relations with the United States in 1854. Magazines and newspapers carried diplomatic and military briefs and anecdotes on Japanese life. Trade goods were also sources for understanding Japan's material culture and, by extension, its commercial potential. Contact with Japanese sailors and students was another way in which New Englanders formulated opinions about Japan. These texts, objects, and people—although small in number—serve as the context for how New Englanders viewed Japanese acrobats in the mid-nineteenth century.

Prior to Commodore Matthew C. Perry's arrival in Japan in 1853, what little information Americans had about Japan came from sixteenth- and seventeenth-century European writers, especially Dutch ones. Starting in the 1540s, European missionaries and merchants developed trade relations with the local Japanese populace and established a scattering of Catholic missions. Missionaries produced most of the early European texts on Japan, focusing on Japanese society and culture and their conversion successes for readers back home. The Tokugawa shogunate, however, found Christianity to be a threat to its authority, and by the mid-seventeenth century expelled or killed all missionaries. Merchants, with the exception of the Dutch, were barred from Japan after continuing to assist European missionaries and their converts. Although they were still able to trade with the Japanese, the Dutch faced many restrictions on their movements and were forced to live on a *deshima* (a manmade island) in Nagasaki's harbor.[1] Little information went in or out of Japan for the next two hundred years.

The signings of the Treaty of Kanagawa (1854) led to an explosion of American writing about Japan. Most writings were travel narratives and focused on a set number of issues common to this genre: history and politics, religious practices, commercial developments, social organization, and artistic expression. Perhaps the most noteworthy author was Commodore Matthew C. Perry, who was from a prominent Rhode Island seafaring family. Although he had been unable to formalize trade relations with Japan in 1854, Perry had obtained a few of his goals in the Treaty of Kanagawa: the U.S. government could send a small diplomatic mission to Shimoda, refuel American ships at Hakodate and Shimoda, and establish a retrieval system for American sailors who were shipwrecked in and around Japan. Many members of his crew kept journals about their experiences, but Perry wrote the official, multiple-volume account of the negotiations for the American public. Like most Americans, his opinion of the Japanese, both before and after his expedition, was riddled with contradictions. For example, he viewed the Japanese as inferiors and was particularly critical of his fellow diplomats' negotiating practices. At the same time, he respected many of the diplomats with whom he negotiated the Treaty of Kanagawa and noted the intelligence and curiosity of the Japanese people in general.[2]

The circulation of Japanese trade goods was another vehicle for providing cultural information to Americans about the country's commercial possibilities and artistic strengths. It took a few years after the signing of the Harris Treaty (1858), which opened Japanese ports to trade, for American markets to feel the effects of formal trade relations with Japan. In part, the American Civil War affected the ability of American consumers to purchase Japanese goods. Japan's reluctance to fully implement the Harris Treaty, which many Tokugawa officials felt would lead to Western domination, also contributed to the delay. By the early 1860s, advertisements for Japanese goods appeared in New England papers, with tea and raw silk dominating exports.[3] The *Hartford Daily Courant* advertised a "private sale" of Japanese tea in the spring of 1862; B. W. Brown's, a local grocery store in Hartford, also began offering tea a little more than a year later. Other Japanese trade goods — ceramics, fans, and lacquerware — would gain popularity among Americans over the course of the late nineteenth century and fuel the development of *japonisme* in the decorative and fine arts.

Japanese visitors to New England prior to 1867 were few, but significant. The first were shipwrecked sailors who were rescued by American whaling or merchant ships, many of which hailed from seaports such as Salem or

New Bedford, Massachusetts. By the 1860s, students came to attend the region's many academies and colleges. The shogunate and domain lords sponsored many of these men to study Western civilization and technology so that they could help to modernize Japan's economy, government, and military and to stop any further European and American encroachments on Japanese sovereignty. American missionaries also sponsored their converts to study in the United States in hopes that they would return to convert their fellow Japanese.[4] Unlike those who believed in biologically based forms of racism, most missionaries and their supporters saw cultural attributes, especially religion, as the main cause for the creation of inferior and superior peoples. For them, it was through conversion that the Japanese could become the equals to Americans and Europeans. Niijima Jo (Joseph Hardy Neesima) had converted to Christianity before arriving in Boston in 1864 where he hoped to pursue his education. Sponsored by Alphaeus Hardy, a local businessman and an active supporter of the Congregational Church's missionary work abroad, Niijima attended Phillips Academy in Andover, Massachusetts, Amherst College, and Andover Theological Seminary before returning to Japan in 1874.[5] During the ten years that he spent in Massachusetts, he frequently wrote to his sponsor's family and many of his American friends and teachers. Overwhelmingly, his letters addressed the generosity that he experienced in Massachusetts and support for his religious and academic pursuits. Niijims also noted his speaking engagements at Congregational churches in New York and New England where he told congregants about life in Japan and asked them to support missionary work abroad.[6]

In the end, what did the circulation of these texts, objects, and people mean to New Englanders (and Americans generally)? During the 1860s, attitudes ranged broadly but within limits, depending on the person's knowledge of Japan and his/her worldview. There also existed a tension between American fascination with and even admiration of the Japanese and people's bigotry. The image of Japan as a "Yellow Peril," a term used in the twentieth century to describe the fear that Americans had about a supposed Japanese invasion of the Pacific Coast through immigration and later military conquest, had not yet appeared. Instead, Japan was a mysterious and exotic place that Americans knew little about. Merchants and capitalists found the possibility of establishing Japanese trade and using the islands to improve trade relations with China attractive and potentially lucrative. Pseudoscientific and popular attitudes about race during the mid-nineteenth century cast the Japanese as racially inferior to people of European descent, which led to questions about the development of their civilization and their ability to modernize. Finally, the ability to convert the Japanese to Christianity—despite past and present government hostilities—inspired devout Christians and missionaries who hoped to uplift "heathens" from their depraved state. Early contact with Japan influenced New Englanders, but to what extent is unclear. Even so, their limited, and at times skewed, knowledge allowed varied responses to the arrival of Japanese acrobats in 1867.[7]

Lives of Japanese Acrobats

Aside from the small number of sources about Japan available to New Englanders prior to 1867—and the ways in which these materials influenced their opinions of Japanese acrobats—there is also the question of what motivated acrobats to temporarily leave Japan. Many of the forces that encouraged acrobats to leave affected all Japanese, including many of the first Japanese farmers and farm laborers who settled in Hawaiʻi and California during the late 1860s. The economic and social instability that predated Perry's arrival had led to periodic civil unrest among the general populace, who were frustrated by the shogunate's inability to take care of their basic needs. After the opening of Japan in 1854, the ruling elite was divided in its view of Japan's relationship with the Western world, with some hoping to close the country off again and others wanting to expand foreign contact. No one was prepared for the economic downturn that followed the opening of Japanese trade ports to European and American merchants in the late 1850s. Unable to manage these crises, the Tokugawa shogunate finally collapsed in 1867. That same year the emperor was reestablished as the primary ruler of Japan in what is otherwise known as the Meiji Restoration.

Within the context of this turmoil, acrobats (*karuwaza*) faced hurdles peculiar to their social position in Japan. Within the Tokugawa class structure, they were outcasts (*hinin* or "nonhuman") because of their occupation and were forced to live on the margins of society. As Mikiso Hane points out in *Peasants, Rebels, Women, and Outcastes*, acrobats faced many restrictions on what they could wear, whom they could marry, and their access to shrines and temples. By the nineteenth century, further regulations enacted on the local and domain level affected their ability to buy land, have windows that faced a street, and be outside their home at night. Although rigid in certain ways, the class structure did permit performers to mingle with people from other classes and to alter their outcast status by changing their occupation.

The arrival of foreigners in the 1850s gave acrobats new audiences to entertain and the possibility of improving their economic situation. Sir

Rutherford Alcock, the British Minister Plenipotentiary to Japan from 1858 to 1861, gave a description of an acrobatic performance at the residence of the American minister in Edo in *The Capital of the Tycoon*. In response to what he saw, Alcock pronounced: "*We* leave spinning of tops, and flying of kites, to children in Europe . . . and the former is followed as a profession in Japan, — and very clever and wonderful are the performances of the professors" (318). This complement was clearly double-edged — top spinning in Europe was not considered a form of high art but a children's game, thus implying the idea that the Japanese were infantile in comparison to Europeans. In the end, however, he enjoyed the performance, which he also described as a "marvel," and wrote extensively about the experience (320).

A few foreigners were so enthralled by the novelty of these performers — and positive that Japanese acrobats would generate a great deal of money — that they wanted to exhibit them in the United States and Europe. For acrobats, traveling abroad to perform was just one step further from entertaining foreigners at home, and had great profit-making potential for them as well. No Japanese were officially permitted to travel overseas during the Tokugawa period (with the exception of the 1860 and 1862 embassies to the United States and Europe respectively), which precluded any plans of these troupes to travel abroad. The signing of the Convention of 1866, however, changed Japan's laws on overseas travel and instituted a modern passport system for the first time. As David C. S. Sissons explains in an article on Japanese acrobats in Australia and New Zealand, the Japanese government had presumed that the new passport system would be used by merchants and students who were traveling abroad to help develop Japan's economy, military, and government apparatus — not by entertainers. To persuade officials, British impresario William Grant turned to his local consulate to pressure the Japanese government to authorize passports for acrobats. He and Richard Risley, another British impresario and circus performer, were successful and received the first passports for Japanese acrobats on 23 November 1866.

It may have horrified Japan's ruling elite, but for a time the popularity of acrobats meant that they were the only contact that outsiders had with the Japanese people. In 1866 and 1867 alone, European and American impresarios recruited at least seven acrobatic troupes to perform outside of Japan. The majority of these troupes sailed directly to San Francisco and then toured the eastern half of the United States. One troupe premiered in London before going to Paris for the Exposition Universelle; by the end of 1867, troupes were also traveling to New Zealand and Australia. Over the next few years, Japanese acrobatic troupes made appearances in theaters and under tents almost everywhere in the world, from Kolkata (Calcutta) to Worcester, Massachusetts.

Each troupe—with some variation—performed feats that were commonplace in Japan and to a certain extent China (where many of these acts originated), but had been unseen elsewhere in the world. Aerialists danced and posed with umbrellas on both a slack and tight rope. Troupes presented a perch act, in which one acrobat balanced a pole on his shoulders and another performer climbed to the top and produced various postures. Foot jugglers, who tossed large objects into the air and balanced them on their feet, were found in every troupe. Top spinning, with tops of many different sizes moving along various objects and being thrown into the air, was popular. Magic was also scattered throughout an evening's performance and consisted mostly of sleight-of-hand tricks, including the famous butterfly trick.[8]

Few people were likely to have imagined the kind of sensation that Japanese acrobats would cause among non-Japanese theatergoers in the late 1860s. The arrival of Japanese acrobats led to one of the first Japan "crazes" of the nineteenth century; audiences filled theaters to capacity and newspapers reported extensively on their performances and daily activities. But these events would not be the last time that Americans were attracted to Japanese culture. Ten years later, Americans would respond similarly toward the Japanese Pavilion at the 1876 Centennial Exposition in Philadelphia. The premiere of W. S. Gilbert and Sir Arthur Sullivan's *Mikado* in 1885 at the Fifth Avenue Theater in New York City also led to increased curiosity about Japanese culture. Throughout the late-nineteenth and early-twentieth centuries, Americans would periodically embrace what they saw as Japan's novelty and exoticism, especially in the arts.

Japanese Acrobats in New England

The first troupe to premiere in New England was Maguire's Imperial Troupe of Japanese Acrobats on 4 March 1867 at the Tremont Temple in Boston. Bostonians filled the theater to capacity during the company's three-week run. The local press celebrated its arrival, giving the troupe extensive commentary and urging readers to attend its performances. In fact, two days after Maguire's premiere, the *Boston Daily Evening Transcript* reported that the troupe was playing to full houses and that one of its competitors—a pantomime version of *Aladdin* at the Theatre Comique—introduced its own "Japanese Jugglers" ("Amusements," 6 March 1987, 2).

Maguire's Imperial Troupe of Japanese Acrobats, which had originally been recruited by another American impresario, Thomas F. Smith, had first appeared in San Francisco in December 1866. In early January 1867, Maguire joined forces with Richard Risley, the British impresario and circus performer mentioned earlier, and introduced San Franciscans to another company, named Prof. Risley and T. Maguire's Imperial Japanese Troupe. Within a month, both troupes set sail for New York City to woo eastern theatergoers and, it was hoped, to earn large profits for themselves and their organizers. Unfortunately, New York's theaters were completely booked. The troupes separated. Risley and Maguire's headed south to Philadelphia, Washington, D.C., and Baltimore; Maguire's went north to Boston, Providence, Worcester, Springfield, Hartford, and New Haven.

Soon after the premiere of Maguire's troupe, three other Japanese acrobatic troupes appeared in New England in 1867 and early 1868: Risley and Maguire's Imperial Japanese Troupe (the same troupe that had traveled to New York City with Maguire's and then performed in Philadelphia, Washington, D.C., and Baltimore); the Flying Dragon Troupe of Japanese Acrobats (also known as the Red Dragon Troupe or Marshall and Doyle's Mikado Troupe); and the Fusiyama Troupe of Japanese Acrobats. Risley and Maguire's Imperial Japanese Troupe performed only in Boston at the Boston Theatre for a little over a week in June 1867. Although it had a successful run, the troupe faced two hurdles. First, its name was too similar to Maguire's Imperial Troupe of Japanese Acrobats, which could cause confusion among theatergoers who might think that they had already seen these performers. Second, the troupe was performing in Boston only two months after Maguire's triumphant run. Audiences might assume that they had already seen everything that there was to see when it came to Japanese acrobatics and decide not to attend Risley and Maguire's performances. Luckily, Risley and Maguire's was able to turn to two common theatrical practices to make its Boston visit a success. To distinguish itself from Maguire's, Risley and Maguire's emphasized in its advertisements and in the local press that its performers were members of the "real" imperial troupe and lived in the shogun's household in Edo. This kind of fabrication was not unusual in nineteenth-century entertainment: other impresarios, most notably P. T. Barnum, had manipulated Americans' love and curiosity about royalty to bring in audiences. Outside its control but beneficial to its success, Risley and Maguire's relied on reports from New York City on its most famous member—Hamaikari Nagakichi—to produce interest (fig. 3.1). Nagakichi, one of the few child acrobats to come to the United States, was otherwise known as "Little All Right," a phrase that he had first shouted after a fall

FIG. 3.1. Carte de Visite of Hamaikari Nagakichi (also known as "Little All Right"), dressed as a frontiersman. *Harvard Theatre Collection, Houghton Library.*

from the slack wire in San Francisco that evolved into a nickname. He was a sensation in San Francisco and New York, where theatergoers were impressed by his agility in a perch act with his adopted father Hamaikari Sadakichi (the lead performer of the troupe; fig. 3.2) and in an aerial routine on the slack wire. A few days before the troupe's appearance in Boston, stories about Nagakichi increased after he fell again at New York's Academy of Music.

The diary of Risley and Maguire's secretary and manager, Hirohachi Takano, gives us further insight into the general workings of this company. Born into a silk merchant family, Hirohachi frequently traveled to Edo and Yokohama where he probably was hired to work for the troupe, but—based on research by theater historian Aya Mihara—it is unclear as to why he chose to join Risley and Maguire's troupe and leave Japan. Hirohachi's entries focus almost entirely on what was going on behind the scenes, in terms of both his personal observations and the business aspects of the troupe.[9] For instance, he mentioned watching President Andrew Johnson, whom he had met in April when the troupe performed in Washington, D.C., in a Boston parade. He also wrote that the troupe had been robbed of its earnings, possibly by its interpreter and former consulate official, Edward Banks. Finally, he listed when the troupe gave matinee and evening performances and periodically mentioned when it had a full house. Unfortunately, Hirohachi did not list the company's proceeds from each performance, which would tell us more about the extent to which Risley and Maguire's tour was profitable.

Unlike the companies that preceded them, the Flying Dragon Troupe of Japanese Acrobats and the Fusiyama Troupe of Japanese Acrobats mostly performed in smaller cities and towns. Both troupes probably turned to these venues in order to maximize profits by entertaining audiences who had not already had the opportunity to attend a Japanese acrobatic performance. Novelty was key to having a full house and, therefore, making profits. By the time these two troupes appeared in New England, Maguire's and Risley and Maguire's had already hit the major New England cities. To make the most of their appearances in the region, the Flying Dragon and Fusiyama troupes had to turn to other locations.

Organized by two men named Marshall and Doyle, the Flying Dragon Troupe of Japanese Acrobats was part of the Grand Asiatic Alliance during the summer of 1867. Besides the Flying Dragon Troupe, the Alliance included two other companies: the Beni Zoug-Zoug Troupe and Dodsworth's Band. The Beni Zoug-Zoug Troupe ("beni" stands for *ibn* or *abna* which means "sons" or "sons of" in Arabic; "zoug-zoug" is meaningless)

FIG. 3.2. Carte de Visite of Hamaikari Sadakichi, lead performer in Risley and Maguire's Imperial Japanese Troupe. *Harvard Theatre Collection, Houghton Library.*

consisted of North African tumblers, another type of non-Western entertainment that was popular in Europe and the United States during the nineteenth and early twentieth centuries. Dodsworth's Band, led by Harvey B.
Dodsworth, was one of the earliest brass bands established in the Untied
States and performed with several New York–based military regiments
starting in the 1830s. After premiering in New York City in July 1867, the Alliance performed in cities and towns of various sizes in Connecticut, Massachusetts (with the exception of Boston), New Hampshire, and Maine. In
a world without air conditioning, it was often too hot to perform in a theater during the summer, so the Alliance used a tent that it could erect in an
empty lot or even a field. The tent also allowed the Alliance to visit towns
that did not have theaters big enough for their performances (acrobatics required high ceilings) or had no theaters at all. Ultimately, by using a tent instead of a theater, the Grand Asiatic Alliance was able to cover more of New
England than any other troupe that visited the region.

The Fusiyama Troupe of Japanese Acrobats was the last company to tour
New England in the late 1860s. It had arrived in San Francisco in early October 1867 and was recruited by three well-known blackface minstrel performers from New York City: Ben Cotton, Sam Sharpley, and Charley
White. After appearing at the Theatre Comique in New York, Fusiyama
began its tour of southern New England by late November. Worried that
the excitement surrounding Japanese acrobats had worn off, Fusiyama's organizers emphasized the novelty and skill of their troupe in comparison to
those that preceded it. In those cities in which other troupes had previously
performed, Fusiyama's advertisements stressed that it was "[e]ntirely different in every Act from any one preceding them," language that was similar
to that used by Risley and Maguire's troupe to distinguish itself from Maguire's earlier that summer (Advertisement, *Providence Evening* 3). Like the
Grand Asiatic Alliance, Fusiyama turned to smaller communities, such as
Middletown, Connecticut, and Webster, Massachusetts, that had not previously hosted Japanese acrobatic performances; it also stopped at a few of
the larger cities in Rhode Island, Connecticut, and western Massachusetts.
However, unlike the Grand Asiatic Alliance, Fusiyama toured New England during the fall and winter months and could only perform in places
that had a hall or theater available.

By the beginning of 1868, four separate Japanese acrobatic troupes had
toured New England over the course of a year. Each troupe was popular
with theatergoers, and in their quest to set themselves apart from each
other, they managed to cover almost the whole of New England. Despite
their successful tours, all four companies moved on to other places to find

fresh audiences. Maguire's troupe went to upstate New York and the upper Midwest before heading south along the Mississippi River to New Orleans. Risley and Maguire's returned to the Academy of Music in New York City in July 1867 and then toured Europe, including performances at the Cirque Napoléon during the Exposition Universelle in Paris. By the fall of 1867, the Flying Dragon Troupe had left the Grand Asiatic Alliance and was touring under the name "Marshall and Doyle's Mikado Troupe of Japanese." It went north to Canada. Finally, the Fusiyama Troupe followed in the footsteps of Maguire's and headed for New York and the Midwest. With the exception of Hamaikari Nagakichi ("Little All Right") who continued to perform in Europe and the United States, these troupes eventually returned home to Japan by the early 1870s.

The Response from New England Newspapers

One writer's review of a Japanese acrobatic troupe's performance is a limited way to assess the reaction of audiences to what they were seeing both on and off the stage. However, by taking the various reviews and articles together, we get a better understanding of how New Englanders reacted to performers and what sorts of attitudes they helped to generate. In many ways, newspapers validated the stereotypes that were circulating in the late 1860s. Attitudes about Japan, however, varied widely, and no one image dominated American rhetoric. What is equally significant is that these transnational migrants were performers. Actors and audiences have a shared knowledge that performances are public events that are separate from what are commonly understood to be everyday interactions. This understanding influenced the ways in which audiences responded to performances and potentially created alternative views.[10]

Newspapers frequently recorded whether there was a full house the previous night, information that demonstrated a troupe's popularity and that inspired others to attend future performances. Frequently, writers stated that a company was "attracting large and enthusiastic audiences," "have been well received wherever they have appeared," and played to "a crowded house" or a "full house" ("Entertainments" 4; "Japanese," 16 April 1867, 8; "Amusements," *Boston Daily Evening*, 6 March 1867, 2; "New England News," 9 January 1868, 2). Boston's *Daily Evening Traveller* noted: "we advise all to go and see them, for 'take them for all in all, we shall not look upon their like again'" ("Amusements," 22 March 1867, 2). Reporters also mentioned when there was, in their view, an unusually small audience. In response to the poor turnout for the Grand Asiatic Alliance in Hartford, a reporter for the *Hartford Courant* wrote: "The Japs and Arabs were not so liberally patronized yesterday as we supposed they would be, though in the evening there was a fair attendance, and the performance gave good satisfaction" ("General City" 5).

Speaking to their popularity, even newspapers from towns in which these troupes did not perform ran articles about them. By January 1867, a report from San Francisco on Risley and Maguire's company had appeared in the *Independent Democrat* from Concord, New Hampshire (Japanese acrobats only visited the New Hampshire towns of Portsmouth and Manchester). Other small-town newspapers reported on Nagakichi's fall in New York City and Risley and Maguire's visit with President Andrew Johnson and Secretary of State William H. Seward in Washington, D.C. A reprinted article from the *San Francisco Bulletin* on Japanese artisans who built a theater for the Hayatake Troupe of Japanese Acrobats inside San Francisco's Metropolitan Theater appeared in at least two small-town newspapers. Led by Hayatake Torakichi from Osaka, the Hayatake Troupe stopped performing after the death of Torakichi in February 1868 in New York City. It never performed in New England.

Although each troupe produced similar routines, the New England press emphasized that the experience of watching these troupes was novel for New Englanders. The day after Maguire's Imperial Troupe of Japanese Acrobats' premiere in Boston, the *Daily Evening Traveller* liked some routines more than others, but concurred that "[t]he entertainment is well worth going to see from its novelty and will prove very attractive" ("Amusements" 4). The *Providence Evening Press* went further in its response to the Fusiyama troupe in December 1867, calling it "unapproachable in their feats" ("Academy" 3). This kind of language was common in the advertisements for these troupes as well. The advertisement for Maguire's troupe in the *Boston Daily Advertiser* during the last week of its run noted that the troupe performed "the most astounding and unparalleled Feats, unequalled by any performers in the world" (Advertisement 1).

Another way that New England newspapers described these troupes' abilities was to compare them to their European counterparts that had toured the United States during the 1850s and 1860s and were also quite popular. The *Boston Daily Advertiser* stated that the routines of Maguire's troupe were similar to those of the Ravels, a well-known French acrobatic troupe, and the Hanlon-Lees, another popular acrobatic company from Great Britain recognized for its pantomimes and trickwork. The *Daily Evening Traveller* believed that Maguire's troupe was better than the Ravels and Charles Blondin, a French acrobat who premiered in Boston with the Ravels in 1855 and later walked over Niagara Falls on a tightrope in 1859. These comparisons highlighted the skill and ability of Japanese performers, putting them side by side with Europeans who were considered the best in their field at the time. More important, by associating Japanese performers with Europeans, newspapers muddied nineteenth-century attitudes about racial difference that had marked Asians as inferior.

Not everything that performers did on the stage was appealing to local reporters (nor, presumably, to New England theatergoers). For instance, the stage manager for Maguire's troupe talked to the audience during each performance, but because his monologue was in Japanese, no one understood what he was saying. The *Daily Evening Traveller* treated him sarcastically: "[a] descriptive lecture is given during the performance, in the Japanese tongue, which is of course readily understood, and fully appreciated by all" ("Amusements," 5 March 1867, 1). The *Boston Daily Advertiser* was much more charitable in its response: "[a] running commentary or descriptive lecture is kept up in the Japanese tongue by one who appears to be the stage manager of the company, and though failing to enlighten the audience serves to keep them in good humor" ("Dramatic and Musical," 5 March 1867, 1). In this particular moment of cultural dissonance, what is interesting in both of these reviews was the lack of race-based language that could have been used to portray Maguire's manager as ignorant and foolish. Instead, both criticize the troupe as they would any group of performers for speaking in its native tongue without an interpreter.

It was the troupes' musical accompaniment that received the most disdain. As with other non-Western musical traditions, Americans perceived Japanese music to be more akin to noise than music. The music provided by Maguire's troupe was simply called "inharmonious" ("Amusements," *Daily Evening*, 5 March 1867, 4). In Worcester, the musical accompaniment for Fusiyama was described in the *Worcester Daily Spy* as "pure Japanese, furnished by a 'Jap' and baffles description" ("Fusi Yami" 2). It can be assumed that the reporter's use of the word "Jap," a derogatory term, in single quotation marks, along with a failure to describe what he/she had heard, made it clear to readers that the reporter did not like Japanese music. His/her word choice, however, also demonstrates that the author's aversion to Japanese music making was tied to a belief in American constructions of racial inferiority and superiority. The *Boston Daily Advertiser* had a particular problem with the music provided by Risley and Maguire's Troupe at the Boston Theatre: "The musicians, whose performances surpass those, either of Gideon's Band or the Cowbellogians, play plaintive airs while their brethren and sisters are dispensing magic, and it is safe to assert that they beat more time than any other musical organization which ever appeared in the theater" ("Dramatic and Musical" 2).

Although producing a much more elaborate description of what s/he heard in comparison to the reviewer in the *Worcester Daily Spy*, this anonymous author's emphasis on percussion was tied to nineteenth-century Western music philosophy that considered percussion to be one of the lowest forms of music making. For European and American music experts, elaborate harmonic structures, which had become the basis of Western music by the end of the seventeenth century, were considered the highest development in musical expression.[11] To convey this attitude, the reporter described the troupe's music in such a way that would be familiar to his/her readers. "Gideon's Band" was a reference to the story in the Old Testament of Gideon, who recruited three hundred soldiers to defeat the Midianites with blaring trumpets, the sound of breaking water pitchers, and the blinding light of oil lamps; it also referred to a very popular blackface minstrelsy song first sung by the Buckley's New Orleans Serenaders in the extravaganza *Mazeppa* (1861). "Cowbellogians" was probably a reference to the "Anvil Chorus" from Giuseppe Verdi's *Il Trovatore* (1855), one of the most popular operas in the United States during the late 1850s. It included the playing of actual anvils.

That these performers were of Japanese descent was also a subject of interest in New England newspapers. Comments went beyond stressing the novelty of watching Japanese acrobats and emphasized that these troupes should be seen as windows into Japanese life. Many reporters included detailed descriptions of the acrobats off the stage, especially their foodways and dress. In the *Newport Mercury* from Rhode Island, a reporter made some general statements about the everyday lives of these performers:

> at home they wear a black cape across their shoulders and a white band about their loins; they sleep on little single mattresses, laid side by side on the floor, use chopsticks and are quite fond of money. Their dress on the stage is much that [as] on the street. The Japs believe in charms, and a dish of salt always sits on a table behind the scenes, and previous to undertaking a perilous feat before the audience, the members of troupe generally taste of the saline substance and scatter a little about (2).

As with previous writers, this author uses the derogatory term "Japs," this time in his description of the superstitious nature of acrobats. Because the Japanese were not Christians, American and European writers almost always put their religious practices and beliefs in a negative light. Of course, European American actors had their own superstitions, such as telling a fellow actor "to break a leg" or "c'est merde" ("it's shit") so that a performance would be a success. Such statements, however, were not treated in the same way as non-European superstitions.

Local reporters also believed that they could comprehend the character of these performers just by observing them. This supposed ability was common among Europeans and Americans who traveled abroad. Although they did not speak the language of the people around them and knew little about their culture and society, European and American writers were confident in their own intellectual ability to decipher another culture. Reporters were simply replicating this practice at home. For example, the *Worcester Daily Spy* called Maguire's troupe "self-possessed and dignified" ("Our Japanese" 2). Not all commentaries, however, agreed on what were the common traits among Japanese acrobats. The *Hartford Courant*, reporting on the same troupe, called them "awkward and uncouth" ("Japanese," 16 April 1867, 2). Sometimes, what reporters saw was interpreted as a national trait, common to all peoples of Japanese ancestry. In August 1867, the *Worcester Daily Spy* noted that the performances of the Grand Asiatic Alliance were a great way for audiences to see the national differences between Japanese and Arabs. "It was decidedly interesting to compare throughout the nervous, feisty Arabs with the staid and deliberate Japanese" ("Japanese and Arabs" 2). Playing to popular stereotypes of the time, the Japanese were seen as much more reserved than their Arab counterparts and, arguably, more "civilized." This type of comparison had started from the beginning of formal American-Japanese relations in the 1850s. Commodore Perry's official narrative described the Japanese as "the most moral and refined of all eastern nations," especially in how women were treated. Although he noted that women were "not as elevated" as in the West, they were far better off than their Chinese or Turkish counterparts (1:364–97).

Based on what was written in a few local newspapers, it can be assumed that New Englanders were aware of the skill of Japanese acrobats prior to their arrival. Presumably, this information had circulated through travel narratives, newspapers (including articles on performances in San Francisco and New York City), or word of mouth. A few people, most likely sailors or merchants, had visited Japan and witnessed these performers there. The *Portsmouth Journal of Literature and Politics* noted the amount of press that the Grand Asiatic Alliance had received in other cities and that little promotional work would be needed. "So much has been said and written about these marvelous people that we consider a long notice at this time unnecessary" ("Wonders" 2). In Providence, a newspaper pointed out that Rhode Islanders had known for some time about the ability of Japanese acrobats: "For scores of years we have read of the wonderful skill and remarkable accomplishments of these singular people, and aside from the mere curiosity attached to the occasion, it will be most gratifying to see the stories of their dexterity verified, and to learn the unique nature of a genuine Japanese entertainment" ("Japanese Jugglers," *Providence Evening* 2). The *Boston Daily Evening Transcript* went a little further with its comments the day after Maguire's Imperial Troupe of Japanese Acrobats premiered in the city: "The troupe is of an unique character, and their demeanor, language and performance introduce the beholder into a phase of Japanese society of which was well known to all classes in our own community" ("Amusements," 5 March 1867, 2). This reporter seemed to believe that, although the acrobats provided a unique theatrical experience, Bostonians already had some knowledge about them, using the word "phase" to denote this group of people.

While little information had previously circulated about Japan, New England reporters built upon what they had already learned in their responses to Japanese acrobatic troupes. In the late 1860s, a wide variety of attitudes abounded, but only one press response was a constant: that local theatergoers should go out to see them. And, for the most part, audiences did. With so few opportunities to see people of Japanese descent (as well as Japanese acrobatics), audiences appeared to have listened to their local newspapers and satisfied some of their own curiosity about these performers.

In July 1867, a writer for the *Whalemen's Shipping List and Merchant's Transcript* from New Bedford, Massachusetts stated: "from appearances the Jap style of amusement would soon be run into the ground in this country" (2). Although two more troupes—Flying Dragon and Fusiyama—toured New England during the latter half of 1867 and into 1868, no Japanese acrobatic troupes performed in New England for the next three years. With their disappearance from New England, Japanese acrobats were no longer mentioned in local newspapers, including articles about their daily lives. But Japanese acrobats had not vanished from New England forever. In 1871, a new company came to New England: Satsuma's Royal Japanese Troupe. In much the same way as the troupes before it, Satsuma's performed in theaters and, during the hottest months of the year, under a tent in cities throughout New England. The press again promoted Japanese acrobatics among its readers, praising performers for their novelty and skill.

Neither was Satsuma's troupe the last company to perform in New England. Throughout the 1870s and 1880s, troupes visited the region as part of combination companies and circuses. By 1886, the Barnum-Forepaugh Circus included Houssabura (also spelled Houssaboro) Sam and his "Suspended Japanese Pendulum Perch," a type of act that involved a performer balancing on an apparatus while kicking objects into the air. At the same time, smaller troupes and individual performers appeared in dime museums and vaudeville. When Toki Murata, a foot juggler and slack-wire aerialist, performed at the Scenic Theater in Pawtucket, Rhode Island, in 1921, the stage manager called him an "old-time performer," a reference to his act's long history on the American stage (Reddy 113). Even the Gentleman's Agreement (1907) and Ladies' Agreement (1920), two treaties that barred the immigration of Japanese male and female laborers respectively, did not affect performers. The passage of the National Origins Quota Act (1924), which curtailed almost all Japanese immigration, also did not stop Japanese acrobats from coming to the United States, although it did limit the amount of time they could remain in the country. It was only the beginning of World War II — when Americans feared and condemned everything that was Japanese, including Japanese Americans — that Japanese acrobats were unable to find work in the United States.

Although these acrobats were probably the first persons of Japanese descent that most New Englanders — and by extension Americans — saw, their travels and performances have been primarily overlooked. Prior to the arrival of these troupes, most audiences knew very little about Japan, and what they had learned came from travel narratives and newspaper articles, trade goods, and a handful of Japanese visitors. The large number of Japanese acrobats who performed in the United States starting in December 1866 allowed Americans from all walks of life to be exposed to "real" Japanese people for the very first time. Local newspapers, while promoting these troupes among their readers, also participated in circulating information. Advertisements and articles played to a variety of images — novelty, inferiority, exoticism, and so forth — all of which had the potential to influence the general public.

But why have Japanese acrobats been forgotten? In part, their erasure is tied to older definitions of migration that focused on particular kinds of individuals (such as laborers) moving across international borders and settling in another nation. As historians over the past decade have discovered, this model is quite limiting and does not address the myriad ways in which people have moved throughout the world. Scholars interested in intercultural contact and *japonisme* have also overlooked these performers, focusing on Japanese and Western travel literature, the decorative or fine arts, or Japanese "high art" theatrical traditions such as Nō or Kabuki, which came to the United States at the turn of the century. But perhaps their erasure was because they were acrobats—performers who were seen as outcasts in their own country and often marginalized in the United States and elsewhere. Their second-class status and transient occupation make their presence in the United States difficult, although not impossible, to trace, especially compared to that of other Japanese visitors, such as students, sailors, and diplomats. Nevertheless, they should be studied because they were among the earliest Japanese visitors to the United States, traveling extensively throughout the country and influencing the general population's opinion of Japan.

NOTES

1. For more information on this period, see Jurgis Elisonas, "Christianity and the Daimyo."

2. There is only one major biography on Perry. See John H. Schroeder's *Matthew Calbraith Perry: Antebellum Sailor and Diplomat.*

3. For a more thorough discussion of Japan's economy prior to and during the early years of the Meiji Restoration, see Ohara Keishi, *Japanese Trade and Industry in the Meiji-Taisho Era*; Shinya Sugiyama, *Japan's Industrialization in the World Economy, 1859–1899*; and J. Richard Huber, "Effect on Prices of Japan's Entry into World Commerce after 1858."

4. For more on missionaries and the recruitment of Japanese students for schooling in the United States, see W. G. Beasley, *Japan Encounters the Barbarian: Japanese Travellers in America and Europe* (119–138), and John E. Van Sant, *Pacific Pioneers: Japanese Journeys to America and Hawaii, 1850–80* (49–53).

5. More biographical information can be found on Niijima in Van Sant, *Pacific Pioneers,* 64–78.

6. To read Niijima's own observations on his life in the United States, see Arthur Sherburn Hardy, *Life and Letters of Joseph Hardy Neesima.*

7. To read about the ways in which Americans have imagined Japan during the nineteenth and early twentieth century, see Mari Yoshihara, *Embracing the East: White Women and American Orientalism*; Ian Littlewood, *Idea of Japan: Western Images, Western Myths.*

8. For further reading on Japanese acrobatics, see Nishiyama Matsunosuke, *Edo Culture: Daily Life and Diversions in Urban Japan, 1600–1868,* 242–244.

9. Mihara has written extensively on Japanese acrobats and their contact with the outside world during the nineteenth century. See her "Professor Risley and Japanese Acrobats II: Their Provincial Tour in England, 1867–1868"; "Little 'All Right' Took the Stage: A Tour of the Japanese Acrobats in Western Europe"; "Professor Risley and Japanese Acrobats: Selections from the Diary of Hirohachi Takano"; "Professor Risley's Life in Japan, 1864–1866."

10. To read more about the potentially complicated ways of reading a performance, see Judith Butler, "Performative Acts and Gender Constitution: An Essay on Phenomenology and Feminist Theory."
11. For more on the racialization of music, see Philip V. Bohlman, "The Remembrance of Things Past: Music, Race, and the End of History in Modern Europe."

WORKS CITED

Primary Sources

"Academy of Music." *Providence Evening Press*, 28 December 1867, 3.
Advertisement, Private Sale—O. P. Case. *Hartford Daily Courant*, 30 May 1862, 4.
Advertisement, B. W. Brown's. *Hartford Daily Courant*, 7 September 1863, 4.
Advertisement, Fusi-Yama Japanese Troupe. *Buffalo Commercial Advertiser*, 10 October 1868, 2.
Advertisement, Fusi-Yama Japanese Troupe. *Milwaukee Daily Sentinel*, 6 May 1868, 1.
Advertisement, Fusi-Yama Japanese Troupe. *Providence Evening Press*, 23 December 1867, 3.
Advertisements, Maguire's Japanese Troupe. *Boston Daily Advertiser*, 22 March 1867, 1.
Alcock, Rutherford. *The Capital of the Tycoon: A Narrative of Three Years' Residence in Japan*. 2 vols. London: Longman, Green, Longman, Roberts, & Green, 1863.
"Alien-Sounding Performers Feel Less Effect than in Last War." *Billboard*, 10 January 1942, 25.
"Amusements." *Boston Daily Evening Transcript*, 5 March 1867, 2.
"Amusements." *Boston Daily Evening Transcript*, 6 March 1867, 2.
"Amusements." *Daily Evening Traveller [Boston]*, 5 March 1867, 4.
"Amusements." *Daily Evening Traveller [Boston]*, 11 March 1867, 1.
"Amusements." *Daily Evening Traveller [Boston]*, 22 March 1867, 2.
"Bengal." *Times of India [Kolkata]*, 8 November 1867, 2–3.
"California Gossip." *New York Times*, 14 June 1867, 3.
"Circus of his Own, A." *New York Times*, 27 March 1887, 10.
"The Condition of Little 'All Right.'" *New York Times*, 14 June 1867, 5.
De Saint-Victor, Paul. "Théatres." *La Presse [Paris]*, 19 August 1867, 2.
"Dramatic and Musical." *Boston Daily Advertiser*, 5 March 1867, 1.
"Dramatic and Musical." *Boston Daily Advertiser*, 11 March 1867, 1.
"Dramatic and Musical." *Boston Daily Advertiser,* 17 June 1867, 1.
"Dramatic, Musical, Etc." *Daily Dramatic Chronicle [San Francisco]*, 3 August 1867, 3.
"Dramatic, Musical, Etc." *Daily Dramatic Chronicle [San Francisco]*, 24 August 1867, 3.
"Dramatic, Musical, Etc." *Daily Dramatic Chronicle [San Francisco]*, 14 September 1867, 3.

"Eastern." *Daily Dramatic Chronicle [San Francisco]*, 23 November 1867, 3.

"Entertainments." *Boston Post*, 13 March 1867, 4.

The First and Only Troupe of Japanese Conjurors and Gymnasts that Ever Have Been Allowed to Visit Europe. London, 1867.

"The Fusi Yami." *Worcester Daily Spy*, 3 December 1867, 2.

"General City News." *Hartford Daily Courant*, 15 August 1867, 5.

"Gideon's Band." Arranged by Charles R. Dodsworth. Philadelphia: Lee & Walker, 1861.

Hardy, Arthur Sherburne. *Life and Letters of Joseph Hardy Neesima*. 1891. Kyoto: Doshisha University Press, 1980.

"The Japanese." *Hartford Daily Courant*, 16 April 1867, 8.

"The Japanese." *Hartford Daily Courant*, 11 July 1871, 2.

"Japanese Acrobats and Gymnasts." *Worcester Daily Spy*, 10 April 1867, 2.

"The Japanese and Arabs." *Worcester Daily Spy*, 20 August 1867, 2.

"The Japanese and Their Doings." *Springfield Daily Republican*, 13 April 1967, 8.

"A Japanese Death and Funeral." *Hartford Daily Courant*, 12 February 1868, 2.

"Japanese Joiners and Their Tools." *New Hampshire Patriot and State Gazette [Concord]*, 11 March 1868, 1.

"Japanese Joiners and Their Tools." *Weymouth Weekly Gazette*, 20 December 1867, 1.

"Japanese Jugglers." *Independent Democrat [Concord]*, 17 January 1867, 1.

"The Japanese Jugglers." *Providence Evening Press*, 2 April 1867, 2.

"The Japanese Jugglers." *Weymouth Weekly Gazette*, 23 May 1867, 1.

"Japanese Out of Circus." *New York Times*, 23 December 1941, 26.

"The Japs." *Hartford Daily Courant*, 28 November 1867, 5.

Kawada, Ikaku. *Drifting Toward the Southeast: The Story of Five Japanese Castaways.* Translated by Junya Nagakuni and Junji Kitadai. New Bedford, Mass.: Spinner, 2004.

"New England News." *Hartford Daily Courant*, 9 January 1868, 2.

"New England News." *Hartford Daily Courant*, 11 January 1868, 2.

Newport Mercury, 29 June 1867, 2.

"Our Japanese Visitors." *Worcester Daily Spy*, 11 April 1867, 2.

"Pacific Coast." *Daily Dramatic Chronicle [San Francisco]*, 19 October 1867, 3.

Perry, Matthew C. *Narrative of the Expedition of an American Squadron to the China Seas and Japan, Performed in the Years 1852, 1853, and 1854 . . .* 3 vols. Washington, D.C.: A. O. P. Nicholson, 1856.

"Poor Little 'All Right!'" *Fitchburg Sentinel*, 10 August 1867, 4.

Reddy. Report on the Scenic, Pawtucket, R.I. 3 February 1921. Vol. 23. Keith/Albee Collection, Special Collections Department, University of Iowa, Iowa City.

"The Renowned Japanese Performers!" 1867. Playbill. Worcester Theatrical Programs. Worcester, Mass.: American Antiquarian Society.

"The State Dinner to the Japanese." *Exeter News-Letter*, 13 May 1867, 2.

Warner, Morris H. *The Barnum Budget; or, Tent Topics of the Season of 1886.* Elmira, N.Y.: Gazette Company Prince, c. 1886.

Whalemen's Shipping List, and Merchant's Transcript [New Bedford], 9 July 1867, 2.
"The Wonders of a Lifetime Coming." *Portsmouth Journal of Literature and Politics*, 24 August 1867, 2.

Secondary Sources

Beasley, W[illiam] G. *Japan Encounters the Barbarian: Japanese Travellers in America and Europe*. New Haven: Yale University Press, 1995.

Bernard, Donald R. *The Life and Times of John Manjiro*. New York: McGraw, 1992.

Bohlman, Philip V. "The Remembrance of Things Past: Music, Race, and the End of History in Modern Europe." In *Music and the Racial Imagination*, edited by Ronald Radano and Philip V. Bohlman, 644–76. Chicago: University of Chicago Press, 2000.

Butler, Judith. "Performative Acts and Gender Constitution: An Essay on Phenomenology and Feminist Theory." In *Performing Feminisms: Feminist Critical Theory and Theatre*, edited by Sue-Ellen Case, 270–83. Baltimore: Johns Hopkins University Press, 1990.

Cipolla, Frank J. "Dodworth." *New Grove Dictionary of Music and Musicians*. 2nd ed. Edited by Stanley Sadie. 29 vols. New York: Macmillan, 2001.

Elisonas, Jurgis. "Christianity and the Daimyo." In *The Cambridge History of Japan*, edited by John W. Hall, 4:301–73. New York: Cambridge University Press, 1991.

Hane, Mikiso. *Peasants, Rebels, Women, and Outcastes: The Underside of Modern Japan*. New York: Rowman, 1982.

Hata, Donald Teruo, Jr. *"Undesirables": Early Immigrants and the Anti-Japanese Movement in San Francisco, 1892–1893: Prelude to Exclusion*. New York: Arno, 1978.

Huber, J. Richard. "Effect on Prices of Japan's Entry into World Commerce after 1858." *Journal of Political Economy* 79 (1971): 614–28.

Jansen, Marius B. *The Making of Modern Japan*. Cambridge: Belknap Press of Harvard University Press, 2000.

LaFeber, Walter. *The Clash: A History of U.S.-Japanese Relations*. New York: Norton, 1997.

Littlewood, Ian. *Idea of Japan: Western Images, Western Myths*. Chicago: Ivan R. Dee, 1996.

Matsunosuke, Nishiyama. *Edo Culture: Daily Life and Diversions in Urban Japan, 1600–1868*. Translated and edited by Gerald Groemer. Honolulu: University of Hawaii Press, 1997.

Mihara, Aya. "Little 'All Right' Took the Stage: A Tour of the Japanese Acrobats in Western Europe." *Ohtani Women's University Studies in English Language and Literature* 23 (1996): 99–114.

———. "Professor Risley and Japanese Acrobats: Selections from the Diary of Hirohachi Takano, a Manager for the Risley Troupe during the World Tour, 1866–1868." *Nineteenth Century Theatre* 18 (1990): 62–74.

———. "Professor Risley and Japanese Acrobats II: Their Provincial Tour in England 1867–1868." *Japanese Language and Culture* 17 (1991): 39–50.

———. "Professor Risley's Life in Japan, 1864–1866." *Japanese Language and Culture* 16 (1990): 61–84.

Moon, Krystyn R. *Yellowface: Creating the Chinese in American Popular Music and Performance, 1850s–1920s*. New Brunswick, N.J.: Rutgers University Press, 2005.

Ohara, Keishi, compiler. *Japanese Trade and Industry in the Meiji-Taisho Era*. Translated by Ōkata Tamotsu. Tokyo: Ōbunsha, 1957.

Plummer, Katherine. *The Shogun's Reluctant Ambassadors: Japanese Sea Drifters in the North Pacific*. Portland: Oregon Historical Society, 1991.

Preston, Katherine K. *Opera on the Road: Traveling Opera Troupes in the United States, 1825–1860*. Urbana: University of Illinois Press, 1993.

Rodecape, Lois Foster. "Tom Maguire, Napoleon of the Stage." *California Historical Society Quarterly* 21 (1941): 154–182.

Schroeder, John W. *Matthew Calbraith Perry: Antebellum Sailor and Diplomat*. Annapolis, Md.: Naval Institute Press, 1991.

Sissons, David C. S. "Japanese Acrobatic Troupes Touring Australasia, 1867–1900." *Australasian Drama Studies* 35 (1999): 73–107.

Sugiyama, Shinya. *Japan's Industrialization in the World Economy, 1859–1899: Export Trade and Overseas Competition*. Atlantic Highlands, N.J.: Athlone, 1988.

Van Sant, John E. *Pacific Pioneers: Japanese Journeys to America and Hawaii, 1850–80*. Urbana: University of Illinois Press, 2000.

Wichmann, Siegfried. *Japonisme: The Influence on Western Art in the Nineteenth and Twentieth Centuries*. New York: Park Lane, 1985.

Yoshihara, Mari. *Embracing the East: White Women and American Orientalism*. New York: Oxford University Press, 2003.

4

Collecting Asia

Cultural Politics and the Creation of the Department of Chinese and Japanese Art at the Boston Museum of Fine Arts

CONSTANCE J. S. CHEN

A t the invitation of marine zoologist Edward Sylvester Morse, Harvard historian Denman Waldo Ross viewed the renowned connoisseur's vast collection of pottery in 1889. After examining several pieces of porcelain that Morse had acquired on his trips to East Asia, Ross declared that the objects he beheld reminded him of an old adage, "a little thing makes perfection, perfection which is not a little thing" (quoted in Walter Muir Whitehill 122). In an increasingly "modern" world that seemed to be suffering from irreparable intellectual and cultural malaise, Ross and other New Englanders were hoping to recapture and reconstitute the feelings of "perfect" serenity and self-assurance that they had once experienced in the preindustrial past. In turn, certain white Americans came to believe that an appreciation for exotic Asian artifacts could provide an opportunity for reviving the quintessential New England character and for resurrecting a vanishing way of life. While Ross remained primarily an European art enthusiast in his lifetime, he nevertheless began to purchase Asian relics, convinced that many were artistic productions of the highest quality, imbued with spiritual and social significance for both Asians and Americans.

At the time of Ross's writing in the late nineteenth century, the world that he and his middle- and upper-middle-class compatriots knew was disappearing. As mechanization and industrialization took hold, Bostonians like William Sturgis Bigelow and Ernest Fenollosa turned to East Asia in search of a panacea to alleviate the growing sense of spiritual alienation and cultural barrenness.[1] This essay examines the manner in which Bostonians' fascination for Asia — and, in particular, Japan — led to the creation of the

Japanese Department of Art at the Boston Museum of Fine Arts in 1890. Instead of chronicling its development by enumerating the acquisition of artifacts, the focus of the discussion will revolve around an analysis of the racial and cultural politics that emerged amid socioeconomic transformations on both sides of the Pacific. The first institution of its kind in the United States, the Japanese Department would be renamed the Chinese and Japanese Department in 1903.[2] In 1927, it would receive yet another new designation: the Asiatic Department (fig. 4.1). Throughout its various incarnations, it was and still is considered by many scholars and collectors to hold "the most important [Asian art collection] in the world."[3] Morse, Fenollosa, and Bigelow would become the founding members of the venerable department, as their personal acquisitions constituted the bulk of the original collection.

The genesis of the Japanese Department occurred at a time when the field of art history was moving toward academicization.[4] The study of Asian art was to be governed by Europeans and white Americans well into the twentieth century. Indeed, the desire to create an art-historical canon derived momentum from European academics and collectors, who demanded definitive points of reference for identifying and classifying objects. As such, the mounting interest for reliable Japanese art histories in the West would produce the likes of *Histoire de L'Art du Japon* in 1900. Even though it had been written expressly for European readers, the book also was well received within Asia. In the process, Western theories of Asian aesthetics held sway throughout the East and the West. Within the United States, the professionalization of art history as an academic field of inquiry developed coterminously with the establishment of museums as authoritative arbiters of cultural habits and meanings. Museum curators worked closely with their counterparts in universities, forming an intricate and powerful epistemological matrix. Before long, the museum would gain power as a geopolitical site that formulated certain exhibitionary orders that were used to assess the cultural traditions of nations and peoples.[5] Because artistic productions were believed to be the windows through which the maker's degree of civility could be gauged, art-historical canons held ideological importance beyond the rarified community of connoisseurs and scholars. In the same manner that a map "anticipated spatial reality, not vice versa" for cultural critic Benedict Anderson, discussions regarding Asian objects dictated how Westerners should perceive the so-called Orient and interact with its inhabitants by constructing and disseminating specific social and moral orders (173).[6] Consequently, the significance of East Asia and its aesthetics would be constantly made and remade, depending upon political needs and circumstances.

FIG. 4.1. The Boston Museum of Fine Arts, at its Copley Square location around the turn of the twentieth century. *Photograph by Baldwin Coolidge. Photograph © Museum of Fine Arts, Boston.*

The growing dominance of the museum culture abetted the fascination for the exotic at a crucial time in American and Asian histories: when both regions were undergoing dramatic social and demographic convulsions brought about by the advent of industrialization and increased American involvement in the Asian-Pacific world. The evaluation of socioeconomic disruptions taking place in the United States and Asia would become intertwined with ideologies of modernity, affecting aesthetic definitions and cultural paradigms. Although critic Edward Said's monumental treatise on the political exigencies of Orientalist discourses suggests an insurmountable and unchanging chasm of opposition between us/the West and them/the East, a distinctive form of Orientalism took place within New England as many Bostonians embraced Otherness by emulating Asian customs and collecting the artworks that personified the values that they sought to understand.[7]

Interestingly enough, the curiosity for the East seemed to be a departure from the widespread anxiety and apprehension in the American West concerning the deleterious effects that Asian immigrants and their traditions might have upon white American civilization. While Nativists deemed the presence of Asian laborers on the West Coast to be a threat to the security and the prosperity of the United States, Japanese and Chinese scholars were, in general, not subjected to the most malevolent and violent manifestations of racism.[8] In specific cases, they were even received into elite social and intellectual circles.[9] The divergent treatment of immigrants symbolized the differences between the East and the West Coasts in terms of white Americans' perception of and relationship with Asians as well as the impact of economics on the formation of racialist discourses.[10] Furthermore, in contrast to Said's contention, New Englanders did not view Asia as a monolithic entity: not all Asian countries were equally worthy of derision or adulation.

As a result of increased interactions with Westernizing Japan, most Americans believed that it was poised to become the leader of a new Asia. On the other hand, China, the recognized power base of the region, was on the decline. The Japanese, therefore, were perceived to be the most advanced and civilized Asians, on a par as their European and American counterparts. It is no surprise, then, that the Boston museum's newly established Asian Division accumulated more Japanese objects than those of any other Asian country — the fact that it began as a Japanese collection is telling. In addition, throughout its history, most of its Asian and Asian American staff members tended to be of Japanese descent rather than the supposedly unscientific and uncouth Chinese.[11] In the end, the creation of the Chinese and Japanese Department at the Boston Museum of Fine Arts derived, in part, from the New England nostalgia for what was considered to be preindustrial "perfection"; this nostalgia, in turn, worked to shape notions of Asia, modernity, and aesthetics.

Transformations in the "Citadel of Brahmanism"

In the 1850s, profound technological and demographic changes would lead to cultural and political turmoil throughout the United States. Boston's prominence as an intellectual leader would diminish with the rise of New York City but it would remain the so-called citadel of Brahmanism (Frederic Cople Jaher 77). Historian Lewis Mumford argued that the new edicts of urbanization and industrialization redirected "man's social needs" and led to "alternative modes of living" that were not always welcomed by white Americans (*Culture of Cities* 4).[12] More important, growing contacts with foreign nations and their citizens led to the infiltration of new and bewildering civic values and aesthetic conventions. Once thought to be the "American Athens," Boston was renamed the "American Dublin" as the city's ethnic-racial makeup began to fluctuate.[13] In the two decades preceding the Civil War, the country experienced a substantial upsurge in immigration from Europe and Asia. Whereas the Chinese went to the western regions to find employment, the Irish émigrés traveled to the northeastern areas.

Although immigrants from Ireland had been present in Massachusetts since the early nineteenth century, their numbers swelled to an unprecedented level as many made the trans-Atlantic journey in search of financial opportunities. The Irish exodus began in the 1840s when unexpected population explosions and agricultural disasters in Europe drove countless men and women to American port cities in the Northeast. Prompted by years of famine and poverty, the Irish left their homeland for work in factories such as the Lowell textile mills in northeastern Massachusetts.[14] In the meanwhile, other émigrés from Ireland chose to settle in the flourishing hub of Boston. Soon enough, xenophobic local leaders began to fear that the corruptive powers of the purported "scum of Europe" would devastate the city: in addition to their willingness to serve as "ready instruments in the hands of bosses," the immigrants supposedly had a penchant and predisposition for criminal activities (quoted from Van Wyck Brooks, *New England* 96).

As Boston's ethnic-racial demographics continued to evolve, the division between the native-born and the unwelcome foreign-born masses intensified. This became especially evident as immigrants began to struggle for political control. By the 1880s, the Irish had become such a powerful voting bloc that they were able to nominate and elect mayoral candidates.[15] It is no surprise, then, that the popular press in Boston was increasingly preoccupied with immigration policies in the United States, reporting with a great deal of interest and trepidation on the "onslaught" of Irish immigrants in the Northeast and the invasion of the Chinese in the West.[16] Anxiety over the encroachment of foreigners escalated as newcomers competed with native-born workers for jobs.[17] However, while the presumably uncivilized Irish laborers were deemed to be a menace and a nuisance, the small number of middle- and upper-middle-class Japanese and Chinese scholars, merchants, and diplomats in residence in the Northeast were, on the whole, accepted and even welcomed. The presence of these particular groups of Asians was not a cause for alarm as they did not vie with Bostonians for work or political rule. All in all, city life had become progressively more and more unbearable for the white American bourgeoisie.[18] In time, mass immigration, the expansion of "steel mills, the mechanization of agriculture, the substitution of petroleum for whale oil, the development of the trade union movement, and the concentration of great fortunes, built up by graft, speculation, war-profits, or the outright donation of priceless lands to great railway corporations, acquisitions which were not called theft" would over-power time-honored social bonds, intellectual frameworks, and community leadership within the burgeoning metropolis (quoted from Mumford, *Brown Decades* 5–6).[19]

Confronted with seemingly dire and calamitous transformations that threatened the very core of their traditional way of life, Boston's patrician leaders concentrated on implementing municipal reforms and public ser-vices in order to retain some semblance of power and to cultivate support.[20] One strategy they utilized to reestablish and reassert their cultural domi-nance was to champion institutions like museums that could instill shared social values and standards among the changing ethnic-racial populace. In the late nineteenth century, it was believed that a museum's primary calling was ostensibly "the higher art education of the people."[21] The act of learn-ing took many forms and had a civic dimension: visits to museums, athe-naeums, and lyceums not only would provide the all-important emotional uplift but also would lead to personal improvements, producing a moral and sophisticated citizenry.[22] Ultimately, the Boston Brahmins hoped that with proper guidance and acculturation, the teeming immigrant masses would be assimilated and "Americanized" (Claghorn, 543).[23]

At the same time, New Englanders likewise were looking for ways to as-suage feelings of emptiness and confusion that they were experiencing in the midst of modernity. In their quest for an antidote to counteract the mounting sense of dislocation, white Americans utilized a variety of approaches. Some returned to long-forgotten colonial ideals: for instance, the preferred architec-tural style of the era reflected the antiquarian nostalgia that had been preva-lent in the 1890s (Mumford, *Brown Decades* 16). On the other hand, countless "sensitive and thoughtful" dwellers of the "little weak world" were led to "new regions."[24] Writer Henry James and his cohort sought to restore "the perfection of human society" by seceding from the United States altogether and traveling across the Atlantic, making Europe their new home (Brooks, *New England* 147). As such, a number of restless young men and women went to London, Rome, Florence, Düsseldorf, and Paris in pursuit of intellectual and spiritual renewal. For these individuals, "the New England mind had cut its ancient moorings . . . [and was awash] in the paths of travel" (Brooks, *New England* 151). The passion for journeys to distant lands would bring some of James's fellow malcontents even farther afield. Instead of the Atlantic, many looked across the Pacific to newly opened Japan for inspiration.

To be sure, nineteenth-century New Englanders were not the first to in-teract with Asians; local residents had been making their way to Asia since the colonial period. In the 1780s, in the wake of their newfound independence from England, Americans established trade with China and India. Soon thereafter, merchants would be bringing back furnishings, lacquerware, silk wallpapers, spices, and other items to satisfy the desire of the middle and upper-middle classes to decorate their homes with fanciful luxury goods from exotic lands (fig. 4.2).[25]

FIG. 4.2. Asian accents could be seen throughout the library in John Robinson's Salem, Massachusetts home. *Photograph by E. N. Peabody, 1876. Photograph courtesy of Peabody Essex Museum.*

At the same time, colleges and universities like Harvard and Yale were sending missionaries to the Orient in hopes of winning over converts.[26] And Transcendentalists Ralph Waldo Emerson and Henry David Thoreau would lead the way in the American discovery of Asian religions when they rejected institutionalized Christianity by turning toward Buddhism for intellectual and cultural insights.[27] However, the predilection for the Far East would reach new heights by the end of the 1800s. In light of its long-standing relationship with the region, Boston would become the crucible for the collecting and discussion of Asian artifacts within the United States.

Just as many white Americans were growing increasingly dissatisfied with their mechanized surroundings and searching the world for rejuvenation, the Meiji government's efforts to bring the West to Japan further facilitated cross-cultural exchanges. Prior to the mid-1850s when Commodore Matthew Perry forcibly "opened" Japanese ports, there was little contact between Japan and the West.[28] After a series of internal revolutions, the Tokugawa Shogunate surrendered to the emperor in 1867. The Meiji Restoration of 1868 ended two centuries of self-imposed isolation dictated by the nation's military rulers. The restoration marked a turning point in Japanese history: it was the beginning of Japan's transition to industrialization, which would strengthen its connections with the Western world.

On 6 April 1868, the emperor issued an edict ordering the Japanese to "abandon absurd customs of former times" and "seek knowledge from all over the world" in order to ensure its national well-being and security (quoted from Jonathan Goldstein 67). According to many so-called forward-thinking men and women, Japan's future would depend upon the acquisition of Western innovations and ideals. Education was central to the development of the Asian country during this juncture. In its attempt to "enlighten" Japan, the liberal majority within the Meiji government sent official teams of delegates to the West to help the Japanese acquire the latest technologies.[29] In spite of the barrage of criticism leveled by political and cultural conservatives (who feared the loss of ancient traditions in the rush to Westernize), white American and European academics were hired to teach science, English, and other subjects at Japanese institutions of higher learning. Michiko Nakanishi Vigden has stated that in the 1870s, the French, the English, and the Germans dominated the judicial and military departments while American influences were felt in the Ministries of Education, Finance, and Foreign Affairs (63). Within the next few decades and until the death of the emperor in 1912, more than three thousand *yatois* or officially recruited foreign employees, were hired by the government to impart Western scientific and technological knowledge to the Japanese. The activities of the *yatois* would not only change the intellectual and cultural landscapes within Japan; they also would galvanize and shape the American interest in East Asia.

New Englanders in Asia and Asian Objects in New England

Growing mutual curiosity between Asians and Americans would serve as the foundation for the establishment of the Japanese Department at the Boston Museum of Fine Arts in 1890. In particular, New Englanders who worked as foreign advisers in Asia became important intermediaries between the East and the West during this initial stage of cultural encounter. One of the very first white Americans to reside in Asia and to have extensive contact with the peoples and cultures of the region was marine zoologist Edward Sylvester Morse.[30] Having heard about the wide variety of brachiopod fossils and live specimens available in Japan, he departed for the country in June 1877. Within a month of his arrival, Morse was invited to teach zoology at Tokyo Imperial University. He would be credited with bringing the Darwinian theory of evolution to Japan, in addition to mentoring the first generation of Japanese life scientists. At the same time, Morse was instrumental in fueling the popular awareness of Asia among the New England bourgeoisie. He was furthermore a prominent figure in devising and molding the trajectory of scholarly discussions; his students revered him as a "master in everything [he had] undertaken."[31]

While Morse initially traveled to Japan to study sea mollusks and to teach marine biology, he soon became fascinated with Japanese art forms, especially porcelain wares. Visiting countless kiln sites and curio stores, the Boston scholar journeyed throughout Asia in order to amass ceramic pieces, hoping to create an encyclopedic collection. For Morse, these objects not only possessed aesthetic importance but also functioned as evidence for unearthing the social and intellectual conditions of their producers. Comparing contemporary Chinese potteries against Japanese ones, he argued that the former were of poor quality even though earlier designs had been imitated by Japanese artists of yore. He thus concluded that fallen China was not the cultural giant that it once was.[32] On his second extended sojourn to Japan, which began in April 1878, Morse found ceramics experts to tutor him. Several years later, he boasted that at a gathering for Japanese pottery connoisseurs, he "got the highest number of correct attributions." (*Japan Day by Day*, 2:399). In spite of his growing interest and proficiency in identifying Asian porcelain wares, the marine zoologist never made Japan the focal point of his scholarly inquiries. For the most part, Morse and other white Americans perceived Japan's primary usefulness as its ability to provide spiritual and aesthetic revelations to the West. As such, its esoteric nature and mystical characteristics were accentuated; the seemingly enigmatic Japanese were lauded for embodying a certain Oriental charm. In the end, however, Asians had to be taught modern ideals by Westerners. Therefore, in many ways, the East was understood to be the opposite of the scientific and forward-looking West.

Morse's passion for Asian cultures would be communicated to his fellow Bostonians through a series of public lectures that he gave. Upon his return to the city in 1880, the Lowell Institute invited Morse to make a few presentations recounting his experiences in Japan. Based upon his personal observations, the talks took place in the winter of 1881 and 1882; titles included "Country Life and Natural Scenery," "City Life and Health Matters," and "Homes, Food, and Toilet." These were introductory addresses designed to familiarize the increasingly curious middle and upper-middle classes with Japan. Morse began his lecture series by delving into the geography of the Asian nation before moving onto reflections concerning cultural and social habits. In "Traits of the People," he touched upon the Japanese fondness for eating on the streets as well as their unfailing courtesy toward each other and foreign visitors. Morse painted a vivid portrait of a society filled with industrious and intelligent individuals, steeped in ancient traditions, in spite of its efforts to modernize. Creating an idealized Japan that was overflowing with teahouses and women in kimonos, he intentionally omitted the tremendous effects of Westernization and industrialization on the country.[33] In the process, he constructed a romanticized version of Japan devoid of modern contaminants. Nonetheless, Bostonians greeted Morse's Lowell Institute Lectures and additional presentations at the Museum of Fine Arts with great enthusiasm; they saw him as their link to Japan as well as the rest of Asia. Morse's public talks generated a great deal of curiosity for the area and would have lasting impacts on the study of Asian art in later decades.

Like many of their wealthy friends, local luminaries John and Isabella Stewart Gardner were in attendance at all of Morse's Lowell Institute Lectures. The Gardners epitomized a particular kind of bourgeois Orientalism during this era: they used their connections with the Orient to highlight their intellectual sophistication and remarkable affluence at a historical moment when cultural authority was in flux.[34] The two became so enthralled with and inspired by Morse's descriptions of Asia that they set off for China, Japan, Korea, and several Southeast Asian countries in 1883 on an expedition that lasted nearly a year.[35] Along the way, they visited countless storefronts and picked up numerous bric-a-brac.[36] The most popular collectibles at the time, porcelain wares, did not appeal to Isabella; instead, she was more tempted by the colorful silks, folding screens, and hanging scrolls that she encountered in various Kyoto shops.[37] In the 1890s, after being widowed, Isabella would use these souvenirs from Asia to adorn her newly built home, Fenway Court. Even though the palatial domicile was to serve as a showcase for her vast European art collection, she continued to purchase Asian relics with the guidance and assistance of curio dealers. Placed strategically throughout Fenway Court, Asian artifacts were used as decorative accents to draw attention to her worldliness and fondness for the exotic.[38]

For the Gardners and other early travelers, Japan seemed to be filled with untold peculiarities. The sights and sounds that Isabella beheld were so completely foreign that they were otherworldly. It was this sense of oddness and strangeness that would make both the Japanese and the cultural productions that they crafted so desirable to her and her fellow connoisseurs. Landing in Yokohama, Isabella exclaimed: "it is a much more beautiful country than I had imagined . . . and as for the dear little people, with their houses and things, they are all like play things."[39] Without even realizing it, perhaps, she had articulated the concept of American exceptionalism that was so prevalent at the time. Potentially threatening Otherness could be contained and controlled by reclassifying it as being exotically diminutive and inferior. During their stay in Japan, the Gardners kept a busy schedule, visiting with fellow American tourists and wandering through Japanese cities such as Tokyo and Kyoto.[40] Isabella was intent on recording every detail of her adventures. In addition to a journal, she kept scrapbooks filled with photographs, pressed leaves, postcards, and various items that she and John picked up along the way. Pictures of sumo wrestlers, women in native dress, rickshaw drivers, and curio shops demonstrated her fascination for what she considered to be the traditional cultural practices of the realm. Meanwhile, her husband, John, became enamored of the geishas, who were astonishingly "very respectable in appearance."[41] All in all, Morse's prior assurance that this was "the land of gentle manners, rational delights, and startling surprises" had been realized (*Glimpses of China* 3). To the Westerners who arrived on its shores, Japan was alluringly and intoxicatingly alien.

Although the Gardners traveled to Asia in search of adventure and purchased knickknacks to add an aura of exoticism to their home, other New Englanders journeyed to the region for the sake of self-enlightenment. As such, they sought to comprehend the social and ideological contexts that produced the very Asian objects that they accumulated. Two of Morse's protégés, William Sturgis Bigelow and Ernest Fenollosa, would come to see

Japan as holding out the promise of spiritual and cultural salvation in the midst of incredible social turmoil in Boston. They longed for a time without the rule of machines and hoped to find a solution to all of the problems brought on by modernization. Believing that industrializing Japan could use its venerable customs to stave off the violent and disruptive intrusion of modernity, New Englanders became ardent supporters of the need to preserve native cultures. In the process, they purchased artworks they deemed to be the physical embodiments of the time-honored rituals they were emulating. More specifically, for Bigelow and Fenollosa, the allure of these relics derived, in part, from the fact that they served as visual reminders of the Buddhist teachings that they were studying. Throughout their extended stays in Japan in the late nineteenth century, both connoisseurs purchased artifacts with the intention of augmenting the growing collections at the Museum of Fine Arts in Boston. In time, these two New Englanders would become important interpreters and disseminators of Asian beliefs and conventions, influencing literary, aesthetic, and political discourses on the Orient.

At Morse's recommendation, Fenollosa first traveled to Japan in 1878 to teach Western philosophy and political economy at local universities and colleges. As with his mentor before him, Fenollosa also was mesmerized by the Asian arts.[42] However, whereas the zoologist hoarded pottery wares, Fenollosa directed his energy toward paintings, both ancient and contemporary. As he immersed himself in the Japanese cultural circles, he became alarmed by the disappearance of age-old arts and crafts: the Japanese were attempting to modernize by shedding their own seemingly outdated practices. With the assistance of like-minded New Englanders, Fenollosa would embark on a lifelong mission to save Japanese antiquities from neglect and ruin. At the same time, he continued to purchase East Asian paintings, focusing on those by Japanese artists. In 1886, Fenollosa would sell his impressive collection to Japanophile Charles G. Weld, a Harvard-trained surgeon who had traipsed through Asia to acquire Japanese swords and sword ornaments. These items would be known henceforth as the Fenollosa-Weld Collection (fig. 4.3). Together with Weld's cache of metalwork, Fenollosa's Chinese and Japanese paintings were loaned out permanently to the Boston Museum of Fine Arts, greatly enhancing the cultural institution's stockpile of Asian relics.

In the meanwhile, Fenollosa's friend and fellow Japanophile, Bigelow, had developed a penchant for Japanese aesthetics during his travels in Europe in the 1870s. *Japonisme* and Chinoiserie were then in vogue in Paris; consequently, he was able to amass several hundred objects via French dealers. In 1880, Bigelow would lend his collection to the Fine Arts Museum in

FIG. 4.3. One of the most prized objects in the Fenollosa-Weld Collection is the scroll "Night Attack on the Sanjô Palace," from the *Illustrated Scrolls of the Events of the Heiji Era (Heiji monogatari emaki)*, shown here in detail. Japanese, Kamakura period, second half of the thirteenth century. Handscroll; ink and color on paper, 41.3 × 699.7 cm (16¼ × 275½ in.). *Museum of Fine Arts, Boston. Fenollosa-Weld Collection, 11.4000. Photograph © Museum of Fine Arts, Boston.*

his hometown.[43] All along, he yearned to see the part of the world that had produced the very artifacts that he so admired. At the conclusion of Morse's celebrated Lowell Institute Lectures in 1882, Bigelow decided to accompany the distinguished scholar to Japan; this would be Morse's third and final trip to the country. Bigelow would later call his decision to journey across the Pacific "the turning point of [his] life."[44] Like many visitors who preceded him, he was in awe of Japan. With Morse and Fenollosa's guidance and assistance, he began to add to his collection of Asian art as soon as he arrived. Together, the three men aspired to bring some of the rarest and finest Asian articles back to the Boston Museum of Fine Arts.[45] Bigelow was an eclectic connoisseur who was enamored with the decorative arts of Japan, purchasing, among other things, *netsukes*, lacquerwares, prints, bronzes, and swords. And as he became increasingly devoted to the study of Buddhism, he turned his attention to the acquisition of religious pieces, especially sculptures and paintings depicting Kannon, the goddess of mercy.

The growth of Western interest in Buddhism occurred simultaneously with the decline of the religion within Asia itself, leading to the re-envisioning of aesthetic and cultural frameworks.[46] In premodern Japan, the selling of Buddhist art was considered to be blasphemous. Since the

Restoration of 1868 and the forcible separation of Buddhist and Shinto practices, ancient relics had become more readily available. Items that had been used in religious ceremonies were redefined as highly coveted objects of art to be sold for commercial purposes. In the process, abandoned temples and shrines became treasure-houses for dealers to loot. This was, indeed, a good time to buy, given that impoverished noble families were eager to sell heirlooms quickly and cheaply. Furthermore, the craze for all things Western in the country had led to disdain for traditional arts and crafts.[47] As a result, Japanese elites scorned Buddhist art as the personification of superstitious beliefs and outdated customs, while working-class men and women feared the corruptive powers of the icons. Because Buddhist artifacts frequently were associated with funerals, they were not popular collectibles until European and white American connoisseurs became captivated by Buddhism. Certainly, entities such as the Boston Museum of Fine Arts took advantage of the availability of these religious materials to help stock burgeoning Asian art collections in the United States.

As its cache of precious and rare pieces grew, the museum began an extensive construction project that would add several new wings to the existing building in Copley Square in order to better display its immense collection from around the world. In 1890, when work on the edifice was completed, Morse, like Fenollosa, Weld, and Bigelow before him, agreed to deposit his vast holding of pottery wares at the institution, effectively creating the Department of Japanese Art. By 1892, Morse's entire collection would be purchased by the museum.[48] With Fenollosa as the curator of the nascent department, Morse was hired to be the Keeper of Japanese Pottery. The latter's most notable duty was to classify the objects from his own collection and to generate a comprehensive catalogue.[49] In 1911, two years after the museum relocated to its newly constructed Huntington Avenue site, the Bigelow and Fenollosa-Weld Collections would become permanent acquisitions: Bigelow donated his entire collection while Weld's was bequeathed in his will in June of that year.[50] By now, the Japanese branch had been renamed the Department of Chinese and Japanese Art. The opening and the subsequent expansion of the Asian division in the late nineteenth and early twentieth centuries signified the redefinition of intellectual and aesthetic discourses; artifacts from the East were no longer mere ethnological curiosities. The fact that Asian works of art were on display at a prominent American cultural institution spoke volumes about the newfound importance placed on these items.

The addition of the extraordinary Bigelow and Fenollosa-Weld Collections would cement the Boston museum's renown as one of the leading forces in the exhibition and discussion of Chinese and Japanese cultural forms. As its possession of Asian goods reached an "unrivalled" level, the organization sought to give "the public greater opportunities for approaching the real meaning of Asiatic art . . . through the publication of catalogues and through lectures on the collection, [which] will afford full facilities in the future to the lovers and students of art in general, for forming a deeper conception of that of the East" (Okakura 6). Members of the community were to be instructed on the potential advantages that Asian traditions might have for modern civilizations through public programs offered by the museum. At that point in time, the pedagogical function of cultural institutions was especially crucial for advancing the bourgeois interest in Asia, as elsewhere there was a dearth of knowledge on the region. As the Chinese and Japanese Division accumulated more and more relics, the Boston Museum of Fine Arts would continue to serve as one of the primary forums for the propagation of popular and academic discourses on Asia.

Preserving Aesthetic Traditions

Just as they were discovering the value of Japanese culture, white American connoisseurs realized that, like their Western counterparts, the Japanese had been all too eager to reject time-honored customs. To the Bostonians' dismay, Japan's unquestioning acceptance of modernization seemed to be harming its very essence and character. Motivated, in large part, by their own reaction to what they perceived to be artistic and spiritual destruction taking place in New England, both Bigelow and Fenollosa emphasized the importance of antiquity for the welfare of modern societies; they hoped to retain the established way of life while moving toward mechanization and urbanization. In so doing, they replicated Orientalist expectations by inventing an idealized Japanese golden age in danger of annihilation. With the support of many Japanese political and cultural conservatives, white Americans endeavored to safeguard ancient Japanese rituals and conventions, which they believed to be the intellectual and social anchors for all industrializing and industrialized civilizations, both Eastern and Western.

In time, Bigelow and Fenollosa were to become two of the most outspoken advocates for the need to preserve historical landmarks and cultural practices in Japan. They would be regarded as cultural saviors in the Asian nation: in 1909, Bigelow was awarded the prestigious Order of the Rising Sun by the Japanese government for his work in helping to sustain Japanese art. Consequently, the two were able to derive authority within Asian and

American art and social circles through their self-appointed role as conservationists. For instance, their influence would be felt keenly within the Boston Museum of Fine Arts: following the advice of its two principal donors and advisers, the Asian Division would make the collecting of Japanese art its principal goal during its early days.[51] This emphasis can be interpreted as the museum's desire to serve as a repository for the Japanese artistic and cultural forms that were deemed to be on the verge of extinction.

Fenollosa and Bigelow arrived in Japan at a historical juncture, when multitudes of Japanese men and women were becoming increasingly troubled by the manner in which the unchecked fervor for the West could overwhelm indigenous Japanese cultures. On his trips to ancient monuments and archeological sites, Fenollosa became aware of the desecration of Japanese national treasures. He lamented the abandonment and renunciation of tradition in the country's rush to Westernize. In keeping with an imperial mandate, Japan as a whole maintained that "the stimulating of the industries within [its] borders is its prime object and no delay can be suffered."[52] The consequences of this goal could be disastrous. Like other concerned cultural conservatives and antiquarians, Fenollosa feared that Japanese artworks would become "cheapened" in the eagerness to compete with the West.[53] This critical stance toward mechanization and industrialization paralleled New Englanders' own dismay at what they saw happening all around them within the United States.

To make matters worse, not only did the Japanese forsake longstanding virtues; they also tried to eradicate their existence altogether by adopting all things European and American. Western ideals were revered in just about every cultural and intellectual arena: musicians used European techniques as the foundation of their compositions and young women were "dressed to kill in new style European clothes."[54] Moreover, traditional ink brushes were abandoned in favor of using pencils.[55] In conjunction, the Japanese government hired Italian art instructors to introduce Western methods — at the risk of causing grievous injuries to Japan's national culture:

> It was deemed necessary to import Italian painters and sculptors to educate a new generation of "civilized artists." For nearly a decade large classes of young men, trained in crayon drawing from Greek casts, oil studies of models with blurring drapery and marble madonnas, were turned loose upon the community to perpetrate travesties of European salons. It became a disgrace to exhibit a sign of "barbarious" Oriental feeling.[56]

Evidently, the Japanese enthusiasm for the West had compelled them to purge their native customs from the popular consciousness. As a result, certain cultural conservatives worried that the nation would be left unprotected against modern decadence as "everything Japanese was to be despised, and foreign tastes and products were to be the rage of the day."[57] In 1886, Fenollosa lobbied the imperial government to use the Japanese Pavilion to display the traditional arts at the 1890 international exposition to be held in Tokyo. However, Prince Hirobumi Ito was more interested in showcasing Japan's progression toward modernity and in highlighting its implementation of Western practices. Consequently, he insisted that the exhibition would focus principally on Japanese industrial arts.[58] Fenollosa was greatly disappointed by the prince's decision and perceived it to be emblematic of the outright repudiation of tradition that was taking place throughout the country. To combat the growing disregard for ancient ideals, he and various Japanese cultural conservatives helped to establish the Art Club of Nobles to rally Japan's elite society to aid his cause. In the process, Fenollosa, Bigelow, and other like-minded New Englanders became fascinated with antiquities, breathing new life into art forms that were then considered to be obsolete by the Japanese themselves. Fenollosa was especially taken with the aesthetics of the Kano and Tosa schools, which depicted early court life and were associated with Buddhist principles; they had been favorite collectibles of the wealthy and the military ruling class of bygone eras.

As self-professed cultural caretakers who were intent on saving Japan's national heritage, Fenollosa and many Asians and Americans became increasingly alarmed with Japan's willingness to sell valuable treasures to the highest bidders. Indeed, what the West "want[ed] was the very birthright which the Japanese had sold."[59] Ironically, while Fenollosa seemed to be sincere in his desire to serve as a guardian of culture for Japan, he also was traveling throughout the country, searching for precious and unique relics to send to the Boston Museum of Fine Arts:

> I bought several pictures dating from 700 to 900 A.D. Already people here are saying that my collection must be kept here in Japan for the Japanese. I have bought a number of the very greatest treasures secretly. The Japanese as yet don't know that I have them. I wish I could see them all safely housed forever in the Boston Art Museum; and yet, if the Emperor or the Mombusho [the Ministry of Education] should wish to buy my collection, wouldn't it be my duty to humanity, all things considered, to let them have it?[60]

Fenollosa felt an ethical conflict. On the one hand, he wanted to protect ancient artworks for the sake of future Japanese generations; in this regard, the items ought to be kept in Asia. At the same time, though, he sensed a great

deal of pressure to make a name for himself in American art circles by bringing valuable pieces back to Massachusetts; his legitimacy and status as a connoisseur and scholar were directly correlated with the kinds of relics he was
able to obtain. In the end, his personal ambitions triumphed and he
justified his efforts to accumulate rare objects as acts of cultural conserva-
tion. Fenollosa contended that he was working on behalf of a modernizing
Japan that appeared to be unconcerned with and uninterested in safeguard-
ing its own heritage.

Fenollosa's emphasis on the obligation of a society to care for its artifacts
stemmed from his belief that art-historical practices were inextricably connected to the social and spiritual well-being of a nation and its people.
Therefore, Japan not only must maintain but also perpetuate its cultural
legacy in view of the fact that it was the very "flower of its civilization."[61]
Art, for the Japanese, both reflected and constituted a way of life:

> Eastern art is . . . not a craze, or a style; it is a life. With us [Westerners] art is
> little more than an affectation, though admittedly a thoroughly wrought out
> one. With Asiatics it is a necessity like language and food. Apart from Eastern
> life it is nothing. To bind it to an analytic law, would be to destroy it. To call
> it decoration would be to erect momentary conceit into a universal canon. It
> is nothing that the West can know under any familiar category. Being Eastern
> life, it has to be studied as such.[62]

Because aesthetic principles were associated with every aspect of the material world, they were the "most sensitive barometer of Oriental culture."[63]
In East Asia, for instance, art was very much a part of the spiritual life of the
people; in turn, its production was imbued with religious significance.[64]
Aesthetics even pervaded the political arena, influenced by and influencing
legislative decisions.[65] Because it was embedded within specific socioeconomic conditions, Fenollosa argued that East Asian art forms should not be
judged by Western standards; this line of reasoning would help to elevate
Asian objects to the status of fine art in the United States and Europe. More
important, the future of the Japanese populace depended upon the preservation of their traditional arts.[66] A nation had to draw strength and inspiration from its cultural past. However, Japan's eagerness to shed itself of its
supposed ancient savagery had led to a period of artistic decay; worse yet, it
had loosened cultural foundations and dislocated moral norms. For Fenollosa and other white Americans who were both critical and fearful of the
rapid changes taking place in the West, Japan had to remain "authentically"
Japanese. Japan, they maintained, could not afford to forsake its own cul-

tural legacies in its desire to Westernize and to attain so-called enlightenment.

Even though the inextricable bond between art and nature constituted one of the most distinctive aspects of Japanese aesthetics, the advent of industrialization had damaged this previously harmonious relationship. As evidenced in the West, the process of modernization had worked to redefine the idea of nature:

> [In accordance with Western notions, nature was deemed to be] a certain phenomenal externality, apart from ourselves, a separateness of standard capable of being photographed. . . . In the East its divorce from human nature has never taken place. The two are one. . . . It is not nature against man, but nature in man. We have become scientific pedants. . . . Nature is what they [the Asians] feel. . . . When the modern criticize Eastern art as unlike nature, it is their own materialistic nature only which they mean.[67]

Once again, the Orient was identified with being otherworldly and one with the cosmos, the opposite of the mundane and rational West. In all likelihood, Fenollosa thought that this sort of Orientalization was high praise for the Asians. What he and other cultural conservatives in New England dreaded was that the development of the arts had been injured and prematurely terminated because contemporary artists tended to emphasize the mere replication of nature instead of attempting to capture its very spirit. Unfortunately, the same was happening all over Japan and elsewhere in Asia. For Fenollosa, then, the Japanese were in danger of losing their intrinsic essence — and thus what had made them unique — in their efforts to become more modern. If white Americans were not vigilant, a similar fate would be awaiting them.

Conclusion

For many late nineteenth-century Bostonians, the union between Japan and the West could be mutually beneficial. They believed that Westerners could not afford to discount what the East had to offer, as the two regions were essentially halves of the same whole. This acceptance seemed a startling deviation from the dominant view of the time: that Asian immigrants had detrimental impacts on the morality and civility of white American culture. According to Fenollosa, differences between the East and the West made them perfect partners: the two were "opposed in ideals which [meant that each] need[ed] the other for complement. Each alone [was] beset with characteristic weakness."[68] Capitulating to the popular discourses of the era, Fenollosa maintained that Asia personified "the feminine" and the West, "the masculine."[69] When the two were merged together, a new entity materialized and "there is no more West and no more East" (Fenollosa, *East and West* 55). Indeed, for Fenollosa, the "fusion of East and West" was a "sacred issue" and must take place forthwith, for each "was doomed to failure in its isolation" ("Coming Fusion of East and West" 122). In essence, "the reasons why any one in the world likes a great work of Japanese art, are precisely the same reasons for which he likes a great work of Europe, — the minor differences disappear."[70] If one studied the history of art, he or she would discover that Eastern and Western beliefs had developed along similar pathways in antiquity. Touting universalism as an alternative, Japanophiles such as Fenollosa thus set out to disprove critics who held that Japanese and Western arts were stylistically and thematically in opposition to each other; they were attempting to redefine the meaning and the place of Asian aesthetics and cultures. However, in so doing, Fenollosa and his cohort perpetuated notions of Eastern inferiority and mystique while upholding Western ingenuity and superiority. For their ideological purposes, the Japan they had come to admire had to remain unchanged and untouched by the passage of time.

Having arrived in Japan in 1882, Bigelow viewed his new life as exemplifying the inevitable amalgamation between the East and the West. By all appearances, he seemed to have melded his New England upbringing and newly acquired Japanese cultural traditions with ease and contentment. Visitors like the Gardners would remark at how quickly he was able to establish a "comfortable house . . . as he interests himself in many things in a very intelligent way." All in all, his life in Tokyo was "busy and interesting."[71] He not only familiarized himself with ancient Japanese customs and rituals; he had taken them up in his daily life. Instead of rejecting the ostensibly inexplicable Other, Bigelow was emulating the Orientals he saw all around him. While visiting their friend in Tokyo, the Gardners observed that he "always carries local colour about with him as he is thoroughly in love with it all — He wears their clothes, when at home — He takes us to shops, where we sit in stocking feet on their pretty clean mats — drink canary coloured tea, eat sweets."[72] To them, their kimono-wearing compatriot appeared to have taken on the persona of an interloper living blissfully in Bohemia. At a historical juncture when the Asian country was discarding its Eastern habits, Bigelow became immersed in an imagined Japan, one without modern pollutants, in order to create a new cultural identity for himself.

The nineteenth-century enterprise to bind the East and the West together embodied bourgeois New Englanders' response to the radical demographic and technological transformations taking place all around them. On the one hand, some upper-middle-class Bostonians used their association with the exotic East to accentuate their erudition and their access to a newly opened region, thereby reinstating their cultural status as tastemakers in a changing world. Other New Englanders hoped for even more: seeking life-altering revelations, they went to Japan in search of "a little perfection," expecting to find a remedy to ameliorate the problems brought on by industrialization. Instead of marginalizing Asians and their everyday practices as baffling and incomprehensible, they sought to incorporate what East Asia had to offer to enhance their spiritual and intellectual lives. During their visits, these Japanophiles endeavored to understand age-old values, amassing aesthetic productions that they wished to employ as bulwarks against modernity. Realizing that the Japanese were readily casting off ancient principles in an effort to embrace Westernization and industrialization, Bostonians like Bigelow and Fenollosa insisted on the cultural and ideological importance of preserving time-honored rituals within a mechanized society. Taking a morally superior stance, their work as conservationists would enable them to gain privileged positions within Asia and the United States.

In the process, New Englanders asserted that the restoration of Japanese antiquity was to be the primary means of retrieving lost Edens and golden ages for both Asians and Westerners. They thus fabricated romanticized images of Asia that did not always reflect historical realities. All too often, the Orient was depicted as the feminine, timeless, and mystical complement to the masculine, evolving, and scientific West. In many ways, the significance of Asia rested upon its distinctively premodern attributes. Nonetheless, in time, white Americans' collecting habits would help to reconstitute Boston's cultural landscape, leading to the establishment of the Japanese Department of Art in 1890: the collection not only reproduced Asia in New England but likewise educated the uninformed public on the benefits of Asian beliefs in the midst of modernization. Just as Japan had to retain its cultural heritage in order to survive the onslaught of industrialization, the United States also had to do everything possible to integrate the past with the present. Ultimately, the Japan craze in nineteenth-century Boston that culminated in the formation of one of the world's most well known Asian art collections represented a complex mix of the exoticization of the Orient, disillusionment with modernity, as well as the redefinition of cultural consciousness for certain white Americans.

ACKNOWLEDGMENTS

I would like to thank Monica Chiu and the anonymous reviewers for their comments in the preparation of this essay.

NOTES

1. T. J. Jackson Lears has characterized the dominant sentiment among the bourgeoisie as being "antimodernist." I would argue that instead of rejecting modernity, New Englanders were, in fact, attempting to come to terms with it by looking to the East.

2. In the September 1903 edition of the *Boston Museum of Fine Arts Bulletin*, the division appeared as "the Department of Chinese and Japanese Art" for the first time.

3. Quoted from art historian Benjamin March, *China and Japan in Our Museums*, 37. This study consists of a survey of various museum holdings within the United States.

4. See, for instance, Donald Preziosi, *Rethinking Art History: Meditations on a Coy Science*; Vernon Hyde Minor, *Art History's History*; and Sally Price, *Primitive Art in Civilized Places*.

5. See Tony Bennett, *The Birth of the Museum: History, Theory, Politics*; Susan Pearce, *Museums, Objects, and Collections: A Cultural Study*; Eilean Hooper-Greenhill, *Museums and the Shaping of Knowledge*; and Carol Duncan, *Civilizing Rituals: Inside Public Art Museums*.

6. Anderson goes on to write that "[i]n other words, a map was a model for, rather than a model of, what it purported to represent" (173).

7. Edward Said's influential work discusses how the West has constituted "the Other" for cultural, ideological, and political purposes. See also James Clifford, *The Predicament of Culture: Twentieth-Century Ethnography, Literature, and Art*. In addition to exploring the ways in which geopolitical frameworks can shape notions of Otherness, both authors take issue with problematic designations like "the West," "the East," "the Occident," "the Orient," "modern," and "primitive."

8. See Robert Lee, *Orientals: Asian Americans in Popular Culture* and Alexander Saxton, *The Indispensable Enemy: Labor and the Anti-Chinese Movement in California*.

9. See Constance J. S. Chen, "Transnational Orientals: Scholars of Art, Nationalist Discourses, and the Question of Intellectual Authority," and K. Scott Wong and Sucheng Chan, eds., *Claiming America: Constructing Chinese American Identities During the Exclusion Era*. While certain Asian scholars were welcomed into American intellectual circles, they often were compelled to abide by Orientalist expectations such as having to dress in native costumes to substantiate

their credibility as cultural insiders. Their influence was thus limited by specific social boundaries and ideological constraints.

10. This class bias was reflected in the Chinese Exclusion Act of 1882 which barred the entrance of laborers for a ten-year period but exempted merchants from the legislation. See Stuart Creighton Miller, *The Unwelcome Immigrant: The American Image of the Chinese, 1785–1882*; Ronald Takaki, *Strangers from a Different Shore: A History of Asian Americans*; and Bill Ong Hing, *Making and Remaking Asian America Through Immigration Policy, 1850–1990*.

11. This was certainly true during the department's earliest days when professional lacquer artists like Rokkaku Shisui and others were brought over from Japan to work at the museum.

12. For additional discussions on the impacts of urbanization, see Sam Bass Warner, Jr., *Urban Wilderness: A History of the American City* and George J. Lankevich, *American Metropolis: A History of New York City*. There have been many monographs devoted to the development of Chicago, including Daniel Bluestone's *Constructing Chicago* and Carl Condit's *The Chicago School of Architecture: A History of Commercial and Public Buildings in the Chicago Area, 1875–1925*.

13. Quoted from Brooks Van Wyck, *New England: Indian Summer, 1865–1915*, 7. See also Oscar Handlin's *Boston Immigrants, 1790-1865: A Study in Acculturation*.

14. Between 1815 and 1845, about one million immigrants of Irish descent came to the United States, and by the 1920s, four million more would join them. By 1870, sixty-three thousand Chinese laborers were accounted for in the western United States. Most of them resided in California and worked as miners, although some also made their way to New England, the South, and the Southwest. These figures are from Ronald Takaki, *A Different Mirror: A History of Multicultural America*, 140, 143, and 194.

15. See Geoffrey Blodgett, "Yankee Leadership in a Divided City, 1860–1910," and Charles H. Trout, "Curley of Boston: The Search for Irish Legitimacy."

16. See, for instance, the 9 January 1881 *Boston Globe* story on the passage of "the New Chinese Treatise," which permitted Americans to regulate the immigration of Chinese laborers into the United States and was a precursor to the Chinese Exclusion Act of 1882. The following day, 10 January 1881, the *Globe* included several reports on the Irish such as "The Young Men of Ireland."

17. A 1 January 1881 editorial in the *Boston Globe* exemplified New Englanders' fear of foreigners. Written as a satire, the author looked a hundred years into the future and predicted that by the year 1981, the country would be overrun by the "Baboon Empire, ruled over by the Emperor Jocko." This "great Mongkee race" would battle for power with the "Chinamen, to whom a rat pie and an opium stew are necessary of civilized existence." Eventually, the "Mongkee laborer" would win out because he had the support of influential Boston philanthropists and was more "frugal and industrious." The physical characteristics given in the newspaper implied that the "Mongkees" were the supposedly uncouth Irish immigrants, who were quickly becoming the ethnic majority in the city. Many

native-born Americans were terrified of the prospect that the Chinese would take possession of the western states while the Irish lorded over the Northeast.

18. See, for instance, Edward S. Morse, "Can City Life Be Made Endurable?" Edward Sylvester Morse Papers, James Duncan Phillips Library (hereafter PL), Salem, Mass. In an address delivered at the annual commencement of the Worcester Polytechnic Institute on 21 June 1900, Morse argued that, for one thing, the noise level in the cities must be reduced.

19. For the importance of social connections in New England circles, see Judith A. Roman, *Annie Adams Fields: The Spirit of Charles Street* and M. A. DeWolfe Howe, *Memoirs of a Hostess: A Chronicle of Eminent Friendships Drawn Chiefly from the Diaries of Mrs. James T. Fields*.

20. See, for instance, Constance K. Burns, "The Irony of Progressive Reform: Boston, 1898–1910."

21. Edward S. Morse, "Museums of Art and Their Influences," an 1892 address at the Beacon Society in Boston. From the Edward Sylvester Morse Papers, PL.

22. Lillian Miller argues that the Athenaeum in Boston was emblematic of the type of cultural and civic institutions being created to encourage aesthetic and intellectual development within the United States. The idea that social well-being could be obtained through cultural transformations was promoted in Chicago and other regions as well during the same era. See Helen Lefkowitz Horowitz, *Culture and the City: Cultural Philanthropy in Chicago from the 1880s to 1917*.

23. In spite of the growing fear of criminal acts committed by new Americans, Kate H. Claghorn concluded that in the end, Italian, German, and Irish immigrants were no more corrupt or licentious than the native-born. Writing at the turn of the twentieth century, she also suggested that with supervision, the newcomers could be successfully assimilated into American society.

24. Phillips Brooks' letter to William S. Bigelow, 2 September 1889, William Sturgis Bigelow Papers, Houghton Library, Harvard University, Cambridge, Mass. (hereafter HL).

25. See Hugh Honour, *Chinoiserie: The Vision of Cathay*; Carl Crossman, *The China Trade: Export Paintings, Furniture, Silver & Other Objects*; Christina Nelson, *Directly from China: Export Goods for the American Market, 1784–1930*; and Craig Clunas, "Oriental Antiquities/Far Eastern Art." For additional discussions on the political and ideological implications of the bourgeois consumption of Asian goods, see John K. W. Tchen, *New York Before Chinatown: Orientalism and the Shaping of American Culture, 1776–1882*.

26. See Samuel C. Bartlett, *Religion in America: Historical Sketches of the Missions of the American Board* and Paul A. Varg, *Missionaries, Chinese, and Diplomats: The American Protestant Missionary Movement in China, 1890–1952*.

27. See, for instance, Wilcomb Washburn, "The Oriental 'Roots' of American Transcendentalism"; Arthur Christy, *The Orient in American Transcendentalism: A Study of Emerson, Thoreau, and Alcott*; and Arthur Versluis, *American Transcendentalism and Asian Religions*.

28. There has been much debate about whether Japan was, indeed, "opened" by Westerners or whether it was on the verge of initiating increased contacts with the West and the rest of Asia. See, for instance, Peter Booth Wiley, *Yankees in the Land of the Gods: Commodore Perry and the Opening of Japan* and Rhoda Blumberg, *Commodore Perry in the Land of the Shogun*.

29. See Peter Duus, *The Japanese Discovery of America: A Brief History with Documents*. For general accounts see, E. Manchester Boddy, *Japanese in America*; Herman Masako, *The Japanese in America, 1843–1973*; and Charles Lanman, ed., *The Japanese in America*.

30. For additional biographical information on Morse, see Dorothy G. Wayman, *Edward Sylvester Morse: A Biography*; Robert Rosenstone, *Mirror in the Shrine: American Encounters with Meiji Japan*; and Christopher Benfey, *The Great Wave: Gilded Age Misfits, Japanese Eccentrics, and the Opening of Old Japan*.

31. Letter from William S. Bigelow to Edward S. Morse, 17 January 1916, the Edward Sylvester Morse Papers, PL. Morse's renown went beyond the academic circles: many amateur connoisseurs wrote to him hoping for assistance in identifying artifacts or in translating Japanese characters. See Morse's 27 February 1886 letter to an unknown recipient, from the Edward Sylvester Morse Papers, PL.

32. On his visit to China, Morse went to a kiln site, which was "as barren as a brickyard. What vivid memories came back of the Japanese potter with his charming surroundings, the offering of tea and cake, the children in the neighborhood bowing as one passed, the potter himself, a courteous soul with a love and knowledge of his craft and the work of the generations preceding him. In contrast, this Chinese pottery is a desolate yard, the ground strewn with pottery fragments, a number of workmen shouting to each other or at me, a horde of ragged men and boys howling vile names" (*Glimpses of China and Chinese Homes* 199–200).

33. During this time period, Meiji men and women were abandoning traditional Japanese garb in favor of Western-style suits and dresses. See G. B. Sansom, *The Western World and Japan: A Study in the Interaction of European and Asiatic Cultures* and Kenneth B. Pyle, *The New Generation in Meiji Japan: Problems of Cultural Identity, 1885–1895*.

34. Mari Yoshihara has argued that the Gardners' collecting habits were emblematic of that particular era's "Orientalist consumption of Asian cultures" (22). Also see Christine Guth, *Longfellow's Tattoos: Tourism, Collecting, and Japan*.

35. Isabella S. Gardner journal entry of 7 September 1883, Isabella Stewart Gardner Museum Papers, Archives of American Art, Washington, D.C.

36. Letter from Isabella S. Gardner to Anna Lyman (Mason) Gray, 5 July 1883, Isabella Stewart Gardner Papers, HL.

37. Letter from Isabella S. Gardner to George Gardner, 24 August 1883, Gardner Family Papers II, Massachusetts Historical Society, Boston (hereafter MHS).

38. See, for instance, Victoria Weston, "Asian Art at the Isabella Stewart Gardner

Museum" and Rollin Van N. Hadley, *The Letters of Bernard Berenson and Isabella Stewart Gardner, 1887–1924*.

39. Letter from Isabella S. Gardner to Anna Lyman (Mason) Gray, 5 July 1883, Isabella Stewart Gardner Papers, HL.

40. On June 26, 1883, Isabella S. Gardner recorded that she and her husband "[s]hopped all day and dined with WSB [William Sturgis Bigelow]." From Scrapbook, Isabella Stewart Gardner Museum Archives, Boston.

41. John Gardner wrote to his nephew, George Gardner, on 5 July 1883, recounting a dinner with astronomer cum writer Percival Lowell, who was then living in Japan. They were all entertained "with music, dancing, tricks and conversation. He [Lowell] wished you could have been there and I am sure you would have enjoyed it immensely." From the Gardner Family Papers II, MHS.

42. For additional biographical information on Fenollosa, see Lawrence Chisolm, *Fenollosa: The Far East and American Culture* and Van Wyck Brooks, *Fenollosa and His Circle*. Fenollosa's influence went beyond the art world. His work on the Noh theater would help to revive interest in the classical cultural form in Japan and the United States. See, for instance, Fenollosa's writings on *The Classic Noh Theatre of Japan* and *"Noh," or Accomplishment: A Study of the Classical Stage of Japan*.

43. Bigelow's massive collection consisted of several hundred pieces of Japanese lacquer as well as embroideries, ivory carvings, and other miscellaneous objects. He donated 509 additional Japanese pieces the following year in 1881.

44. Letter from William S. Bigelow to Edward S. Morse, 15 November 1917, the Edward Sylvester Morse Papers, PL.

45. Morse hoped that "[w]e shall see a little of the life of old Japan; I shall add a great many specimens to my collection of pottery; Dr. Bigelow will secure many forms of swords, guards, and lacquer . . . so that we shall have in the vicinity of Boston by far the greatest collection of Japanese art in the world" (*Japan*, 2:238).

46. See Carl T. Jackson, *The Oriental Religions and American Thought* and Thomas Tweed and Stephen Prothero, eds., *Asian Religions in America: A Documentary History*.

47. Bigelow claimed that "[a]fter the [Meiji] restoration, in 1868, two causes brought old and good works of art in large quantities into the market. First, the selling out at any price of impoverished noblemen & gentlemen. Second, the sudden frantic mania for every thing foreign among the Japanese. In those days you could have swapped a beaver hat for a gold lacquer box anywhere. . . . Of course the foreigners bought it up." See Bigelow's letter to Henry Cabot Lodge from Tokyo, 30 September 1883, Henry Cabot Lodge Papers, MHS.

48. According to one account, the collection had been valued at $100,000 but Morse settled for $76,000. See Whitehill (122).

49. See Edward S. Morse, *Catalogue of the Morse Collection of Japanese Pottery*.

50. The *Boston Museum of Fine Arts Bulletin* declared that the Bigelow gift was especially impressive; it consisted of more than 26,000 pieces in all, representing

every artistic epoch, from the earliest to the most recent: "Japanese prints, lacquer, swords, metal work and Chinese glass are extensive and of the highest interest, as are the wood sculptures, both Buddhist and purely decorative" ("The Bigelow Gift" 48). Weld's bequest gave the museum thousands of additional objects such as armor and swords. Among the artifacts were also 838 Japanese and Chinese paintings that had been collected by Fenollosa ("The Weld Bequest"). In 1911, the museum had already moved to its new location on Huntington Avenue. By the early twentieth century, the institution had outgrown its Copley Square building. Construction on a new edifice began in 1907, and the grand opening took place in November 1909.

51. The discrepancy between the number of Japanese and Chinese objects is telling: in 1929, there were 4,393 Chinese pieces compared with 88,074 Japanese items. See Benjamin March, 37–38.

52. Letter from Prince Horibumi Ito to Ernest Fenollosa, 15 September 1886, Ernest Fenollosa Papers, HL.

53. Ernest Fenollosa, "The Future of Japanese Art Industries," n.d., Ernest Fenollosa Compositions, HL.

54. Mary McNeil Fenollosa journal entry, 22 January 1898, the Fenollosa Papers, Museum of the City, Mobile, Ala.

55. See John M. Rosenfield, "Western-Style Painting in the Early Meiji Period and its Critics."

56. Ernest Fenollosa, "Contemporary Japanese Art," n.d., Ernest Fenollosa Compositions, HL.

57. 57. Ernest Fenollosa, "Can Japanese Art be Revived?" n.d., Ernest Fenollosa Compositions, HL.

58. Letter from Prince Horibumi Ito to Ernest Fenollosa, 15 September 1886, Ernest Fenollosa Papers, HL. According to the prince, "though the Exhibition is to be principally for the representation of native productions invitations will be given to foreign producers to contribute to it such of their ward as are likely to become articles of merchandise and purchase in this country, and this will be clearly intonated to all exhibitors from beyond the seas, so that it will in reality be an industrial exhibition."

59. Ernest Fenollosa, "Contemporary," n.d., Ernest Fenollosa Compositions, HL.

60. Letter sent from Tokyo from Ernest Fenollosa to Edward S. Morse, 27 September 1884, Edward Sylvester Morse Papers, PL.

61. Fenollosa argued that "[i]n the East . . . art has almost always been the flower of its civilization." From "The Difference Between Eastern and Western Art," n.d., Ernest Fenollosa Compositions, HL.

62. Fenollosa, "Difference" n.d., Ernest Fenollosa Compositions, HL.

63. Fenollosa, "Contemporary" n.d., Ernest Fenollosa Compositions, HL.

64. Ernest Fenollosa, "The Relation of Art to Religion," n.d., Ernest Fenollosa Compositions, HL.

65. "In the West politics are about as far as fourth removed from the sphere of art,

but in the East art enters like everything else into its very life. . . . In the East either the political life of the administration absorbs art and directs it, or else art is in opposition, and the political arts give it the stamp of their ideas. . . . This is why every political era in Eastern history stamps a new character upon its art." From Fenollosa, "Difference," Ernest Fenollosa Compositions, HL.

66. 66. Ernest Fenollosa, "Bijutus Kiokwai-Uyeno," lecture given on 28 October 1896, Ernest Fenollosa Compositions, HL.

67. Fenollosa, "Difference," Ernest Fenollosa Compositions, HL. See also Fenollosa's lecture at the Essex Institute in Salem, Massachusetts, on 20 April 1891. Entitled, "Some Lessons of Japanese Art," the Japanophile stated emphatically that "[n]o divorce [should exist] between man and nature." A copy of this talk can be found in the Ernest Fenollosa Compositions, HL.

68. In "The Symbolism of the Lotos," Fenollosa argued that "the West has a wonderful knowledge of means, but a poor conception of the worthiness of ends. It knows no value in itself upon which to expand its wealth. The East has a clearer conception of ends, of spiritual values; but an imperfect grasp of the means of attaining, of preserving them" (581). The article appeared in *The Lotos* which was the reincarnated form of *New Cycle*. In 1895 and 1896, Fenollosa became an integral part of the "monthly magazine of literature, art and education." In fact, for many months, the running of the journal was "a family affair." For additional details, see Chisolm's aforementioned work, *Fenollosa: The Far East and American Culture*.

69. Ernest Fenollosa, "The Influence of Japanese Art," n.d., Ernest Fenollosa Compositions, HL.

70. Ernest Fenollosa, "The Duty and Opportunity of Japan Toward the Whole World," 1896, Ernest Fenollosa Compositions, HL.

71. Quoted from John Gardner's 5 July 1883 letter to George Gardner, Gardner Family Papers II, MHS.

72. Isabella S. Gardner letter to Anna Lyman (Mason) Gray from Yokohama, 5 July 1883, Isabella Stewart Gardner Papers, HL.

WORKS CITED

Anderson, Benedict. *Imagined Communities: Reflections on the Origin and Spread of Nationalism*. London: Verso, 1983.

Bartlett, Samuel C. *Religion in America: Historical Sketches of the Missions of the American Board*. New York: Arno, 1972.

Benfey, Christopher. *The Great Wave: Gilded Age Misfits, Japanese Eccentrics, and the Opening of Old Japan*. New York: Random House, 2003.

Bennett, Tony. *The Birth of the Museum: History, Theory, Politics*. New York: Routledge, 1995.

"The Bigelow Gift." *Boston Museum of Fine Arts Bulletin* 9, no. 53 (1911): 48–50.

Bigelow, William S. Letter to Henry Cabot Lodge. 30 September 1883. Henry Cabot Lodge Papers. Massachusetts Historical Society, Boston.

———. Letter to Edward S. Morse. 17 January 1916. The Edward Sylvester Morse Papers. James Duncan Phillips Library, Salem, Mass.

———. Letter to Edward S. Morse. 15 November 1917. The Edward Sylvester Morse Papers. James Duncan Phillips Library, Salem, Mass.

Blodgett, Geoffrey. "Yankee Leadership in a Divided City, 1860–1910." In *Boston, 1700–1980: The Evolution of Urban Politics*, edited by Ronald P. Formisano and Constance K. Burns, 87–110. Westport, Conn.: Greenwood, 1984.

Bluestone, Daniel. *Constructing Chicago*. New Haven: Yale University Press, 1991.

Blumberg, Rhoda. *Commodore Perry in the Land of the Shogun*. New York: Lothrop, Lee & Shepard Books, c. 1985.

Boddy, E. Manchester. *Japanese in America*. San Francisco: R & E Research Associates, 1921.

Boston Globe. January 1, 1881.

Boston Museum of Fine Arts Bulletin 1, no. 4 (1903).

Brooks, Phillips. Letter to William S. Bigelow. 2 September 1889. William Sturgis Bigelow Papers. Houghton Library, Harvard University, Cambridge, Mass.

Brooks, Van Wyck. *Fenollosa and His Circle*. New York: Dutton, 1962.

———. *New England: Indian Summer, 1865–1915*. New York: Dutton, 1940.

Burns, Constance K. "The Irony of Progressive Reform: Boston, 1898–1910." In *Boston 1700–1980: The Evolution of Urban Politics*, edited by Ronald P. Formisano and Constance K. Burns, 133–64. Westport, Conn.: Greenwood, 1984.

Chen, Constance J. S. "Transnational Orientals: Scholars of Art, Nationalist Discourses, and the Question of Intellectual Authority." *Journal of Asian American Studies* 9, no. 3 (2006): 215–42.

Chisolm, Lawrence. *Fenollosa: The Far East and American Culture*. New Haven: Yale University Press, 1963.

Christy, Arthur. *The Orient in American Transcendentalism: A Study of Emerson, Thoreau, and Alcott*. New York: Columbia University Press, 1932.

Claghorn, Kate H. "Our Immigrants and Ourselves." *Atlantic Monthly* 86 (1900): 535–48.

Clifford, James. *The Predicament of Culture: Twentieth-Century Ethnography, Literature, and Art*. Cambridge, Mass.: Harvard University Press, 1988.

Clunas, Craig. "Oriental Antiquities/Far Eastern Art." *Positions* 2, no. 2 (1994): 318–55.

Condit, Carl. *The Chicago School of Architecture: A History of Commercial and Public Buildings in the Chicago Area, 1875–1925*. Chicago: University of Chicago Press, 1964.

Crossman, Carl. *The China Trade: Export Paintings, Furniture, Silver & Other Objects*. Princeton, N.J.: Pyne, 1972.

Duncan, Carol. *Civilizing Rituals: Inside Public Art Museums*. New York: Routledge, 1995.

Duus, Peter. *The Japanese Discovery of America: A Brief History with Documents*. Boston: Bedford, 1997.

Fenollosa, Ernest. "Bijutus Kiokwai-Uyeno." Lecture given on 28 October 1896. Ernest Fenollosa Compositions. Houghton Library, Harvard University Cambridge, Mass.

———. "Can Japanese Art be Revived?" n.d. Ernest Fenollosa Compositions. Houghton Library, Harvard University, Cambridge, Mass.

———. *The Classic Noh Theatre of Japan*. Edited by Ezra Pound. Westport, Conn.: Greenwood, c. 1959.

———. "The Coming Fusion of East and West." *Harper's* 98 (1898–1899): 115–22.

———. "Contemporary Japanese Art." Ernest Fenollosa Compositions. Houghton Library, Harvard University, Cambridge, Mass., n.d.

———. "The Difference Between Eastern and Western Art." Ernest Fenollosa Compositions. Houghton Library, Harvard University Cambridge, Mass., n.d.

———. "The Duty and Opportunity of Japan Toward the Whole World." Ernest Fenollosa Compositions. Houghton Library, Harvard University Cambridge, Mass., 1896.

———. *East and West: The Discovery of America and Other Poems by Ernest Fenollosa*. New York: Crowell, 1893.

———. "The Future of Japanese Art Industries." Ernest Fenollosa Compositions. Houghton Library, Harvard University Cambridge, Mass., n.d.

———. "The Influence of Japanese Art." Ernest Fenollosa Compositions. Houghton Library, Harvard University Cambridge, Mass., n.d..

———. Letter to Edward S. Morse. 27 September 1884. The Edward Sylvester Morse Papers. James Duncan Phillips Library, Salem, Mass.

———. *"Noh," or Accomplishment: A Study of the Classical Stage of Japan*. London: MacMillan, 1916.

———. "The Relation of Art to Religion." Ernest Fenollosa Compositions. Houghton Library, Harvard University, Cambridge, Mass., n.d.

———. "Some Lessons of Japanese Art." Lecture given at Salem, Massachusetts, 20 April 1891. Ernest Fenollosa Compositions. Houghton Library, Harvard University Cambridge, Mass.

———. "The Symbolism of the Lotos." *The Lotos* 9 (1896): 577–83.

Fenollosa, Mary McNeil. Journal entry. 22 January 1898. The Fenollosa Papers. Museum of the City, Mobile, Ala.

Gardner, Isabella S. Journal entry. 26 June 1883. Scrapbook. Isabella Stewart Gardner Museum Archives, Boston.

———. Journal entry. 7 September 1883. Isabella Stewart Gardner Museum Papers. Archives of American Art, Washington, D.C.

———. Letter to George Gardner. 24 August 1883. Gardner Family Papers II. Massachusetts Historical Society, Boston.

———. Letter to Anna Lyman (Mason) Gray. 5 July 1883. Isabella Stewart Gardner Papers. Houghton Library, Harvard University, Cambridge, Mass.

Gardner, John. Letter to George Gardner. 5 July 1883. Gardner Family Papers II. Massachusetts Historical Society, Boston.

Goldstein, Jonathan. "Edward Sylvester Morse (1838–1925) as Expert and Western Observer in Meiji Japan." *Journal of Intercultural Studies* 14 (1987): 61–81.

Guth, Christine. *Longfellow's Tattoos: Tourism, Collecting, and Japan.* Seattle: University of Washington Press, 2004.

Hadley, Rollin Van N. *The Letters of Bernard Berenson and Isabella Stewart Gardner, 1887–1924.* Boston: Northeastern University Press, 1987.

Handlin, Oscar. *Boston Immigrants, 1790–1865: A Study in Acculturation.* Cambridge, Mass.: Harvard University Press, 1941.

Hing, Bill Ong. *Making and Remaking Asian America Through Immigration Policy, 1850–1990.* Stanford: Stanford University Press, 1993.

Honour, Hugh. *Chinoiserie: The Vision of Cathay.* New York: Dutton, 1961.

Hooper-Greenhill, Eilean. *Museums and the Shaping of Knowledge.* New York: Routledge, 1992.

Horowitz, Helen Lefkowitz. *Culture and the City: Cultural Philanthropy in Chicago from the 1880s to 1917.* Lexington: University Press of Kentucky, 1976.

Howe, M. A. DeWolfe. *Memoirs of a Hostess: A Chronicle of Eminent Friendships Drawn Chiefly from the Diaries of Mrs. James T. Fields.* Boston: Atlantic Monthly Press, 1922.

Ito, Horibumi. Letter to Ernest Fenollosa. 15 September 1886. Ernest Fenollosa Papers. Houghton Library, Harvard University, Cambridge, Mass.

Jackson, Carl T. *The Oriental Religions and American Thought.* Westport, Conn.: Greenwood, 1981.

Jaher, Frederic Cople. "The Politics of the Boston Brahmins: 1800–1860." In *Boston, 1700–1980: The Evolution of Urban Politics,* edited by Ronald P. Formisano and Constance K. Burns, 59–86. Westport, Conn.: Greenwood, 1984.

Lankevich, George J. *American Metropolis: A History of New York City.* New York: New York University Press, 1995.

Lanman, Charles, ed. *The Japanese in America.* New York: University Publishing Company, 1872.

Lears, T. J. Jackson. *No Place of Grace: Antimodernism and the Transformation of American Culture, 1880–1920.* Chicago: University of Chicago Press, 1981.

Lee, Robert. *Orientals: Asian Americans in Popular Culture.* Philadelphia: Temple University Press, 1999.

March, Benjamin. *China and Japan in Our Museums.* With an introduction by Frederick P. Keppel. New York: American Council, Institute of Pacific Relations, 1929.

Masako, Herman. *The Japanese in America, 1843–1973: A Chronology and Fact Book.* Dobbs Ferry, N.Y.: Oceana Publications, 1974.

Miller, Lillian. *Patrons and Patriotism: The Encouragement of the Fine Arts in the United States.* Chicago: University of Chicago Press, 1966.

Miller, Stuart Creighton. *The Unwelcome Immigrant: The American Image of the Chinese, 1785–1882.* Berkeley and Los Angeles: University of California Press, 1969.

Minor, Vernon Hyde. *Art History's History*. Englewood Cliffs, N.J.: Prentice Hall, 1994.

Morse, Edward S. "Can City Life Be Made Endurable?" Lecture given at the Worcester Polytechnic Institute, 21 June 1900. The Edward Sylvester Morse Papers. James Duncan Phillips Library, Salem, Mass.

———. *Catalogue of the Morse Collection of Japanese Pottery*. With an introduction by Terence Barrow. Cambridge, Mass.: Riverside Press, 1901.

———. *Glimpses of China and Chinese Homes*. Boston: Little, 1902.

———. *Japan Day By Day*. Vol. 2. Atlanta: Cherokee Publishing, c.1917.

———. Letter to unknown recipient. 27 February 1886. The Edward Sylvester Morse Papers. James Duncan Phillips Library, Salem, Mass.

———. "Museums of Art and Their Influences." 1892. The Edward Sylvester Morse Papers. James Duncan Phillips Library, Salem, Mass.

Mumford, Lewis. *The Brown Decades: A Study of the Arts in America, 1865–1895*. New York: Dover, 1931.

———. *The Culture of Cities*. New York: Harcourt, Brace, 1938.

Nelson, Christina. *Directly from China: Export Goods for the American Market, 1784–1930*. Salem, Mass.: Peabody Museum of Salem, c. 1985.

"The New Chinese Treatise." *Boston Globe*, 9 January 1881.

Okakura, Kakuzo. "Japanese and Chinese Paintings in the Museum." *Boston Museum of Fine Arts Bulletin* 3, no. 1 (1905): 5–6.

Pearce, Susan. *Museums, Objects, and Collections: A Cultural Study*. Washington, D.C.: Smithsonian Institution, 1992.

Preziosi, Donald. *Rethinking Art History: Meditations on a Coy Science*. New Haven, Conn.: Yale University Press, 1989.

Price, Sally. *Primitive Art in Civilized Places*. Chicago: University of Chicago Press, 1989.

Pyle, Kenneth B. *The New Generation in Meiji Japan: Problems of Cultural Identity, 1885–1895*. Stanford, Calif.: Stanford University Press, 1969.

Roman, Judith A. *Annie Adams Fields: The Spirit of Charles Street*. Bloomington: Indiana University Press, 1990.

Rosenfield, John M. "Western-Style Painting in the Early Meiji Period and its Critics." In *Traditions and Modernization in Japanese Culture*, edited by Donald H. Shively, 181–219. Princeton, N.J.: Princeton University Press, 1971.

Rosenstone, Robert. *Mirror in the Shrine: American Encounters with Meiji Japan*. Cambridge, Mass.: Harvard University Press, 1988.

Said, Edward. *Orientalism*. New York: Vintage, 1978.

Sansom, G. B. *The Western World and Japan: A Study in the Interaction of European and Asiatic Cultures*. New York: Knopf, 1951.

Saxton, Alexander. *The Indispensable Enemy: Labor and the Anti-Chinese Movement in California*. Berkeley and Los Angeles: University of California Press, 1971.

Takaki, Ronald. *A Different Mirror: A History of Multicultural America*. Boston: Little, 1993.

——. *Strangers from a Different Shore: A History of Asian Americans*. New York: Penguin, 1989.

Tchen, John K. W. *New York Before Chinatown: Orientalism and the Shaping of American Culture, 1776–1882*. Baltimore: Johns Hopkins University Press, 1999.

Trout, Charles H. "Curley of Boston: The Search for Irish Legitimacy." *Boston, 1700–1980: The Evolution of Urban Politics*, edited by Ronald P. Formisano and Constance K. Burns, 165–95. Westport, Conn.: Greenwood, 1984.

Tweed, Thomas, and Stephen Prothero, eds. *Asian Religions in America: A Documentary History*. New York: Oxford University Press, 1999.

Varg, Paul A. *Missionaries, Chinese, and Diplomats: The American Protestant Missionary Movement in China, 1890–1952*. Princeton, N.J.: Princeton University Press, 1958.

Versluis, Arthur. *American Transcendentalism and Asian Religions*. New York: Oxford University Press, 1993.

Vigden, Michiko Nakanishi. "Letters to Edward Sylvester Morse Part I: From David Murray." *Journal of Kanto Gaknin Women's Junior College* 88 (1992): 55–65.

Warner, Sam Bass, Jr. *Streetcar Suburbs: The Process of Growth in Boston, 1870–1900*. Cambridge, Mass.: Harvard University Press, 1962.

——. *Urban Wilderness: A History of the American City*. New York: Harper, 1972.

Washburn, Wilcomb. "The Oriental 'Roots' of American Transcendentalism." *Southwestern Journal* 4 (1949): 141–55.

Wayman, Dorothy G. *Edward Sylvester Morse: A Biography*. Cambridge, Mass.: Harvard University Press, 1988.

"The Weld Bequest." *Boston Museum of Fine Arts Bulletin* 9, no. 52 (1911): 34–36.

Weston, Victoria. "Asian Art at the Isabella Stewart Gardner Museum." *Orientations* 26, no. 11 (1995): 41–50.

Whitehill, Walter Muir. *Museum of Fine Arts Boston: A Centennial History*. Vol. 1. Cambridge, Mass.: Harvard University Press, 1970.

Wiley, Peter Booth. *Yankees in the Land of the Gods: Commodore Perry and the Opening of Japan*. New York: Viking, 1990.

Wong, K. Scott, and Sucheng Chan, eds. *Claiming America: Constructing Chinese American Identities During the Exclusion Era*. Philadelphia: Temple University Press, 1998.

"The Young Men of Ireland." *Boston Globe*, 10 January 1881.

Yoshihara, Mari. *Embracing the East: White Women and American Orientalism*. New York: Oxford University Press, 2003.

🍃 5

Bridges and Chasms

Orientalism and the Constructions of Asian Indians in New England

BANDANA PURKAYASTHA AND ANJANA NARAYAN

Even a casual reading of U.S. immigration laws of the early twentieth century leaves no doubt about the political will to racialize and exclude people of Indian origin from the United States. In 1917, the United States created a "Pacific barred zone" that included the Indian subcontinent, and barred people from that zone from migrating to the United States. In 1921, eligibility for citizenship was defined in terms of Caucasian origin; yet, when an Indian, Bhagat Singh Thind, claimed citizenship based on his Caucasian roots in 1922, "Caucasian origin" was redefined as "white, as the common person on the street understands it" (quoted in Kitano and Daniels 100). Following the decision of *U.S. v. Thind*, those Indians who had already acquired citizenship were stripped of it. Indians were now brought under the purview of state laws that barred aliens from owning property or land. To seal the process, in 1924, the United States passed the National Origins Act, prohibiting the immigration of people who were ineligible for U.S. citizenship. Such overt race/nationality-based laws were not rescinded until 1965. The Asian Indian presence in New England reflects these larger political trends in the United States: a long hiatus in the early twentieth century, marked by the presence of fewer than one hundred Asian Indians, followed by rapid growth when these migration bans were rescinded in the post–civil rights era.

The restrictions on Indians were not merely responses to their phenotype. Ideologies about "other" religions and cultures were central to this project of marginalization. In this chapter, we trace the conflicts over the ideological construction of Hindu Indians — the religious-majority group among Indians — in two key periods: at the onset of the twentieth and twenty-first centuries. Until 1920, all Indians — irrespective of religious affiliation — were officially categorized as belonging to the unacceptable race category, "hindoo." Several groups of Indians attempted to challenge such racialized categorization. Currently, in the twenty-first century, the conflict is twofold. On one level, there is a sociopolitical struggle to establish and claim the right to be Americans, the right to exercise the freedom of religion and exist as Hindus in America. On the other level, there is a struggle within the ethnic group over the construction of "Hindu": who gets to define the ideologies and practices that demarcate this religionationalist category?

Our discussion of the constructions and conflicts over the categorization and racialization of Indians in New England can be partially captured within the framework of the concept of Orientalism, delineated in the latter part of the twentieth century by Edward Said. Orientalism emphasizes how the social imagination and representations of the "Oriental other" constructs and sustains the power of the "Occident." We depict Orientalist tropes that have been prevalent in the United States, and describe the modes of resistance against such Orientalism. We begin this discussion by focusing on the Hindu monk, Swami Vivekananda, who, more than any other individual, challenged the power of evangelical missionaries and political authorities to define "hindoos" as barbaric and uncivilized. Vivekananda is widely credited with publicly proclaiming the tenets of Hinduism in different parts of the United States; as an iconic leader who spoke about Hinduism and challenged the racist discourses of his times, Vivekananda's teachings continue to resonate with many Indian-origin groups in the twenty-first century as they continue to struggle against contemporary racism.

The first part of the chapter describes Vivekananda's visit to New England against the backdrop of his visit to the United States. While he encountered significant racism in the United States, Vivekananda was warmly received by a segment of New England intellectuals who were already somewhat familiar with the Hindu perspective and eager to discuss religious and ideological concepts that had been presented by the Transcendentalists. As a result, he was able to forge intellectual and social networks with some influential New Englanders. In the second part of the chapter we move on to examine the contemporary conflicts and struggles to claim space for practicing Hinduism in the United States, and we document how Vivekananda's message is being reclaimed and reconstructed to create different sorts of bridges and chasms in the United States.[1]

Real and Imagined Indians: Early Encounters

According to Susan Bean, in the centuries leading up to the 1890s, many Yankee traders, especially in the Salem-Peabody area, made vast fortunes by trading with India. Yet the United States imposed stringent political restrictions until the 1920s, including a rule stating that migrants could not stop or change the means of transportation en route to the United States. Herbert Barringer, Robert Gardener, and Michael Levine record historical data from the U.S. Census that shows there were only 84 Indians in the United States in 1850. By 1900, another 595 Indians arrived; by 1924, when the Nationalities Act was passed, there were 8,663 Indians in the United States (Purkayastha 15). New England was home to an insignificant proportion of this population. Even Yale University, originally founded with money from the India trade, had few Indian students. A search by Bandana Purkayastha of the colleges in Connecticut shows that most of the Indian students were Christian missionaries (*Asian Indians* 32–33). In fact, the first Indian to graduate from Yale in 1906 was a Christian minister.

According to Jane Jensen, even though there were very few Indians in the United States, the lives and beliefs of Indians were the subject of many public discussions, sustained and structured by political and missionary interests. During the nineteenth century, the establishment of British colonial power in India was justified by a discourse emphasizing a "civilizational mission" of the British in India that highlighted the flaws of Indians and Indian society. For instance, when Bengal became the headquarters of the colonial power, the colonialists frequently described Indians as effeminate Bengalis, according to Catherine Rolfsen (15).This language is reminiscent of the gendered, racialized imagery describing other Asian males; it emphasized the need to civilize the Indian population and to root out their savageries and exotic customs (Yen Le Espiritu 88).

The British colonial political discourse was paralleled by the discourse of evangelical missionaries and the early feminists in the United Kingdom and the United States. In the United States, evangelical Christian missionaries justified their right to save Indian heathens by repeatedly emphasizing the depravity and licentiousness of the Indians. Through their speeches, writings, and commissioned illustrations, they defined "hindoo" life in terms of idolatry, infanticide (including accounts of mothers feeding their children to crocodiles), young females who became the sexual prey of older men, and the burning of widows (Burke 215–23). Such stories provided the justification for their ongoing need to raise money to bring civilization to heathens.[2]

In general, the intellectuals of the Northeast were not active participants in such overt racialized discourse. Jane Jensen states that New England intellectuals developed a deep interest in Indian religions in the early nineteenth century, at about the time the New England–India trade developed. She describes how Boston society became interested in Indian literature and in Indian religions, especially Hinduism, Buddhism, and the Brahmo Samaj movement. Intellectuals at universities such as Harvard began to cultivate an active scholarship and also initiated a nascent Indian art collection at the Boston Museum of Fine Arts. The theosophical writing of Ralph Waldo Emerson and Henry David Thoreau, as well as Walt Whitman's poems (such as "Passage to India" and "Leaves of Grass"), are reflective of this trend. These earlier writings of the Transcendentalists, on the "life of the spirit" (developed on the basis of earlier encounters with Hinduism), prepared the ground for Vivekananda and his message.

The Monk and His Message

According to Amiya Sen, Vivekananda arrived in the United States in 1893 to attend the World Parliament of Religions in Chicago. Vivekananda was neither the only Indian/Hindu at the parliament, nor was he the first Indian religious emissary to the United States. Yet he stood out at the parliament because, beginning with his first speech, he decried fanaticism and emphasized that all religions were just many paths to the same goal, an assertion that challenged a central plank of contemporary Christianity. Rolfsen argues that the parliament was intended to showcase the universal applicability of Christianity, while acknowledging the presence of a few other religions (Rolfsen 27). Vivekananda's speeches repeatedly challenged this notion. In a speech delivered on 15 September, he said: "I am a Hindu. I am sitting in my own well and thinking the whole world is my well. The Christian sits in his little well and thinks that is the whole world" (Vivekananda 7). On 20 of September, his speech included the following admonition: "You Christians, who are so fond of sending out missionaries to save the soul of the heathen — why do you not try to save their bodies from starvation?" (Vivekananda 39). In the concluding session on 27 September, he said, "The Christian is not to become a Hindu or a Buddhist, nor a Hindu or Buddhist to become a Christian, but each must assimilate the spirit of the others and yet preserve his individuality" (Vivekananda 47). Thus, he directly challenged the idea of Christianity as the sole universally applicable religion and also questioned the proselytizing agenda of many missionaries.

Vivekananda repeated his message about religion in other parts of the United States. Mary Louise Burke's multivolume work, *Swami Vivekananda in the West: New Discoveries*, documents the details of his talks. Three main themes are evident throughout these discourses: descriptions of a universal religion, facets of Vedanta and Hinduism, and the status of Indian women — all of which were a constant source of conflict.

In his lectures in New England and around the country, Vivekananda persistently challenged the hegemony of the orthodox, Orientalist missionaries who framed their version of Christianity as a universal religion by denigrating all other religions as misguided sets of superstitions. Vivekananda recast the framing of a true universal religion by arguing that a universal religion accepts that truth can be expressed in a thousand ways: such a religion assumes that existing religions are but many paths that lead ultimately to the same ocean, therefore sectarianism, bigotry, and feelings of religious superiority have no place in a universal religion.

Vivekananda addressed a second theme that challenged these missionary accounts of Hinduism. He described Vedanta and the practices of Hinduism, a nonsectarian religion that emphasized the divinity of the individual (instead of the individual's penchant for sins); this religion combined realization of god with social upliftment of the masses (Amiya Sen 34). He emphasized four paths for practicing religion: through work (*karma-yoga*), through faith (*bhakti-yoga*), through controlling one's mind through exercises and disciplines (*raj-yoga*), and through acquiring knowledge/wisdom (*jyana-yoga*).

In the third broad theme, concerning women in Indian "hindoo" society, Vivekananda repeatedly challenged the racialized, gendered images about victimized and sexually depraved Indian women. These images, he claimed, were the staple of the "civilizing" missionaries and colonialists who wanted to justify their presence in India as emancipators and liberators of "heathen" or backward people.

Vivekananda's ideas attracted several kinds of reactions. He was received with appreciation by some intellectuals (primarily East Coast liberals associated with the Unitarian and Congregational churches) and lionized by many socialites who thought of him as a romantic ideal. More typically, however, he was vilified vociferously by evangelical missionaries. The latter saw Vivekananda's descriptions of a universal (or rather, an "other") religion, his criticisms of colonialism, and the proselytizing efforts of missionaries as challenges to Christianity (Burke 349). By the end of his visit, he was the first Indian to generate widespread discussion and debate about Hinduism and "Hindoos" in America.[3] His legacy in America includes the record of his talks and the establishment of a series of centers, later called Vedanta Societies, to keep alive his ideas on religion and philosophy (Melendy 26). Two of these Vedanta Societies are located in Massachusetts and Rhode Island.

Vivekananda in New England

Vivekananda spoke to many audiences in New England on the themes mentioned earlier. According to Burke, during Vivekananda's stay at Metcalf,

Massachusetts, he spoke to Mrs. Sanborn's guests at Breezy Meadows and also to the Ladies Club in Salem, where his discourses were received positively. But he also addressed hostile feminist groups, who challenged him to explain the ill treatment of Indian women. He lectured several times in Boston, at the Procopiea Club, at the Harvard Philosophy Club and at a class on metaphysics, at the Twentieth Century Club (whose members were the leading American intellectuals of the time). In addition, he spoke at Annisquam, Holliston, Lawrence, Lynn, Medford, Melrose, Northampton, Plymouth, Salem, Sherborne, and Swampscott. In 1896, he also lectured at Hartford, Connecticut, on "The Universal Religion." Thousand Islands, on the St. Lawrence River (officially in New York State), was the site of his "Inspired Talks," an elaborate discussion on the principles of Vedanta.

There were two groups of people in New England who were receptive to Vivekananda's ideas: socially prominent, progressive-minded families, and some professors of religion/philosophy. Sen classifies people like Sara and Ole Bull, John and Mary Wright, the Hales, the Legetts, Sanborns, and Josephine MacLeod as part of the first receptive group; they organized his visits and talks and tried to thwart some of the most vicious attacks made on him. A couple of the members of this group, like Christina Greenstidel (Sister Christine) and Sara Ellen Waldo, became his disciples. This group was attracted to the idea of a universal religion that would not profess superiority over others.

The tenets of Vedanta, including Vivekananda's description of the fourfold yogas (paths) also attracted this group. The message of Vedanta that Vivekananda described did not involve belonging to a "church" or a creed; it was nondenominational in character, and it offered a way of moving beyond the sectarianism and bigotry that was practiced in the name of religion (Eastern and Western Disciples). The central idea of his universal religion was to move to a more inclusive, more universal practice of religion; that is, to promote harmony between creeds and unity in variety (rather than unity through homogeneity), without giving up the religion with which an individual hitherto identified. As Vivekananda said in one of his speeches at the World Parliament of Religions, "The Christian is not to become a Hindu or a Buddhist, nor a Hindu or Buddhist to become a Christian" (*Chicago Addresses* 49); rather, each individual has to live by values that recognize every person's individuality and humanity. In a speech delivered at Hartford, Connecticut, in 1896, he said, "We must learn to love those who think exactly opposite to us. We have humanity for the background, but each must have his own individuality and thought. Push the sects forward and forward until each man and woman are sects unto themselves" (Burke 479).

Some members of Harvard's philosophy department were also receptive to his ideas. When Vivekananda addressed them in March 1895, the department included the two most influential metaphysicians of the time: William James, a pluralist and pragmatist, and Josiah Royce, an idealist. We know that Vivekananda's talks on Vedanta philosophy were generally received positively, as they led to the offer of a chairship at Harvard (Burke 551). While he refused this offer, he had greatly influenced the student community: American idealist, William Hocking, later wrote that he rethought his philosophical foundations after listening to Vivekananda at Harvard (Burke 88).

Vivekananda's reception among the established intellectuals was more complex. At the time of his visit, Josiah Royce and William James were concerned about challenges to the foundations of Christian theology arising from Darwin's theory of evolution. Both philosophers accepted the main features of Darwin's framework and were thus not immersed in tenets of contemporary Christian theology. Moreover, Royce professed he was an admirer of Indian thought; he had studied them through the works of Schopenhauer, Max Mueller, and Paul Duessen, and he added Sanskrit quotations in some of his publications. However, Vivekananda's ideas about *advaitic* vedantism posed a challenge to the philosophical frameworks of these intellectuals.[4] James, while respectful of Vivekananda, summed up his view of Eastern religions by stating, "the Hindoo and the Buddhist . . . are simply afraid of more experience, afraid of life" (39). Similarly, Royce concluded, "Hindoo philosophy, extensive as are its literary monuments, is in its essential doctrine always brief and unfruitful. Life for the Hindoo is an ill" (353). Thus, unlike Hocking (who was a student), neither established philosopher was willing to rethink his ideas and framework in light of the encounter with a different epistemology. As a result, the structure of the prevailing *intellectual* hierarchy, and the philosophers' own positions of authority, remained unchallenged; they professed an interest in "Indian thought," but summarily dismissed the "hindoo's" views when it came to rethinking their philosophical bases.

While Vivekananda's interactions with these first two groups, of socially prominent families and professors of religion/philosophy, were generally positive, his encounters with certain missionaries were marked by conflict and acrimony on their side. The more sustained attacks by the more orthodox sections of evangelical Christian groups began soon after his Chicago lectures. For example, in March 1896, Vivekananda was attacked publicly in Detroit by a number of "Christians" especially a Reverend Thoburn, who accused Vivekananda of being an imposter and a rascal. As part of his concern that large numbers of women were coming to listen to Vivekananda,

Thoburn insisted, "Hinduism has gone into partnership with sin. No vice is rebuked at her alters . . . if our American women only knew what slaves the religions of India made of their sisters there, they would be slow to crowd the audience of a mystic pundit who dares to champion such degrading superstitions. . . . Hinduism enamours only those who have never gotten close to it" (Burke 25–26). Burke described how Vivekananda was accused of being a charlatan, a person secretly educated at Harvard and Oxford (implying that these institutions were the source of his ideas), a lawyer, a man who decried American women, and a person who lied consistently about the real nature of Hinduism.

These attacks increased as Vivekananda continued to talk about Hinduism, challenging the Orientalist images of exotic and heathen Indians. The tenets of the universal religion that he laid out, with coexistence rather than conversion as the foundation of religions, were viewed with alarm by institutions whose ideologies and resources depended on propagating the latter view. The tone of the attacks in Detroit and Chicago continued in New England. In this geographical region, however, the countervailing forces of acceptance by the first and second groups minimized the impact of the missionary attacks.

Apart from attempting to challenge the depictions, Vivekananda challenged the racialized depictions of "hindoo" women. In New England (as in other parts of the East Coast), he was invited to speak before Ramabai circles and these networks were highly critical of "hindoo" women's status.[5] Because Orientalist depictions of Hinduism were partly based on a series of gendered imageries about oversexual *and* victimized, subordinated "hindoo" women, Vivekananda had begun to counter this Orientalist version by asserting that Hindu women were celebrated as mothers. The Ramabai circles specifically challenged Vivekananda's depiction by pointing to the abject condition of child widows and Indian women. While there is no doubt that the plight of child widows (and, indeed, all widows who lacked economic independence) at the turn of the twentieth century was miserable, the Ramabai circles had taken Ramabai's depiction of upper-caste Hindu widows and generalized their condition to all Indian women.

Vivekananda countered the broader attack on Indian womanhood by addressing the gendered *and* racist content of the messages through the trope that Indian women were worshipped as mothers. He pointed out that, unlike any other religion, Hinduism was replete with female goddesses and strong female imagery and that mothers were highly regarded across India. By using this argument, he attempted to counter the amalgam of charges about effeminate (yet sexually predatory) men and subordinated (yet sexually depraved) women — racist ideologies that have been used against all Asian groups. Shamita Basu argues that if we follow Vivekananda's descriptions of Indian mothers, we find that he depicted them in terms of an asexual metafeminine principle, which encapsulated a signifier of the divine. This reasoning is perfectly consistent with his main theme of the principles of a universal religion. Yet, in his attempt to refute the Orientalist discourse about Indian women (and men), Vivekananda was caught in the problematic situation of trying to create an effective alternative discourse to challenge the essentialisms inherent in Orientalist depictions without resorting to a similar stance himself. That he did not succeed in breaking out of the bounds of essentialism is an illustration of the power of the hegemonic group to set the terms of discourse in ways that force challengers to respond in narrowly defined terms.[6]

In contemporary times, Vivekananda's repeated assertions about the high status of Indian mothers have been interpreted as his essentialist views about women (King 93). Nonetheless, we know from the rest of his work that he did not view women in India or the United states in one-dimensional terms. As he reflected upon the charges raised by the Ramabai circles, he wrote to Sarala Devi, a leading nationalist leader in Calcutta, "If talented and bold women like yourself, versed in Vedanta, go to England and preach . . . speak [to] America, if an Indian woman in Indian dress preach[es] there . . . there will rise a great wave which will inundate the whole Western world . . . you have power, wealth, intellect and education, will you forego this opportunity?" (quoted in Basu 158). Clearly, along with Vivekananda's notion of the mother-ideal, his perspective on ideal Indian womanhood could be equally expressed by highly erudite, bold, talented, activist women like Sarala Devi.[7] As Radha Kumar has documented in *A History of Doing*, Sarala Devi was one of the leading female organizers of the nationalist uprising against the British in India at the turn of the century (Kumar 39). She was a well-known national figure who had organized both men's and women's units to challenge the political power of the British. Vivekananda, who was well aware of the many prominent Indian women who were active in the public sphere, clearly felt that the people in the West needed to meet and hear from Indian women like her as a way to counter the constant refrain of subordination in Orientalist discourses.

Overall, an assessment of Vivekananda's experiences in New England and the United States reveals attitudes and ideas about Indians that helped shape laws severely curtailing the migration possibilities and life chances of Indians in the United States. Vivekananda's spirited challenge to the overtly racist rhetoric of evangelical missionaries and that of more secular groups concerned about Indian women can be read as part of the history of struggles of "hindoos" with Orientalism in the United States. Equally important, however, though less recognized, is the partial acceptance of Vivekananda's ideas by the Harvard professors; they were willing to invite him to talk, but were not willing to recast their frames of thinking based on the challenges he posed. This latter issue reveals a more subtle form of rejection, where a person may be acknowledged as having some good ideas, but there is no attempt to reorganize the intellectual realm and to recast it in light of the new ideas the "other" person has raised. In this situation, the intellectual hierarchy (and civilizational superiority) was maintained: the ideas of the Harvard professors continued to be developed on their preset routes; Vivekananda and the ideas he spoke about remained on the fringes, as part of "Eastern thought."

As Vivekananda was not an immigrant, these encounters do not reveal the kind of everyday restrictions and degradations Indian Sikh migrants, who arrived by the early twentieth century, faced as they settled in different parts of the United States. But the general resistance to the message and the messenger, evident through Vivekananda's experiences, reveal an important aspect of racialization. Once "imagined people" are created, these controlling ideologies act as surrogates for real people. Such ideologies are used to justify multiple ways in which people's social, religious, work, and political lives continue to be restricted through laws and practice.[8]

Contemporary Exchanges

The Orientalist discourse and social structures — interactions and institutions — that racialized "hindoos' at the turn of the twentieth century have changed in form and substance over the last half century. The civil rights movement in the United States ushered in major structural shifts that benefited Indians significantly. The dismantling of the overt race-based immigration laws in 1965 enabled Indians and other people of Asian origin to migrate to the United States. And, in spite of its limited fiat, the ideology of multiculturalism created new spaces for practicing different cultures in the United States.[9] Currently, unlike in the early twentieth century, there is greater acceptance of the idea that groups should be able to practice their multiple cultures; that is to say, practice their religions, eat their preferred foods, and perform their "ethnic" music, dances, and arts. However, under what conditions and circumstances they can do so is structurally limited in ways that, as we discuss in this section, force groups to alter their practices to fit the norms of what is "comfortable" and "normal" for the dominant group. Thus, these structural changes do not signal an end to Orientalism. They simply indicate a change in the actors and the kind of social structures that shape contemporary forms of Orientalism.

Because overt race-based immigration restrictions were rescinded in 1965, a relatively large number of Asian Indians were able to migrate to the United States. In the post-1965 era, Indians arrived via the Atlantic, and many settled in the Northeast. By 1980, the Northeast had the largest concentration (33 percent) of Indians in the United States. In 1980, Massachusetts and Connecticut were the two New England states with "significant" Indian populations, of 8,387 and 4,995 respectively. According to Anjana Narayan, this number has risen to 41,935 in Massachusetts and 23,905 in Connecticut, according to Census 2000 (13). The New England states show a concentration of highly educated migrants; unlike the concentration of Indians in New Jersey and New York, these Asian Indians mostly reside in suburban locations. The majority of this population is Hindu in its religious affiliation.

Vijay Prashad has argued that contemporary migrants are subject to new forms of Orientalism. If the Orientalist ideology of the early twentieth century was evident through overt rejection of Indian practices or simply displaying them as grotesque aspects of an alien culture, in the contemporary knowledge-based U.S. economy, selected Indian ideas and practices are co-opted, used, and packaged in ways that profit individuals and groups in the United States. While "India" and "Indian culture" appear to be acceptable and lauded in the United States — because of the marketing ploy of selling products by appealing to an exotic culture (Halter 6) — these vastly modified "Indian" artifacts or practices, such as yoga, are not usually controlled by the initiators or longtime practitioners of these ideas; the "Indian" commodities marketed here are developed and marketed to suit American tastes and lifestyles and generate profits for American businesses.

The organization of multiculturalism encapsulates similar trends. New immigrants have some freedom to express aspects of their cultures, as long as these fit in with existing rules. For instance, Hindu immigrants are expected to alter their religions and cultures to fit existing rules in the United States about when, where, and how — on Sundays, in temples, as congregations — they should practice their religions. Two recent empirical studies, by Purkayastha and Joshi, illustrate how such limited acceptance negatively affects the post-immigrant generation who have to contend with the rejection and marginalization of their religions, as well as the ongoing stereotypes about the deleterious effects of their religion on women. Thus, much like Vivekananda's encounters with the Harvard philosophers, some U.S. cultural space is created for accommodating "new" cultures, but no deep alterations to this space or understanding are under way to truly include religiocultural practices that are different from Christianity.

Our research shows that Indian-origin Americans have been responding to the new structures of Orientalism in a variety of ways.[10] Three sets of activities are featured here, although multiple forms of adaptations and resistances exist as a continuum. The first stream of activities emanate from Hindu temples and the second from Hindu student groups in colleges and universities. Both are adaptive religiocultural nationalistic in character; they attempt to fit into the boundaries of multiculturalism and religion set by mainstream society by altering the content of their practices. The third type of activities is generated by decentralized nuclei of academics, activists, and community members who challenge and breach the boundaries set by the mainstream as well as the cultures being developed by many of the first two Hindu groups. Vivekananda's messages, which are selectively used by some of these groups, provide a lens for understanding how subgroups challenge their marginalization.

Claiming Geographical Spaces

According to Web-based sources, there are nine temples in New England ("Hindu temples" 2006); some of these temples have multiple deities representing different regional versions of Hinduism; others are temples of sects where a particular guru and group's practices are featured. In addition to these, there are two Vedanta Societies in New England, but these are organizationally and ideologically different from the temples (these societies are described in a later section). Since the 1980s, these temples have been primarily commissioned by groups of Hindu immigrants in professional careers. While temples in India (which range from humble edifices to large town-size complexes) mark sites that have become sacred through myths, histories, centuries of common practice, or charitable giving, in the United States, the location, size, and form of temples reflect local zoning laws and locally dominant norms about what is "allowed" as public forms of worship. Conventional Hindu temples in India do not operate in a congregational mode, but in New England, as in the rest of the United States, temples have, perforce, become "Hindu congregations" with clearly identifiable memberships, in order to comply with the 501(c) 3 definitions of religious organizations.[11] Some temples in New England are based on a *guru-sisya* (teacher-disciple) relationship, where the guru or leader, most often male, is venerated by his band of followers. These temples are gathering places for these devotee-congregations, upholding a structure of faith-based "missions" much like evangelical Christianity (without similar emphases on proselytization).

As Prema Kurien has pointed out, homogenized religious practices and a simplified, neopatriarchal articulation of Hinduism have become characteristic of many such religious institutions in the United States. The way of practicing religion is interpreted as "performing *pujas*"; such faith-based worship is mediated, invariably, by male Brahmin priests. While most temples do not overtly discriminate on the basis of caste, the appointment of the priest symbolically sets up a social hierarchy. Moreover, this Brahmin priest performs *pujas* according to what is customary for his group, further sustaining the preeminence of certain caste and gendered functions. Unlike in India, where practicing religion would not inevitably involve going to a temple or using a priest—because practices vary by class, caste, culture, community, age, and sex—the requirements in the United States intersect with the wishes of some sections of the Indian community, who set up temples as "the" places of religious worship for Hindus in the United States. Another key transformation of the cultural content is the representation of a benign, domesticated image of the divine. Most temples feature male gods, while female goddesses are typically portrayed as "wives" of the gods. Although some Christian leaders decry the worship of rebellious "dark goddess" Kali/Shakti, that form is not evident in any Hindu temple in New England (Grillo B4). While a core principle of Hinduism is the concept of the active female principle (*shakti*) which, along with the passive male principle (*shiva*) reflects the universe, no temple in New England depicts this nonbinary duality in any form except through the images of gods and their wives.[12]

These temples resist one aspect of contemporary Orientalism. By claiming the right to build Hindu temples and worship in them, they challenge the expectation of assimilationists that immigrant groups will give up "ethnic places of worship" and join the modern, "superior" institutions of the mainstream. Yet, just as they exercise their right to religious freedom (freedom to worship), the actual process of establishing places of worship involves a series of compromises based on what is allowed in the United States. Groups who establish temples actually adapt, ideologically and organizationally, to the boundaries set by the mainstream.

Temples initiate many cultural activities to instill cultural pride and teach religious practices, because part of their objective is to teach Hinduism to the next generation. In the process, they invent new ceremonies, such as the gift-giving tree in December (to parallel Christmas and Hanukkah), institutions such as the Hindu Sunday schools, and new lessons on "how to do *puja*." (*Puja* is treated as a singular practice, ignoring the vast multitude of practices that differ by caste, region, community, family, sex, age, and occupation of the worshipper in India).

As part of their attempt to instill Hindu pride, New England–based temple newsletters often feature selections from Vivekananda's religiocultural nationalistic messages, especially his call to be proud Hindus. His quotations are featured very regularly, so that he is widely recognized as one of the "founders" of Hinduism in America. Yet this adoption of Vivekananda and his messages by temples is highly ironic: Vivekananda was extremely critical of the kind of religion that focuses on rituals and devotion to deities in temples while ignoring the sufferings of people. In a widely quoted critique of (exclusively) faith-based practice in general, and ways of performing *puja* in particular, Vivekananda asserted that he despised the many so-called Hindus who spent their time debating whether "the bell should be rung on the right side or left, whether the sandal paste mark should be placed on the forehead or some other part of the anatomy: people who spend their days in such wretched thoughts are truly wretched" (quoted in Radice 12). He was equally critical of the amount of money that was spent on temples, stating: "ten million rupees are spent to open and close the temple doors . . . and all the time the living perishes for want of food, for want of education" (quoted in Radice 13). Yet, despite their co-optation of Vivekananda as an icon, temples continue to offer instructions in the performance of rituals such as *pujas* and they continue to raise large sums of money to build new temples or extend existing temples in the United States.

Overall, in their quest to assert Hinduism within the preset, Christianity-inspired template in the United States, temples have radically altered the content of Hinduism. The form of Hinduism the temples promote alters the diverse, decentralized character of Hinduism; instead, it emphasizes a centralized, homogenized form, based on membership in temples. Equally important, by marking temples as "Indian community places," temples and temple-based communities consciously or unwittingly create a segregated "community space" that, in fact, keeps out Indians who practice other religions.

Claiming Virtual Space

The second stream of religiocultural activities rapidly growing in New England is that fostered by Hindu student groups. Founded in 1990 by the Vishwa Hindu Parishad (World Hindu Council) of America, the Hindu

Student Council (HSC) has a national organization and chapters in more than sixty U.S. universities. It is well represented in all the leading educational institutions in New England and operates within the structures of college-based student groups. Through its Web sites, Hindu student groups construct ideologies of what they propagate to be a "superior" Hindu civilization and challenge the negative racial categorization of their cultures in the racist depictions of India, Indians, and Hindus.

The Hinduism professed by the HSC emphasizes two main tropes. The first is that Hinduism is a universal religion; that is, like Christianity and Islam. Practitioners of Hinduism are located around the globe, and the religion has global appeal. The second trope emphasizes the high status of Hindu women in Hindu society. Both these tropes respond to the main types of racialization that students are most familiar with. As Joshi explains, the constant refrain of Christianity as a universal — hence superior — religion is confronted by the HSC, which constructs universalizing tropes of its own. Similarly, ongoing Orientalist depictions of Indian women (irrespective of religion) and Indian immigrant women by sections of academia, media, and proselytizing groups are challenged by the HSC, which asserts its versions of strong and venerated Hindu women.

The HSC also uses Vivekananda's messages to resist Orientalism. The Web sites feature Vivekananda's assertions of a universal religion, his call to Hindu males to rise up and act, and his talks about the high status of Hindu mothers. As Purkayastha and Joshi's studies show, there are large groups of young people in the mainstream who grow up with overt and covert stereotypes about the negativity of their "religion" and "customs." To these young people, Vivekananda's messages, especially the messages challenging the basis of religio-racialization, remain very relevant and inspirational. The HSC can make claims about Hinduism by quoting a savant who spoke about Hinduism in the United States, and these proclamations about Hinduism can be used by individuals to challenge the claims of those sects of Christians who claim exclusive rights to a superior universal religion.

As with the temples, in spite of the seemingly transformative nature of their messages, the HSC conforms to the Orientalist boundaries imposed upon it. Both the structure of its arguments and its emphases reflect its conformity to mainstream boundaries. For instance, Vivekananda is repeatedly deployed by the HSC for his depiction of religion as action, as a call to "social upliftment." As middle-class Americans well socialized about the value of résumés that include community service, these second-generation individuals are quick to adopt a religious discourse that emphasizes social service as religion. A key component of Vivekananda's call to action was predicated on individuals using community service to wean themselves away from material bounty. He argued that "a contentless frame of words and sophistry with perhaps a little flavor of a kind of social scavenging" did not meet the standards of social upliftment as a way of practicing religion (quoted in Basu 149). The HSC version of Vivekananda's call to action obliterates this need to reject materialism. Thus the sanitized versions of Vivekananda's discourse, delivered in simplistic sound bites to comfortably fit the lives of middle-class students in the United States, are, like the marketing of yoga or *ayurveda*, a way of fitting Hinduism within the parameters of the U.S. capitalistic-political system.

Vivekananda's message to Hindu *males* to become active in upholding Hinduism is repeatedly evoked by the HSC; this message provides a good way to refute the implicit charges of the effeminacy of Asian males so central to racist tropes. The masculinist virile version of Hinduism that HSC projects also includes an overt rejection of the Orientalist tropes about subordinated Indian/Hindu females. In fact, the HSC asserts its superiority over other religions — especially Islam — by pointing out that Hindus worship female goddesses. It also claims that Hindu women are accorded very high status for their maternal status, an argument it traces to Vivekananda. But a closer examination of the HSC presentation of Vivekananda reveals how it misinterprets or selectively deploys Vivekananda's messages. His call to action to Hindu males was a call to reject temple-based, institution-based rituals, to break out of their caste-based social isolation and to act to mitigate people's suffering. This call was directed toward males rather than females *in India*, because Vivekananda saw Indian males as the primary upholders of hoary rituals and useless "religious" traditions. The care-work that Vivekananda essentialized to women was, in his understanding, a continuation of women's family work, in community spaces, as they took care of the needy and vulnerable. He expected males to break out of ritualistic religious practice and embrace the feminine care ethic of religion. Shorn of the historical lineage of the message, the HSC's depictions of males and females introduce new gender hierarchies, while claiming to follow Vivekananda's teaching.

While many of the HSC discussions claims Vivekananda as their source, these messages about women are misleading: as Basu, Amiya Sen, Radice, Burke, and others have consistently pointed out, Vivekananda's characterization of women as mothers was made by a monk (thus an asexual view of women) to challenge the trope of depraved Oriental women as well as the binary conceptualization of women achievers in "the West" versus the subordinated, nonachieving mothers of India. In making these claims about "the" Hindu women, the HSC ignores the thousands of Hindu traditions and practices that coexist in India and that women's statuses are diverse there, varying by culture, class, age, and region. Vivekananda, who traveled all over India, repeatedly talks about this variety of practices and different statuses of men and women in his writings. Equally important, Vivekananda was vocal about contemporary social ills visited upon women, a discussion missing from the ethnonationalistic messages of the HSC.

These misrepresentations cumulatively contribute to an essentialist view of males and females that mires the HSC in the very boundaries it wishes to transgress. The HSC's message about superior women in "our Hindu ideology" is couched solely in terms of women's family (private sphere) roles, and portrays a perfect gender hierarchy in the message's call to men to defend the faith and for women to inspire and incite men to fight for their faith. The HSC is critical about racist representations of Indian women in academia, often referring to racist depictions by earlier generations of feminist scholars as the illustration of racism in academia. Yet, not a single HSC Web site acknowledges two generations of Indian-origin feminist work in the United States that has already developed stringent critiques of racist discourses about Indian and Indian immigrant women and men. The lack of reference to Indian female intellectual leadership in challenging the Western intellectual hierarchical realms contributes to upholding the Orientalist idea that "Indian" women's roles are confined to the private or community spheres only. Challenging the boundaries of Orientalism requires breaking out of existing intellectual frameworks. The HSC discourses fail to do so.

Vivekananda's insistence on considering all religions equal is also strikingly absent in these overt claims of Hindu superiority. Instead, the HSC plays on the contemporary ideologies about Muslims as terrorists and seeks to construct India as a Hindu nation, Islam as a foreign religion in India, and themselves as the legatees of a pristine Hinduism. According to the version of history presented on the Web sites, the invasion of India by Muslim conquerors is seen as marking the end of the glorified ancient Hindu society and the beginning of a subsequent period of decay. Good Hindus are urged to fight Muslims.

It is interesting to document how the HSC's accounts of Islam diverge from Vivekananda's views. Vivekananda was very clear in denouncing sectarian interpretations that emphasize Islam as the only path, a standard he applied to Christianity and Hinduism as well. Nonetheless, he praised

> Mohammed, [as] the prophet of equality, of the brotherhood of man. . . . There is no question of race, caste, creed, colour, or sex. The Sultan of Turkey

may buy a negro from the mart of Africa . . . but should he become a Mohammedan and show sufficient ability and merit, he might even marry the daughter of the Sultan. Compare this to the ways in which the Negroes and American Indians are treated in this country! And what do the Hindus do? If one of your missionaries touchesthe food of an orthodox person, he would throw it away. Notwithstanding our grand philosophy, you note our weakness in practice. (quoted in Basu 129)

Similarly, he repeatedly claimed, as Nemaisadhan Bose has pointed out, an Indo-*Islamic* past as part of Indian heritage, just as he spoke about the advantages of children who have Muslim fathers and Hindu mothers. Indeed, Tattwajanananda's book on the architecture of the temple at Belur, designed by Vivekananda, shows how Vivekananda consciously combined features of this Indian Islamic heritage (along with features of Buddhism, Hinduism, and Christianity) in its architecture. Vivekananda's discourse on this syncretic heritage is missing from the HSC's account of Hinduism.

Overall then, the activities in the temples and among the HSC, while differing in degree and specific emphases, are illustrative of forms of adapting to existing social structures in the United States. Ideologically, both groups repeatedly draw on Vivekananda's talks from the late nineteenth century to counter some of the racial marginalization they are attempting to challenge. Their strategies create some forms of resistances against Orientalism, while transforming the form and content of cultures to fit preexisting policies and institutions. At the same time, both groups create and uphold new gender, caste, class, and interreligious hierarchies, while claiming a superior status for Hinduism.

Challenging Orientalist Boundaries

In contrast to the temples and the HSC agenda, a third stream of decentralized activities by Indians in New England continues to challenge Orientalist tropes *and* sectarian forms of Hinduism. A variety of people are involved in this process: academics who challenge the Orientalist tropes; activists (who organize campaigns against sectarianisms, those who challenge narrowly defined identities and create pan-ethnic coalitions, such as those who work for human rights); as well as other organized groups, which sustain multi-identity, multi-issue social networks and reject narrowly defined social identities. This third stream analyzes Orientalism and challenges its framework.

The core principle guiding the third stream, which ultimately creates a deeper form of resistance to Orientalist tropes, can be summarized with reference to the work of one well-known New Englander of Indian origin, Amartya Sen, whose ideas have the greatest reach in contemporary times. Sen has pointed out that a central objective of Orientalist tropes is to sustain the idea of a singular, overarching identity of "the other." Indeed, the latest tropes attempt—through discourses about clashing civilizations and security regimes intent on racial profiling—to impose a singular dominant religious identity on people, irrespective of their national origin, class, education, occupation, sex, age, interests, passions, and politics, and to create security regimes based on such ideas. Thus, Sen notes that "increasing reliance on religion-based classification of the world also tends to make the Western response to global terrorism and conflict peculiarly ham-handed. Respect for other people is shown by praising their books, rather than taking note of the many-sided involvements and achievements, in nonreligious and religious fields, of different people in a globally interactive world" (12). He argues that the power of hegemonic groups to reduce people to exactly one identity is the basis of the ideology of clashing civilizations. Such neo-Orientalist discourses no longer classify "others" in regional or national-origin terms; they rely on civilizational discourses to establish their power and to define and diminish the lives and work of "the others" all over the world. Sen points out that civilizational discourses coopt all forms of modern thinking and human achievements in science, technology, medicine (indeed, all enlightened and humane ideas) as specifically Western characteristics. Meanwhile, the "non-West"—including the embodiments of the non-West living in Western societies—is left to sort out its identity within the realm of religion alone.

Amartya Sen and other scholars have correctly identified that those who challenge such ideologies solely *in terms of the debate set by the hegemonic group* end up resorting to assertions of narrow cultural nationalisms. Unable to breach the boundaries established by the mainstream, such cultural nationalistic groups focus their energies inward and begin to reinvent "traditions" as a way of gathering ethno-gendered power. Cultural nationalists often impose new boundaries on people, most often on women within the ethnic group, and force them to live by narrow ethno-nationalistic standards. We argue that the temples and the HSC are engaged in constructing such narrow ethno-nationalisms.

If some Indian Americans in New England are engaged in constructing new identities that conform to Orientalist boundaries, others are involved in creating ways of breaching these boundaries. For instance, documenting multifaceted involvements and achievements of people of many religions as part of an "Indian" identity have engaged the talents and energies of a number of scholars. In a manner reminiscent of Vivekananda's claim of an Indo-

Islamic heritage, Sen's *The Argumentative Indian: Writings on Indian History, Culture and Identity* challenges the sectarian Hindu version emerging in the United States by presenting a multicultural, multireligious, multilingual, non-heteronormative history of India.[13] Groups that uphold multireligious traditions through their actions, such as Vedanta Societies (the "temples" created to promote the teachings of Vivekananda) that continue to conduct services to mark the holy days of *all* major religions, are part of this third stream. Individuals and groups engaged in interfaith networks, and all the groups (like the Bengali Association of Greater Hartford) that organize religious activities in nonsegregated spaces, are also part of the effort to maintain porous boundaries between religions and between people of different religious backgrounds.

The idea of "Indian culture" as a pregiven (which is implicit in much of the temple and HSC discourses) has also been challenged by many New England–based Americans of Indian origin, who recognize the role of class formation, gendering, caste ascription, occupation, religious and regional affiliation, generation, and racialization as factors shaping Indian-ness.[14] These scholars often challenge singular assertions of U.S.-based identities such as Indian, South Asian, or *desi* and have discussed and documented the power hierarchies that become embedded in such labels when the boundaries of these identities are reified. Similarly, Indian scholars and activists have been engaged in challenging the deleterious effects of gender hierarchies within ethnic communities, while criticizing the racialized gendered imageries of Indian women. This latter group has been very critical of the essentialized representations of "Hindu" women in the temple and HSC discourses. Such boundary-breaching is not confined to scholarly writing alone; Indians in New England have become active in organizing movements on Asian American issues, immigrant rights, antiracism, hate crimes, civil liberties, human rights, women's issues, and other activism that, irrespective of the issues, keep other local, national, and global dimensions of people's familial, cultural, economic, social, and political identities salient.

Thus the substance of Vivekananda's messages — the need to get beyond narrowly defined religious walls and respect all religions as many coexisting paths to the same truth; the need to build and sustain relationships with people instead of proclaiming the superiority of one group and its practices over others; the need to break out of the pattern of ritualistic practices in order to serve all those who require aid, without any expectation of reward — are all implicit in the writings and activities of the third group. Overall, the work of the third stream moves us beyond thinking about singular identities and membership of all Indians in all-enveloping religious groups. By challenging one-dimensional identities and pointing to plural social identities and networks, this last stream challenges the ideologies and structures of ethno-nationalism and Orientalism.

Conclusion

Examining the conflicts over the places of "hindoos" in the United States at the turn of the twentieth century and of Hindus at the turn of the twenty-first century provides us with some insights about the persistence of Orientalism in the United States. While the forms of Orientalism, driven by contemporary sets of material and political circumstances, are clearly different between the two periods, Orientalism persists in the United States today. By comparing two periods that are separated by a century, this account shows the ways in which Indian-origin groups continue to struggle to claim their religious space in America.

The ban on Indian "Hindoo" migrants for nearly half a century means that some of the conflicts that started during Vivekananda's visit and were in abeyance in the intervening decades are gaining new momentum now. Indians' religious conflicts are similar to those of the Jews, who struggled for centuries to create their space on "America's sacred ground." The first half of this chapter made clear that most of the American mainstream was unwilling to accept Vivekananda's message a century earlier. The second half demonstrates that the mainstream is still not ready to be wholly inclusive; multiculturalism has not created sufficient space for Hindu Indians who are affected by the racialized gendered construction of themselves. Thus we find contemporary Indian origin groups reaching back to a century ago, when there were public debates about the merits of Hinduism. Vivekananda's messages and his iconic status as "the Hindu monk" who brought Hinduism to America become the bedrock on which various groups attempt to build their own modes of resistance.

While Orientalism attributes backward, unchanging, unitary forms of identity on "others," the forms of resistance depicted here illustrate the chasms that result from the championing of one-dimensional identities and the bridges that may be built by adopting and working for more humane visions.

NOTES

1. By restricting ourselves to Hindus alone, we are aware that we are diverting attention from the experiences of Indians who practice Islam, Sikhism, Christian-

· ity, Jainism, Buddhism, and Zorastrianism. Nonetheless, by examining the process through which groups are imagined and marginalized, and how such Orientalist imaginaries and structures are rejected and resisted, we hope to illustrate facets of the ongoing forces of racism, fundamentalism, and cultural nationalism that shape the experiences of all Indians in the United States, irrespective of their religion.

2. The conflation of these missionary and political discourses is best illustrated in Katherine Mayo's infamous book of 1926, *Mother India*.

3. For a detailed historical account of Vivekananda's visits to different cities and the public discussions his talks generated, read Mary Louise Burke's *Vivekananda in the West*, vols. 1–4.

4. Advaitic vedantism is drawn from the concept of advaita, developed by the philosopher/teacher Shankara in the eighth and ninth centuries. It is the idea of nonduality of what is real and permanent in an otherwise eternally changing universe. See Killingley's chapter "Vivekananda's Western Message from the East" for an overview or read Vivekananda's *Collected Works* for a fuller description of this subject.

5. By the 1890s, the Indian activist Pandita Ramabai, who had converted to Christianity after her husband's death, had established a few societies in the United States to raise money for widows' homes she established in India. The networks among women who were involved in social work, especially those who wanted to address the plight of women, led to the formation of more societies, known as Ramabai circles. Pandita Ramabai was well known in India for her highly critical book about the plight of upper-caste Hindu child widows (Prashad 2000); when her message was circulated in the United States, the class delimitation of her thesis was discarded and her statements were taken to represent "Indian" or "Hindu" women. Ramabai actively sought money from Western countries to establish homes (shelters) for these widows in India. For more on racism of white feminists, see Geraldine Forbes's *Women in Modern India*, Inderparl Grewal's *Home and Harem*, and Teresa Hubel's *Whose India?*

6. Carol Breckenridge and Peter van der Veer, as well as Ashis Nandy, have discussed how the hegemonic group is often able to set the terms of discourse in ways that force marginalized groups to respond within preset parameters. This chapter illustrates how some of the racialized Orientalist discourses were generated and how Indians have tried to attend to the hegemonic discourses and the parameters of the discourse.

7. Vivekananda also broke through norms of Hindu orthodoxy to establish the Sarada Math (an organization for female "missionaries"). Throughout his life, he publicly expressed his reverence for Sarada Devi (who was the wife of Vivekananda's guru/teacher Ramakrishna) as the embodiment of the female signifier of the divine and urged all his disciples to regard her as the Divine Mother.

8. Vivekananda's experiences were not unique. The poet Rabindranath Tagore encountered similar structures of overt and subtle resistance to his ideas when he

visited the United States a decade later: Tagore was vilified by the mainstream, but was accepted, in limited ways, by some sections of the intelligentsia (Datta and Robinson 1997). Indeed, Tagore's experiences in the United States along with meeting Okakura Tenshin (the Japanese art historian and curator), led to their thinking about a pan-Asian identity, a cultural form that Tagore later explored at Santiniketan in India.

9. While expectations of assimilation have not disappeared, there is some attempt to organize the displays and performances of "different cultures" in multiple public venues in the United States. Multiculturalism recognizes that different cultural groups should be allowed to express their cultures in civil society instead of assimilating to WASP standards. The expectation is that multiculturalism will lead to cultural exchanges—explorations of literatures, arts, foods, performances, and so forth—among groups. By equating cultures to races, the power differences between cultures, particularly the ability of the dominant group to create the structures that shape how different cultures may be expressed, is often made invisible.

10. Anjana Narayan has conducted ethnographic research on some temples in New England. She has also completed research on the messages that Hindu student groups in New England (and other parts of the world) publicize through their Web sites. Bandana Purkayastha has studied first- and second-generation Indian groups, covering themes of migration, transnationalism, gendered racialization, and resistances through organized movements. Also see our *Living Our Religions: Hindu and Muslim South Asian American Women Narrate Their Experiences*.

11. 501(c) 3 is the Internal Revenue tax code that governs which organizations can claim not-for-profit status. This code requires organizations to set up a governing body, written rules, and formal membership guidelines. Religions like Hinduism, which philosophically do not require formal membership in religious institutions, are then forced to change the meanings and organization of Hinduism in order to conform to the Christian principles that governed the creation of these laws.

12. 12. Many religious leaders could argue that the deities in U.S. temples reflect what is "typical" for the linguistic-cultural communities they serve (whether the communities are mostly from southern India or western India); in any event, there is nothing wrong with such domesticated images as there is no "typical" deity for all Indian Hindus.

13. Also see Jyoti Puri's *Encountering Nationalisms*; Geeta Patel's *Lyrical Movements, Historical Hauntings*; Neela Bhattacharya Saxena's *In the Beginning is Desire;* and Anjana Narayan and Bandana Purkayastha's *Living Our Religions*.

14. In addition to Puri, Patel, and Saxena, see Narayan, "Ethnic Organizations"; Shankar and Srikanth; Srikanth; Prashad; and Purkayastha, *Negotiating Ethnicity*.

WORKS CITED

Barringer, Herbert R., Robert W. Gardner, and Michael J. Levin. *Asians and Pacific Islanders in the United States*. New York: Russell Sage Foundation, 1995.

Basu, Shamita. *Religious Revivalism as Nationalist Discourse : Swami Vivekananda and New Hinduism in Nineteenth-Century Bengal.* New Delhi: Oxford University Press, 2002.

Bean, Susan. "Yankee Traders and Indian Merchants, 1785–1865." In *Festival of India in the United States, 1985–1986*, 131–37. New York: Abrams, 1982.

Breckenridge, Carol, and Peter van der Veer. *Orientalism and the Postcolonial Predicament.* Philadelphia: University of Pennsylvania Press, 1993.

Brekke, Torkel. "The Conceptual Foundation of Missionary Hinduism." *Journal of Religious History* 23 (1999): 203–14.

———. *Makers of Modern Indian Religion in the Late Nineteenth Century.* Oxford: Oxford University Press, 2002.

Bose, Nemai Sadan. "Swami Vivekananda and the Challenge to Fundamentalism." In *Swami Vivekananda and the Modernisation of Hinduism*, edited by William Radice, 281–299. New Delhi: Oxford University Press, 1999.

Burke, Marie Louise. *Swami Vivekananda in the West: New Discoveries.* 6 vols. Kolkata: Advaita Ashram, 1983.

———. *Swami Vivekananda in the West: New Discoveries.* 2nd ed. Vols. 2, 4, and 5. Kolkata: Advaita Ashram, 1985.

Dutta, Krishna, and Andrew Robinson. *Selected Letters of Rabindrantha Tagore.* Cambridge: Cambridge University Press, 1997.

———. *Rabindranath Tagore, Myriad Minded Man.* London: Vintage Books, 1995.

Eastern and Western Disciples. Reminiscences of Swami Vivekananda. Calcutta: Advaita Ashram, 1961.

Espiritu, Yen Le. *Asian American Women and Men: Love, Labor, Laws.* Thousand Oaks, Calif.: Sage, 1997.

Forbes, Geraldine. *Women in Modern India.* Cambridge: Cambridge University Press, 1996.

Grewal, Inderpal. *Home and Harem: Nation, Gender, Empire and Cultures of Travel.* Durham, N.C.: Duke University Press, 1996.

Grillo, Thomas. "Baptist Book Spurs March by Hindus." *Boston Globe*, 3rd ed., 22 November 2001, B4.

Halter, Marilyn. *Shopping for Identity: The Marketing of Ethnicity.* New York: Schocken Books. 1990.

"Hindu Temples in New England." 16 August 2006. http://www.hindumandir.us/east-coast.html#RI.

Jensen, Joan. *Passage from India: Asian Indian Immigrants in North America.* New Haven, Conn.: Yale University Press, 1988.

Joshi, Khyati. *New Roots in America's Sacred Grounds: Religion, Race, and Ethnicity in Indian America.* New Brunswick, N.J.: Rutgers University Press, 2006.

Killingley, Dermott. "Vivekananda's Western Message from the East." In *Swami Vivekananda and the Modernisation of Hinduism*, edited by William Radice, 138–157. London: Oxford University Press, 1998.

King, Richard. *Orientalism and Religion: Postcolonial Theory, India and "the Mystic East."* London: Routledge, 1999.

Kitano, Harry, and Roger Daniels. *Asian Americans: Emerging Minorities*. Englewood Cliffs, N.J.: Prentice Hall, 1995.

Kurien, Prema. "Gendered Ethnicity: Creating a Hindu Indian Identity in the U.S."
American Behavioral Scientist 42, no. 4 (1999): 648–70.

———. "Multiculturalism and Ethnic Nationalism: The Development of an American Hinduism." *Social Problems* 51, no. 3 (2004): 362–85.

———. *A Place at the Multicultural Table: The Development of an American Hinduism*.
New Brunswick, N.J.: Rutgers University Press, 2007.

———. "Religion, Ethnicity and Politics: Hindu and Muslim Indian Immigrants in
the United States." *Ethnic and Racial Studies* 24, no. 2 (2001): 263–93.

Leong, Russell. "Before and After Orientalism: From the Oriental School to Asian
American Studies." *Amerasia Journal* 31 (2005): v–xviii.

Nandy, Ashis. *The Intimate Enemy: Loss and Recovery of Self under Colonialism*. Delhi:
Oxford University Press, 1983.

Narayan, Anjana. *Asian Americans in Connecticut, Census 2000: Citizenship, Employment, Poverty, Income and Education*. Storrs: University of Connecticut, Asian
American Studies Institute , 2004.

———. "Ethnic organizations and Ethnic Identities: Websites as a Tool for Creating
Transnational Ethnic Identities." Ph.D. diss. University of Connecticut, 2006.

Narayan, Anjana, and Debrashmi Mitra. *Asian Americans in Connecticut, Census
2000: Race and Ethnicity, Household, Family*. Storrs: Univerisity of Connecticut:
Asian American Studies Institute, 2004.

Narayan, Anjana, and Bandana Purkayastha. *Living Our Religions: Hindu and Muslim South Asian American Women Narrate Their Experiences*. Sterling, Va.: Ku-
marian Press, 2008.

Patel, Geeta. *Lyrical Movements, Historical Hauntings: On Gender, Colonialism and
Desire in Miraji's Urdu Poetry*. Stanford, Calif.: Stanford University Press, 2002.

Prashad, Vijay. *The Karma of Brown Folk*. Minneapolis: University of Minnesota
Press, 2000.

Puri, Jyoti. *Encountering Nationalism*. Malden, Mass.: Blackwell, 2004.

Purkayastha, Bandana. *Asian Indians in Connecticut*. Research Paper Series, No. 2.
Storrs, Conn.: University of Connecticut, Asian American Studies Institute,
1999.

———. *Negotiating Ethnicity: Second-generation South Asian Americans Traverse a
Transnational World*. New Brunswick, N.J.: Rutgers University Press, 2005.

———. "Skilled Migration and Cumulative Disadvantage: The Case of Highly Qualified Asian Indian Immigrant Women in the U.S." *Geoforum* 36 (2005): 181–96.

Purkayastha, Bandana, and Mangala Subramaniam. *The Power of Poor Women's Informal Networks: Lessons in Social Change from South Asia and West Africa*. Lanham, Md.: Lexington Books, 2004.

Radice, William, ed. *Swami Vivekananda and the Modernisation of Hinduism*. Delhi:
Oxford University Press, 1999.

Rolfsen, Catherine. "Resistance, Complicity and Transcendence: A Postcolonial

Study of Vivekananda's Mission in the West." Master's thesis, Queens University, Ontario, Canada, 2005.

Said, Edward. *Orientalism*. New York: Vintage Books, 1978.

Saxena, Neela Bhattacharya. *In the Beginning Is Desire*. Delhi: Indialog Books, 2004.

Sen, Amartya. *The Argumentative Indian: Writings on Indian Culture, History, and Identity*. New York: Farrar, Straus, and Giroux, 2005.

———. *Identity and Violence: The Illusion of Destiny*. New York: Norton, 2006.

Sen, Amiya. *Swami Vivekananda*. New Delhi: Oxford University Press, 2000.

Shankar, Lavinia, and Rajini Srikanth. *A Part, Yet Apart: South Asians in America*. Philadelphia: Temple University Press, 1998.

Sinha, Mrinalini. *Selections from Mother India*. New Delhi: Kali for Women, 1998.

Srikanth, Rajini. *The World Next Door: South Asian American Literature and the Idea of America*. Philadelphia: Temple University Press, 2004.

Tattwajnanadana (Swami). *A Symphony in Architecture: A Visitor's Guide towards Better Understanding of the Spirit and Architecture of the Temple*. Belur: Ramakrishna Mission, 2001.

Vivekananda (Swami). *Chicago Addresses*. 17th printing. Calcutta: Advaita Ashram, 1974.

———. *The Complete Works of Vivekananda*. 8 vols. Calcutta: Advaita Ashram, 1963.

———. *Inspired Talks*. New York: Ramakrishna-Vivekananda Center, 1978.

6

New WORLD Theater Archives

Asian American Women Playwrights in Western Massachusetts

LUCY MAE SAN PABLO BURNS

In the early 1990s, Roberta Uno, founding artistic director of New WORLD Theater, created a collection currently called the Roberta Uno Asian American Women Playwrights Scripts Collection at the University of Massachusetts Amherst.[1] Housed at the W. E. B. Du Bois Library, this extraordinary collection currently contains more than two hundred plays as well as supplementary materials documenting the work of Asian American women playwrights. While the collection contains the writings of many contemporary playwrights, such as Alice Tuan, Jeannie Barroga, and Velina Hasu Houston, it also houses rare materials by early writers, including those of Gladys Ling-ai Li, a Hawaiʻi-based playwright whose play was staged in New York as early as 1924.[2] My discussion of the emergence of this particular archiving project is embedded in multiple understandings of the term "archive" and of the processes of "archiving" within the specific context of Asian American women playwrights. I use "archive" and "archiving" here to mean the gathering of objects, in this case plays by Asian American women, for preservation and centralization of access. I deploy these terms to refer equally to the process by which an institutional entity emerges as a source of and material site for plays by Asian American women. Such a history of the Uno Collection is thus grounded in an understanding of archival projects as always already engaged in entangled structures of poetics, power, and politics. [3]

The Uno Collection is unique in that it is one of the few institutions to specifically archive the plays of Asian American women playwrights.[4] Crucial here is that it is directly attached to a theater company and a university. The works of Asian American women playwrights may be found in other collections, such as the East West Players (housed at the University of California, Los Angeles) and the Asian American Theater Company (housed at the University of California, Santa Barbara). These companies' official archives primarily store scripts of plays that have been produced in their season productions while individual theater companies usually oversee and fund their own preservation and documentation processes.[5] Centralized archiving institutions such as the New York Public Library's Performing Arts Library have, over the years, amassed an equally formidable collection of diverse dramatic materials. A repository of plays/performance texts by Asian American women, I will suggest, figures the very dynamics of archival formation, not simply as a site of preservation but rather as a venue for theorizing processes of production, dissemination, and appropriation. I analyze the emergence of the Uno Collection primarily through an engagement with debates around archivization in Asian American Studies and Performance Studies. To do so, I delineate a strategic overview of the contents of this archive, highlighting a few key works and artists. Such an effort moves beyond the language of summary to signal an "imagined community" of Asian American women playwrights made possible through the creation of the Uno Collection, a community otherwise effaced within the vastness and whiteness of American theater. My essay closes with a set of provocations that emerges from the formation and institutionalization of archives such as the Uno Collection.

Genealogies, Archives, Politics

While this essay tells the story of the specific emergence of the Uno Collection, I first briefly rehearse issues central to the question of "archive" in both Performance Studies and Asian American Studies. In doing so, I intend to frame the story of the Uno Collection within and outside the politics of established archival practice. The foundation of the Uno Collection extends and complicates such inherited genealogies of archival formation in Asian American and Performance Studies. The emergence (temporally and spatially) of the Uno Collection in western Massachusetts foregrounds the archival convergences and divergences of Asian American Studies and Performance Studies. I am especially interested in some of the shared archival preoccupations of these two fields and their intersection with a community-based project such as the Uno Collection. As Performance Studies scholar Diana Taylor writes, "What makes an object archival is the *process whereby it is selected, classified, and presented for analysis*" (19; emphasis added). For Taylor the emergence of an object as "archival" is an active and conscious undertaking that involves deliberate classification, selection, and presentation. Taylor's insistence on the active, embodied, and historical practices of archival formation is key to my concerns on the practice of archiving and its relationship to performative expressions of community and self-identity. As I will demonstrate, the process of building the Uno Collection, and by extension any archive, is one of calling up a community into being.

Archiving practices in the fields of Theater and Performance Studies and Asian American Studies have elaborated common concerns around what and who gets archived. In Theater and Performance Studies, the question of what constitutes archival objects is complicated by performance and embodiment that are not captured in text-based materials. Taylor's critically acclaimed *The Archive and Repertoire* propels debates on archive and performance within Theater and Performance Studies. She critiques the process that led up to the dominance of texts as *the* objects that make up the archive. She proposes the "repertoire" as an alternative concept for the archival formation, underscoring the embodied and textured forms of recording and performing history. Useful here is Taylor's emphasis on how the social relations produced by historical conditions directly influence what gets constituted as archival objects. More specifically, Taylor has provocatively argued that European colonialism (as historical condition) produced domination and hegemony as determining social relations that naturalized the written text and writing as objects worthy of archiving. That is, the colonial archive's privileging of text-based materials routinely suppressed other forms of expressions. By offering the idea of the repertoire, Taylor proposes an alternative that shifts a text-based paradigm toward the inclusion of embodied expressions of self- and community identity.

Such a shift in archival practices has been prominent in Asian American Studies, a field formation preoccupied with the (re)collection of silenced and lost voices, disappeared and distorted by racism in U.S. society. More generally, Asian American Studies has vigorously promoted a "community-based" first-voice perspective that prioritizes the point of view of Asians in America. Academics play a key role in the recovery and constitution of archives as they can be made to mobilize the resources of the university to support the community. Asian American Studies encourages projects that break down the hierarchical relationship between academia and community, that are driven by community needs, and that make a recognizable impact on the community. Scholarship production within Asian American Studies must be understood as a transformative project that should be accessible and relevant to the community. As the field of Asian American Studies dynamically changes and adjusts, its commitment to recovery projects and to community continues even as it struggles to account for what Lisa Lowe calls Asian America's "heterogeneity, hybridity, and multiplicity."[6] At stake here is a sustained interrogation of the ideological entailments that fuel and fracture Asian American Studies' historical attachment to the very idea of the community and the archive. Thus, any invocation of the Uno Collection must necessarily engage its situatedness at the cusp of multiple archival initiatives: a performance studies project that focuses on the inclusion of embodied self and community expressions and an Asian American Studies project that attempts recovery amidst the detritus of historical racism and elision.

The Uno Collection provides a key instantiation of the force of multiple archival logics. As I elaborate later, the Uno Collection disrupts, even transforms, what Asian American Studies historian Stephen Sumida has termed the hegemony of the "Californic-paradigm" or the "Pacific-dominated" paradigm within Asian American Studies (86). Sumida's description of Asian American Studies' earlier trajectory productively critiques the dominance of scholarship and institutional formations that "originate" in California, the *unmarked* point of origin for the Asian American Studies imaginary. His formulation challenges Asian American Studies scholars to examine closely privileged intellectual and political constructs such as the concept of community, so key to any teleology of minority development. Sumida's call for a re-imagining of Asian American Studies de-links location, majority, and longevity as primary categories for the composition and emergence of community. Within such re-imaginings, the concept of community becomes primarily a space of the imagination, anchored to narratives that may or may not be attached to more conventional geographies of Asian migration.

The Uno Collection is an artist-centered archiving process in which the artists determine the contents of the collection. It is an exemplar of the multiple forms through which a community chooses to record (or disappear) itself. Here, the artist chooses what she submits to the archive, thereby maintaining partial control of the archiving process and what it might mean to her. It is also thus a vivid and strikingly "living archive."[7] In this context, this "living archive" refers to how these materials are attached to a place of production. The allusion to "liveness" foregrounds the continued process of archival evolution (if you will), and the life of the works archived in it. Of equal significance is that the Uno Collection is directly connected to a theater-producing institution, one that supports and manages the "liveness" of the archive. From its inception, the Uno Collection was designed to expand and remain active. The Uno Collection's affiliation with an educational institution that incorporates the contents of the archive into the curriculum clearly authorizes some of the frames though which the works and the artists in this archive, and the archive itself, may be understood and interpreted. In other words, the Uno Collection is housed within a structure that can produce knowledge about itself, even as it continues to emerge as a space of knowledge formation. In what follows, I detail Uno Collection's histories of emergence within a multiracial theater company and an Asian American–led organization drawn from the hub of Asian American communities in New England.

A New WORLD, A New Archive: Global Theater in Rural Massachusetts

to have my work archived means
i have a voice beyond myself
to have my work archived
with other Asian American women writers means
i am part of a community of women
diverse in experiences, cultures, generations
and artistic expressions
to have my work archived means
it is possible that some distant day
a young sister struggling for her voice,
might stumble upon us and realize,
hey, these women have lived and found a way to tell their stories
i can do it too
to have my work archived means
my voice is part of the colorful, unruly, eurythmic choir that is Americana
—Nobuko Miyamoto

I imagine my words blending among sister playwrights, as safe as a locket, as independent as stone. My daughters and my daughters' daughters will move on, but I smile knowing they have a glimpse of who I once was.
—Louella Dizon

Any discussion of the Uno Collection of plays by Asian American women must include an understanding of the organization that formed and continues to coordinate this project in process. As mentioned earlier, this archive project was initiated and established by the NWT's founding director

Roberta Uno. One may well ask, what is a nearly thirty-year-old-theater by, about, and, for people of color doing in the hinterlands of western Massachusetts? Perhaps such a question no longer needs to be asked, but in 1979, when playwright, director, and premed student Roberta Uno had just dreamed up the idea of a multiracial, global theater company, it was one that did not seem to belong in a rural western Massachusetts town.[8] Uno notes the racial context of the Pioneer Valley in the early years of NWT:

> I founded the New WORLD Theater in 1979, at the University of Massachusetts at Amherst, as a student-organizing project, when students of color numbered a marginal 6 percent at the University and were minimally reflected in campus life or curriculum. The founding vision was to create a theatrical space that would offer a contemporary program of works by Black, Latino, Asian, and Native Americans, a repertory that was completely invisible within the existing arts environment of the region. The theater was founded while apartheid was still the rule in South Africa, and it drew parallels between supporting the anti-apartheid movement and combating racial and cultural de facto segregation in America. ("Introduction," *The Color of Theater* 7)

From its inception, New WORLD Theater, formerly named Third World Theater, filled a lacuna in the academic curriculum; it asserted narrative and aesthetic points of view that were underrepresented and directly excluded in the canon of American theater. NWT's mission exceeded strict university boundaries. After all, those who worked at the university belonged to other social networks outside of the university. Hence, this artistic organization serviced and found its support from those in the local community who sought and believed in the labor of culture in calling up a community.

In its early years, NWT productions primarily operated within the politics of inclusion through representation. In other words, they staged plays to present stories and experiences of people of color not typically dramatized on American stage. Their productions confronted and defied racism in the larger American society and in its microcosm, American theater. An artistic team of actors and designers, who were students as well as nonuniversity theater artists living in western Massachusetts, usually made up NWT's artistic, technical, and administrative staff. Yet from the very beginning, Uno was clear that the NWT project was not primarily about *integration*. She did not see this project as solely about claiming its rightful place within an existing canon or caliber of standards in American theater. As Uno elaborates,

New WORLD Theater, as a theater of artists of color, was never an *integra-tion* project, we were a *desegregation* project — and that is an important distinc-tion. We never intended to join the existing structure of American theater or higher education. Nor did we aspire to reform those structures. Our goal was, as artists, to gain access to the means of production, however temporally, and transform the environment. We knew we were the people who weren't sup-posed to be there in the first place. And we have been creating "guerrilla" transformations of spaces — formal theater space and informal community space — for twenty-two years. ("Being Present: Theater and Social Change" 71)

NWT was focused on setting its own sets of standards that accounted for what mainstream white American theater did not. It was, and continues to be, a project of paradigm transformation, and thus was not an exclusionary project. To this day, NWT supports all theater artists who imagine a new world, who offer a vision of transformation. True to its desire to disrupt standards, the renaming from Third World Theater to New WORLD The-ater signaled a forward-looking and more capacious politics. While "Third World" described the politics that imagined the emergence of NWT, "New WORLD" signified a dynamic politics of always imagining new ways of being, creating, and relating.

NWT's multidimensional programming commitments that included producing and presenting theatrical works simultaneously involved collect-ing playscripts and supplementary materials and occasionally artist inter-views. Artistic director Uno taught University of Massachusetts Amherst courses — such as "Third World Theater," "American Theater and Race," and "Contemporary Plays by Women of Color" — that integrated the theater's season productions into the course curriculum. These courses were lab-oratories for theorizing a radical genre of work, where frameworks and approaches included inquiry into modes and means of production and cir-culation. NWT also presented touring works by artists, in addition to pro-ducing and developing new works.[9] Hence, visiting artists gave classroom lectures, offering the students an opportunity to engage with the perform-ance, dramatic literature, and aesthetic in the works of contemporary artists of color. It also trained students in skills such as oral history by assigning, for example, artist interviews that become part of the archival collection. At a personal level, I directly benefited from this pedagogical practice as a stu-dent and a teacher in training. Our intellectual and artistic training urged us to reimagine the archival process as one of transparency and collaboration, as opposed to one of surveillance and cataloguing.[10]

Initially, Uno had reservations about establishing an archive of this significance in western Massachusetts. She had been collecting scripts and did not necessarily have a consistent system of storing these materials. She was also working on her first anthology of plays by Asian American women, *Unbroken Thread*. Uno considered sending the scripts to a place where the materials would be more accessible to a geographical and institutional center that had a large, established Asian American community, as well as an academic institution that already supported Asian American Studies.[11] Ultimately however, Uno's choice to build this archive at the University of Massachusetts Amherst (in western Massachusetts) is a statement about Asian American community formation in the United States: "We are everywhere, and such spaces [the university, western Massachusetts, the archive] belong to us as well" ("Introduction," *Unbroken Thread* 3). Thus the Uno Collection is not only archiving an emergent culture (the practice of theater making by Asian American women); it is also a cultural practice in itself. The creation of the Uno Collection accessed and showcased Asian American communities in marginal locations; in doing so, it also created future communities of alliance through its collection of Asian American writings.

As noted earlier, formations such as the Uno Collection, the East of California Caucus, and Asian American Studies in the South interrupt a "Californic paradigm" or "Pacific-dominated" paradigm within Asian American Studies. These projects make us attentive to the literal presence of Asian Americans in places outside of California, Hawai'i, and the Pacific Coast of the United States, where large concentrations of Asian Americans reside. However, they also challenge the categories of analysis that hinge on majoritarian politics. They make us rethink the terms in which we seek to be included or visible. The political project then, as Uno asserts, is to acknowledge and create the community where you are and resist reifying "centers" of community formation. This differentiated relationship to Asian America emerges from a political practice of coalition and an understanding of racial formation (and its representation) as relational. In other words, the process by which Asian American subjects and communities become racialized is in direct relation to other racialized communities.

In my consideration of the politics of the archive and archiving through the Uno Collection, the notion of performance as ephemeral provides another possibility for rethinking community, specifically in regards to the link between belonging and time. The presumption is that a community forms over time and hence deserves recognition and acceptance. Performance and the university setting urge a rethinking of longevity and fixity as hegemonic values guiding our principles of what constitutes community and the politics of community. Student contributors to the establishment of the Uno Collection accurately demonstrate my point. Those of us who worked with Uno were students temporarily making our home in a largely unfamiliar western Massachusetts. [12] My involvement with the archive and the theater taught me to acknowledge and engage with the local community that supported the existence and operations of the university. Our contributions in helping to establish the Uno Collection were small but significant to the project of Asian American theater. My current research in Filipino migrant labor and performance studies grew out of these early understandings of access and institutionalization and informs my insistence on the acknowledgment of how temporary work contributes and ultimately transforms our notions of labor (regarding production and product) as well as social relations. [13]

From Object to Archive: A Sampling of the Works in the Uno Collection

It is an honor to have work archived. The cultural marketplace defines the label of Asian American Woman Playwright as passive, lyrical, long-suffering, ornamental, dragony. I tend to write against dominant norms, drawing from my edgier voice. So I am glad to be included in the AAWP Uno collection, as it gathers varied works that exist despite the marketplace.

My earlier writing is naïve and furious, perhaps an overcompensation for invisibility. Later works drift away from "Asian American" ethnicity as a primary concern, though women are always placed in the center of the drama. To be archived is to be able to follow an organic progression; it takes the pressure off of having to exist through meeting market-imposed categories.

— Alice Tuan

I remember UM-A [University of Massachusetts Amherst] folks reminding me via many letters and phone calls that I should submit any updates or ephemera relating to my plays. And I remember hauling out, from my own haphazard filing system, boxes of scripts and agonizing whether or not to "rewrite" this one, or maybe that one, before sending it to any archives. . . . once production is achieved, a stage play performed — in a moment — stamps a memory, instant, affecting, impressionable. Without further documentation, that moment would be difficult to re-create. Archiving all these amazing works by fellow Asian American women playwrights has, with this collection, moved us all into an uncarved niche of theater history.

— Jeannie Barroga

Although it is beyond the scope of this essay to provide an account of each archival entry, the following discussion is a glimpse of the richness of the materials collected in the Uno Collection.[14] Playwrights whose works are housed in the Uno Collection include some of those who have published and often produced plays, including Velina Hasu Houston (*Tea*; editor of *The Politics of Life: Four Plays by Asian American Women* and *But Still, Like Air, I'll Rise*), Jeannie Barroga (*Walls, Bubblegum Killers*), Diana Son (*R.A.W. 'Cause I'm a Woman, Stop Kiss*), Bina Sharif (*Ancestor's House*), and Brenda Wong Aoki (*The Queen's Garden*). Contents archived are records of scripts in varying stages — early drafts, versions that are finalized for production, and published plays.[15] Because the archive is attached to a theater company, it also contains records of Asian American women artists who have developed works at NWT. For example, Leilani Chan's *E Nana I'ke Kumu / Look to the Source*, thúy lê's *bodies between us*, and Chitra Divakaruni's *Clothes* (adapted by Divakaruni from her short story with the same title, choreographed by Aparna Sindhoor and performed with Purva Bedi) found support in their early forms at NWT. These are examples of the direct imbrications of archival practice and the politics of production. In other words, the process of archiving is already implicated within the struggle for the limited resources for actual staging of plays, a material concern that continually plagues the genre of theater by people of color.

In its archiving of plays by early Asian American women playwrights such as Gladys Ling-Ai Li, Betsy Inoue, and Wai Chi Chun, the Uno Collection performs the task of what Josephine Lee, Imogene Lee, and Yuko Matsukawa call "re/collecting early Asian America." Its commitment to "re/collecting" is not simply one that any archival project undertakes. Specifically for Asian Americans, whose "presence" in the United States is often relegated as "contemporary" or "recent" phenomenon, the project of "re/collecting" becomes a political project that challenges the very ownership of and belonging to history. To "re/collect" the works of early Asian American women playwrights is not just to amass minoritized voices; rather such a process of "re/collection" mandates the very rethinking of forces of temporality, authorship, and community formation within histories of archives and documentation.

"Asian American woman playwright" as archival object already signals a deviation from conventional notions of a "playwright." The inclusion of pieces by Asian American theater artists who work in performance collectives or ensembles, for example, further expands the conventional definition of a "playwright" as a single author writing plays. These performance collectives include a wide range of community collaborations, such as the Vietnamese American theater ensemble Club O'Noodles, spoken-word pan–Asian American collectives I Was Born with Two Tongues and Mango Tribe, and the multiracial dance theater ensemble Maura Nguyen Donohue's In Mixed Company. One of the prized materials in the Uno Collection is the work of early women of color performance collaborations among Jessica Hagedorn, Ntozake Shange, and Thulani Davis (*mississippi meets the amazon*), and those among Hagedorn, Robbie McAuley, and Laurie Carlos, also known as Class Thought (*teenytown*). With the inclusion of these ensemble pieces, the Uno Collection acknowledges multiple forms of authorship and diverse modes of creative process. The playwrights sought out and invited to submit their works to the Uno Collection do not strictly nor necessarily develop or produce their plays with Asian American, multiracial, or women's theaters. NWT's commitment to its profile as a multiracial theater company is attentive to the possibilities and the limits of strict cultural nationalism that may operate within the logic of ethnospecific cultural projects. Uno, as well Velina Hasu Houston, for instance, has openly pointed to the ethnocentrism within Asian American cultural communities and in Asian American theaters in particular.[16]

The practice of collective creation and multiracial collaboration takes a different form and significance in the work of the activist-theater group Sining Bayan, which produced many unique archival materials now housed in the Uno Collection. The scripts written by Sining Bayan made their way into the archive through Ermena Vinluan, a Filipina American political activist and multimedia artist. From 1972 to 1981, Sining Bayan staged plays about the struggle of Filipino people in the Philippines and in the United States and was relentless in its criticisms of martial law and imperialism. Sining Bayan was the cultural arm to the radical political organization Katipunan ng mga Demokratikong Pilipino/KDP.[17] This group's original productions dramatized the pressing political concerns of Filipinos in the United States. These concerns included the history of Filipino labor and labor organizing in the United States, the U.S. military's and Philippine central government's joint intervention in the Southern Philippines's search for land rights, and the fight for the acquittal of two Filipina nurses of murder charges in Chicago. The inclusion of the Sining Bayan materials alongside more recognizable dramatic productions makes the Uno Collection not just an archive for and about Asian American women. Its reach extends to include larger questions of imperialism and nation formation. I close this essay with some thoughts that return us to the relationship of archiving and performance to rearticulate what I see as the Uno Collection's interventions.

Coda

While I believe that the Asian American feminist voice is and must be a vital part of the overall American theatre voice as well as the global theatre voice, sociopolitical challenges remain that complicate the recognition of that voice. Special archives that focus on that voice aid in keeping those voices from being lost in history.
—Velina Hasu Houston

I return now to the crucial question of the politics of archival formation as debated within feminist performance theory. The Uno Collection was instituted at the height of these debates, and any engagement with its history must thus necessarily trace its engagement (or lack thereof) with contemporary discussions of gender, performance, and archival formation. In the 1990s, stimulating conversations among feminist performance theorists centered on the impossibility of archiving performance. Peggy Phelan provocatively argued for an understanding of performance as that which is unrepeatable and thus cannot be archived. In Phelan's *Unmarked*, she challenges the dominance of a text-based Theater and Performance Studies, arguing for a shift toward the body-in-performance.[18] The body-in-performance interprets performance as a "representation without reproduction" (148). Theater scholar Elin Diamond situates Phelan's body-over-text within the genealogy of poststructuralism's declaration of the death of the author. The turn to the body-in-performance raises questions of authenticity and the "real," as well as where the true interpretation of performance may lie. Phelan's "representation without reproduction" is informed by radical queer studies' critique that imagines an alternative to the normative notions of reproduction, lineage, and generation naturalized in the project of visibility and representation. Taylor's *The Archive and the Repertoire*, as previously noted, builds upon these conversations in the 1990s and argues for "repertoire" as a practice of memory-keeping and remembering that exceeds the materiality of the written text.

Phelan's theory of the body-in-performance provokes us to ask, "What are we archiving when we archive performance?" Within the context of the Uno Collection, I am wary of the oversimplification of the turn to the body-in-performance, where performance and embodied expressions displace conventional archival objects such as written materials. A polemical distinction between archive and embodiment advocates for a privileging of performance without accounting for the process of selection of what gets performed. An approach to performance that makes primary the body-in-performance must also account for the inescapable fact that what gets performed is necessarily what becomes the basis of what gets archived (through scholarly work, reviews, publication, and so forth). Rather, one could ask more productively how Phelan's anti-representational theory informs the politics and poetics of ethnic theaters, including NWT and the Uno Collection, which focus on representing stories that have been deliberately silenced. Is the Uno Collection a recuperative project that maintains its unreconstructed attachment to materials and objects as well as to the project of preservation? Or is it merely reproducing the repressive categories of representation that produced its conditions of possibility in the first place?

This essay has been an attempt to address these questions and to suggest that the Uno Collection and its artist-centered process of archiving propose alternatives beyond recuperation and a disavowal of subjectivity. Even as we generatively critique the desire for fixed subjectivity offered through the recovery of lost archives, equally we must be attentive to a more complicated theorization, not abandonment, of agency, representation, and alternative social formation. A project such as the Uno Collection can only remind us that the struggle for agency, representation, and alternative social formation remains a powerful political project, a "new WORLD" archive of possibility and collaboration.

ACKNOWLEDGMENTS

The initial idea for this essay was presented at New WORLD Theater's 2005 Intersections IV conference (under the leadership of artistic director Andrea Assaf). I thank Priscilla Page for inviting me to participate in a panel on the Uno Collection. This essay also benefited from comments by Cindy Garcia, Priya Srinivasan, and Sansan Kwan. Lastly, I recognize Roberta Uno for her tireless envisioning of a new world.

NOTES

1. For the rest of this essay, I will refer to New WORLD Theater as NWT and the Roberta Uno Asian American Women Playwrights Scripts Collection as the Uno Collection.
2. For more on Gladys Ling-ai Li, see Roberta Uno's "Ling-ai Li: Remember the Voice of Your People's Gods" and Sucheng S. Huang's bio-bibliography entry in *Asian American Playwrights: A Bio-Bibliographical Critical Sourcebook*. For Li's play, "The Submission of Rose Moy," see *Paké: Writings by Chinese in Hawai'i*.

3. For a nuanced understanding of archival hermeneutics, see Anjali Arondekar, "Without a Trace: Sexuality and the Colonial Archive" and her *For the Record: On Sexuality and the Colonial Archive*.

4. Worth mentioning here is the Native American Women Playwrights Archive (NAWPA) at the King Library, Miami University at Ohio. For more information about NAWPA, see http://staff.lib.muohio.edu/nawpa/index.php. Of course, a playwright's work could be archived in several different places. For instance, Velina Hasu Houston, a hapa, Afro–Asian American playwright, has her own collection, The Velina Hasu Houston Collection, archived at the Huntington Library's Art Collections and Botanical Gardens in San Marino, California, in addition to having a smaller number of pieces housed in the Uno Collection.

5. Objects in the archives include scripts, playbills, artistic notes from the director and designers, production reviews, as well as budget reports and official company meeting minutes. Scripts and other materials that have been submitted for production consideration in these theaters, but were rejected, are not included in the official archival roster.

6. See Viet Nguyen's *Race and Resistance: Literature and Politics in Asian America* and Kandice Chuh's *Imagine Otherwise: On Asian Americanist Critique* for works that take to task uncritical invocations of the notion of community. These works question the celebratory uses of community as well as the presumed progressive politics it is made to connote.

7. I say "partial" control as any archiving process already involves shared operation. Having (partial) control of the means of production, or more accurately the right to self-determination, is an abiding principle in NWT's projects.

8. For more about NWT's history, see Uno and Kathy Perkins' introduction to *Contemporary Plays by Women of Color*; Uno's "Being Present: Theater and Social Change"; Uno's introduction to the section on "Drama" in *Bold Words*; Uno's introduction to *Unbroken Thread*. Also see a special issue of *MELUS*, called "Ethnic Theater," celebrating NWT's tenth anniversary, edited by and with an introduction by Uno. Theses about New WORLD Theater include: Donna Beth Aronson's "Access and Equity: Performing Diversity at the New WORLD Theatre"; and Nona E. Chiang's "Speaking Up, Speaking Out: Negotiating an Asian American Cultural Identity at New WORLD Theater."

9. Arts administrator Sansan Wong observes that NWT often was, significantly, the first touring invitation for many Asian American artists (especially solo performers) in the 1980s and 1990s.

10. Other scholars who have found research support from the Uno Collection include theater historian Esther Kim, dance studies scholar Yutian Wong, and Japan-based literary scholar Iwao Yamamoto.

11. Before the 1990s, various faculties have been teaching courses about Asian immigration to the United States and Asian American communities at the University of Massachusetts Amherst. There had been early efforts to increase the presence of Asian American Studies in the curriculum through the labor of professors such

as Sally Habana-Hafner (international education), James Hafner (geography), Bob Suzuki (School of Education), and Lucy Nguyen (Southeast Asian Studies and the director of the United Asian Learning Resource Center), and through the support of Lee Edwards, the former dean of humanities. Mitzi Sawada, professor of history at Hampshire College, and Peter Kiang, professor of sociology at the University of Massachusetts Boston, assisted in the galvanizing efforts toward a more formalized and sustained curriculum building of Asian American Studies in the early 1990s. Graduate and undergraduate students and staff actively collaborated with faculty in these efforts as well. Now, the University of Massachusetts Amherst offers a certificate program in Asian American Studies and the Five Colleges (Amherst College, Hampshire College, Mount Holyoke College, Smith College, and the University of Massachusetts Amherst) have been granting dissertation fellowships and postdoctoral fellowships. A significant number of faculty with expertise in Asian American Studies have been hired steadily in the Five Colleges since the early 1990s; in addition, a joint, multicampus faculty position has been filled.

12. Students who worked on the Uno Collection in its early years include Hillary Edwards, Sangeeta Rao, Megan Smith, Patti Chang, Esther Kim, and many others.

13. Dance Studies and Asian American Studies scholar Priya Srinivasan draws out further interesting tensions between corporeal influences and kinesthetic traces among and between classical Indian dancers and modern dance choreographers in the early twentieth-century United States. Through her discussion of these early dancers as contract and temporary laborers, she argues for a transformation of our notions of labor, especially in Asian American Studies. See "The Bodies Beneath the Smoke; or, What's Behind the Cigarette Poster: Unearthing Kinesthetic Connections in American Dance History."

14. 14. A complete list of the Uno Collection contents may be accessed through http://www.library.umass.edu/spcoll/ead/mums345.htm. The Web site listing of the archive contents is a new phase of the collection that is now managed by NWT literary associate Priscilla Page. Page builds upon the notion of the Uno Collection as a "living archive" through her theater courses and her proposed graduate concentration on multicultural theater in the University of Massachusetts Boston's theater department. NWT's project to transform theater and academic institutions continues.

15. It is beyond the scope of this essay to analyze the role publication plays within the archival process. Some questions worth considering, however, include: Is there a difference between a performance text and dramatic literature? What is the role of publication in transforming a playscript into dramatic literature?

16. See Velina Hasu Houston's introduction to *The Politics of Life* and Uno's foreword in Hasu Houston's second edited collection *But Still, Like Air, I'll Rise*.

17. *Katipunan ng mga Demokratikong Pilipino* translates as the Union of Democratic Pilipinos.

18. Also see Phelan's "Reciting the Citation of Others; or, A Second Introduction" in *Acting Out: Feminist Performances*.

WORKS CITED

Arondekar, Anjali. *For the Record: On Sexuality and the Colonial Archive*. Durham, N.C.: Duke University Press, 2009.

———. "Without a Trace: Sexuality and the Colonial Archive." *Journal of the History of Sexuality* 14, nos. 1–2 (Winter 2005): 10–27.

Aronson, Donna Beth. "Access and Equity: Performing Diversity at the New WORLD Theater." Ph.D. diss., Florida State University, 2003.

Barroga, Jeannie. E-mail interview. 31 May 2008.

Chiang, Nona E. "Speaking Up, Speaking Out: Negotiating an Asian American Cultural Identity at New WORLD Theater." Master's thesis. University of California, Los Angeles, 2001.

Chuh, Kandice. *Imagine Otherwise: On Asian Americanist Critique*. Durham, N.C.: Duke University Press, 2003.

Diamond, Elin. *Unmaking Mimesis: Essays on Feminism and Theater*. New York: Routledge, 1997.

Dizon, Louella. E-mail interview. 4 June 2008.

Hasu Houston, Velina. *But Still, Like Air, I'll Rise: New Asian American Plays*. Philadelphia: Temple University Press, 1997.

———. E-mail interview. 7 July 2008.

———. *The Politics of Life: Four Plays*. Philadelphia: Temple University Press, 1993.

Huang, Shucheng S. "Ling-ai (Gladys) Li." In *Asian American Playwrights: A Bio-Bibliographical Critical Source*, edited by Miles Xian Liu, 185–88. Westport, Conn.: Greenwood, 2002.

Kim, Esther. *A History of Asian American Theater*. Cambridge: Cambridge University Press, 2006.

Lee, Josephine, Imogene Lee, and Yuko Matsukawa, eds. *Re/Collecting Early Asian America: Essays in Cultural History*. Philadelphia: Temple University Press, 2002.

Li, Ling-ai (Gladys). "The Submission of Rose Moy." *Hawaii Quill Magazine* 1 (June 1928): 7–19. Reprinted in *Paké: Writings By Chinese in Hawaii,* edited by Eric Chock and Darrell H. Y. Lum, 50–64. Honolulu: Bamboo Ridge, 1989.

Lowe, Lisa. "Heterogeneity, Hybridity, Multiplicity." *Diaspora* 1, no. 1 (Spring 1991): 24–42.

Miyamoto, Nobuko. E-mail interview. 10 June 2008.

Nguyen, Viet. *Race and Resistance: Literature and Politics in Asian America*. New York: Oxford University Press, 2002.

Phelan, Peggy. "Reciting the Citation of Others; or, A Second Introduction." In *Acting Out: Feminist Performances,* edited by Lynda Hart and Peggy Phelan, 13–31. Ann Arbor: University of Michigan Press, 1993.

———. *Unmarked: The Politics of Performance*. New York: Routledge, 1993.

Srinivasan, Priya. "The Bodies Beneath the Smoke or What's Behind the Cigarette Poster: Unearthing Kinesthetic Connections in American Dance History." *Discourses in Dance* 4, no. 1 (2007): 7–48.

Sumida, Stephen. "East of California: Points of Origin in Asian American Studies." *Journal of Asian American Studies* 1, no. 1 (1998): 83–100.

Taylor, Diana. *The Archive and Repertoire: Performing Cultural Memory in the Americas*. Durham, N.C.: Duke University Press, 2005.

Tuan, Alice. E-mail interview. 10 June 2008.

Uno, Roberta. "Being Present: Theater and Social Change." In "How Do You Make Social Change?" *Theater* 31, no. 3 (Fall 2001): 62–93.

———. "Introduction: Asian American Theater Awake at the Millennium." In *Bold Words: A Century of Asian American Writing*, edited by Rajini Srikanth and Esther Y. Iwanaga, 323–32. New Brunswick, N.J.: Rutgers University Press, 2001. 323–32.

———. "Introduction." In *Unbroken Thread: An Anthology of Plays by Asian American Women*, edited by Roberta Uno, 1–10. Amherst: University of Massachusetts Press, 1993.

———. "Introduction: The Color of Theater." In *The Color of Theater: Race, Culture, and Contemporary Performance*, edited by Roberta Uno and Lucy Mae San Pablo Burns, 1–17. New York: Continuum, 2002.

———. "Introduction to Special Issue: Preliminaries." In *MELUS* 16, no. 3 (Autumn 1989–Winter 1990): 1–3.

———. "Remember the Voice of Your People's God." *Dramatist's Guild Quarterly* (1995): 18–23.

Uno, Roberta and Kathy Perkins. *Contemporary Plays by Women of Color: An Anthology*. New York: Routledge, 1996.

Wong, Yutian. *Choreographing Asian America*. Middletown, Conn.: Wesleyan University Press, forthcoming.

Vietnamese American Community Cultural Development and the Making of History in Boston

SHIRLEY SUET-LING TANG AND JAMES ĐIỀN BÙI

From 2001 to 2005, a variety of grassroots creative expressions of Vietnamese diasporic history and culture became increasingly visible in public spaces throughout the Fields Corner neighborhood in Boston, Massachusetts. These creative expressions revealed a hidden dimension of Vietnamese American community development. They were products of new collaborations between Viet-AID—the nation's first Vietnamese American community center—and various civic and cultural groups constituting their multiracial and multigenerational community. They were testimony to the efforts and visions of a younger generation of activists and artists who chose not to define "development" simply as housing, land redevelopment, or business investment. They presented a different sort of vision of urban community development: a vision within which the multicultural, multilingual, and multigenerational diversity of people living and interacting in the same neighborhood were acknowledged and appreciated, as well as their lived experiences, collective memories, and cultural traditions. While Viet-AID's organizers devoted many of their resources to political organizing within the Vietnamese American community, especially through the Viet-Vote campaign (which will be discussed in the following section), they also undertook new initiatives that promoted interracial and intergenerational relations across the neighborhood. Their call for the long-term, holistic development of Fields Corner focused not only on the civic engagement of an older generation of Vietnamese who were already politically active, but also on the mobilization of a broad-based, multicultural constituency toward shared community visions and political actions. As Viet-AID's cofounder and former executive director Hiep Chu recently noted, "If the community in Fields Corner and Dorchester is diverse and strong, we need to work with everybody. We're not revitalizing the neighborhood just for the Vietnamese" (quoted in Smith). Grassroots creative expressions offered a rich inventory of the ways in which the expanding Vietnamese diaspora, complex demographic changes, and the limits in local conditions of U.S. urban cities converged in producing new understandings of culture, politics, and development in the Vietnamese American community.

Unlike traditional forms of development involving mostly adult community members, creative productions functioned as vital components of a public sphere that was created by a younger generation of Vietnamese Americans from the grassroots. Typically excluded from access to other discussions of development, young people responded to community issues by claiming one of the few domains available to them with their own cultural creativity and contestation. Their creativity reflected what Alice Walker referred to as cultural heritage or what Audre Lorde has called "living consciousness" and "a vital necessity of our existence" (36, 39). In their work, we see glimpses of how Michelle Wallace describes cultural productions as sharing "the primary goal of liberatory and profound (almost necessarily nonviolent) political transformation" and as being "inherently critical of current oppressive and repressive political, economic and social arrangements" (215). In Boston's Fields Corner, Vietnamese American artists and activists shaped and refined the role of the cultural worker who dared to tap the power of creativity. They were arguing for the nurturing of new cultural workers who were capable of emboldened visions for sustainable community development and who would be able to play a critical role in terms of what Asian American artist and scholar Margo Machida suggested in her mid-1990s discussion of Asian American artists: they would have "a telling impact on an increasingly plural conversation — aesthetic, cultural, historical — that is integral to the development of America" (68).

The implication that sustainable development involves a complex process of engaging in "an increasingly plural conversation" that is aesthetic, cultural, and historical with multiple groups of people underscores the theoretical and practical importance of cultural development in racially mixed communities like Fields Corner. Grassroots creative expressions are not just mirror images or artistic reflections of other development projects. In addition to educating the community about shared memories and common experiences among different groups, these cultural productions also play crucial roles as expressions, interactions, and imaginations, all of which are integral to healthy, holistic, long-term community development. Within Viet-AID's framework of community development from the early to mid-2000s, creative productions emerged as one of the important sites where new spaces, new activists, new voices, and new visions were created and nurtured.

The very presence of such creative work in common places of Boston's Fields Corner clearly shows that cultural development matters as much as dominant development approaches that target political macrostructures, economic growth, and housing development. The case about "culture" has been made in the past decade by cultural studies scholars such as Lisa Lowe, who has argued that it is within the cultural sphere that individuals and collectivities are transformed, and that culture is the very medium through which people connect with pasts, make meanings of presents, and imagine futures. Lowe states,

> Culture is the medium of the *present* — the imagined equivalences and identifications through which the individual invents lived relationship with the national collective — but it is simultaneously the site that mediates the *past*, through which history is grasped as difference, as fragments, shocks, and flashes of disjunction. It is through culture that the subject becomes, acts, and speaks itself as "American." It is likewise in culture that individuals and collectivities struggle and remember and, in that difficult remembering, imagine and practice both subject and community differently" (2–3; emphasis in original).

A growing body of recent scholarship on art and community development has further argued that art and cultural projects function as tools for rebuilding community pride, remaking neighborhoods, and revitalizing economies in disinvested communities.[1]

Though offering a richly engaging perspective on culture, this body of recent scholarly research on culture and development falls short in addressing one of the most frequently asked questions by grassroots development practitioners and social activists: what kind of concrete "liberatory and profound political transformation" is actually being produced through cultural creativity and contestation (Wallace 215)? We also ask this question; but rather than viewing political and socioeconomic gains as the ultimate goals of community development, we argue here that it can be more productive to view cultural creations as critically linked to the historical struggles of the past as well as to the material realities and the political obligations of the present. Boston's Vietnamese American experience is especially telling in this regard. Specifically, we explore how local meanings and consequences of intense transnational sensibilities, which include the realities of multiracial and multigenerational neighborhoods, simultaneously influence how directions of community development were being envisioned and created.

We place our analysis of young people's strategies/visions of community development within the history-making process of Dorchester's Vietnamese American community. We pay attention to the individual historical actors (particularly to the 1.5 generation and second generation) and their specific artistic expressions and creative collaborations in order to illuminate the significance of the cultural sphere in understanding what development means. In the Fields Corner case, what has yet to be addressed are the ways that community organizers drew on both nationalist homeland sentiments and cultural identities to reach Vietnamese elders while simultaneously exploring a broader, multidimensional, transcultural, and transnational framework for "development" that emphasized the bringing together of people from multiple racial, linguistic, and age groups. We begin by highlighting some key markers in the development of Fields Corner's Vietnamese American community to situate the essay in relation to the history of Vietnamese Americans.

The Cultural-Historical Context of Fields Corner

With the fifth-largest Vietnamese American community in the United States, Boston has been the site of several notable, history-making efforts. In 1986, one of the first Vietnamese American priests was appointed to lead a Vietnamese Catholic parish in the United States at St. Peter's Church in Dorchester. Since 2002, the University of Massachusetts Boston regularly began offering one of the few Vietnamese American Studies courses in U.S. higher education. In 2004, Boston hosted the founding national conference of Vietnamese Student Associations that created the Union of North American Vietnamese American Student Associations (uNAVSA).[2]

Particularly important markers of local Vietnamese American community history are the founding in 1994 of Viet-AID, the first Vietnamese American community development corporation in the United States; and the opening in 2002 of the nation's first Vietnamese American Community Center, a remarkable $4.6 million, two-story, newly constructed facility that houses Viet-AID, the *Au Co* bilingual preschool, a community library, and office/program space for several other organizations, projects, and coalition activities.[3] The Center is located on a formerly abandoned lot in the heart of Boston's Fields Corner neighborhood with Vietnamese-inspired design elements incorporated into the building's architecture. A commemorative stone in the atrium lobby reads, in part, "Built of Bricks, Concrete, Steel, and Dreams, this center houses our history, community, and vision."

In our prior study, "The Local/Global Politics of Boston's Viet-Vote," we and coauthor Peter Kiang provided an analysis of the voter education and registration efforts of an ongoing coalition of organizers and advocates in Boston's Vietnamese American community known as Viet-Vote. We noted that those Viet-Vote targeted areas yielded an impressive 941 percent increase in Vietnamese voter participation in the fall 2003 city elections (compared to 1999 voter participation percentages) for the three local wards in Boston's Dorchester–Fields Corner neighborhood.[4] Our analysis also showed that the average age of the Vietnamese voter in these wards was fifty-five years. In this modest example of making Vietnamese American history in Boston, the elder refugee population had emerged as the politically active voting group within the Vietnamese community, even though the activities of the Viet-Vote campaign had been carried out primarily by college students and young professionals.

Viet-Vote's voter education efforts reflect a story of civic engagement with both local and transnational meanings in diasporic context. While the Viet-Vote campaign worked to connect desires for Vietnamese voice, power, and representation with critical local issues ranging from crime prevention and jobs to affordable housing and bilingual education, a complementary strategy focused on gaining recognition of the flag from the former Republic of Viet Nam as the "official" flag of the Vietnamese community in the City of Boston. To understand how this complex, critical framework of community development evolved over time, we must examine the broader, long-term organizing and capacity-building efforts in the community: for example, the establishment of the country's first Vietnamese American community center in Fields Corner; the intergenerational, bilingual sharing of stories through cultural/community development projects; and the hard-earned street solidarity with other minority groups. This chapter, then, may be read as a preliminary analysis of some of these fresh, history-making visions and practices of development as a younger generation of Vietnamese American activists and artists sought sophisticated interventions through grassroots cultural creations during the 2000s.

A Bridge Generation

To a large extent, the key Vietnamese American leaders who garnered broad support for the Vietnamese American Community Center in the 1990s and early 2000s were those who had the bilingual and bicultural skills to navigate both American and Vietnamese cultures and politics. Many had arrived in the United States as teenagers or young adults during the peak years of Southeast Asian refugee resettlement in the late 1970s and early 1980s and became the first in the refugee community to graduate with college degrees. Their higher education status and socialization in the United States, as well as their empathy toward the older generations' political struggles for "freedom" in Vietnam, enabled this 1.5 or "bridge" generation to achieve a nuanced understanding of both the U.S. political system and Vietnamese anticommunism. Within the Vietnamese community, they knew that their work was continuously defined by homeland politics. As executive directors of the Vietnamese American Civic Association in the 1980s, Long Nguyen and Hiep Chu each attempted to shift the weight of that orientation by emphasizing citizenship and voter education. Older generations, however, given their years of military service for the former Republic of Viet Nam as well as the punishing rule by the victorious communist government, remained emotionally and ideologically committed to exile politics. Most of the community's elders regarded local politics as secondary to their patriotic struggle for democracy and human rights in their homeland.[5]

Another local community history-making moment and important marker of Vietnamese American political engagement occurred in 1992.[6] That year, Boston City Councillor Albert "Dapper" O'Neil refused to apologize to the Vietnamese community after making racist remarks about it that were broadcast in the evening news. Referring to the growing Vietnamese residential and commercial section in Fields Corner, he told Boston's police superintendent while participating in a neighborhood parade, "I just passed up there. I thought I was in Saigon for Chrissakes" (quoted in Sege's "Vietnamese Find Their Voice," B1). Two hundred members of Boston's Vietnamese community and allies from throughout the city then rallied at Boston's City Hall to call for racial equality and a public apology from O'Neil.[7] But with fewer than one hundred Vietnamese Americans registered to vote in Boston at that time, and with most Vietnamese residents still struggling in poverty amid refugee realities, their capacity to exert local political pressure directly through votes or campaign contributions was minimal, despite their outrage over such blatant and official disrespect.[8] For the bridge generation, the city councillor's utter neglect of its demands quickly confirmed a need for political awareness and mobilization consistent with their education and socialization as minorities in U.S. schools as well as their interactions with other Asian American community groups. They concluded that Vietnamese Americans must redefine community development goals and work together toward empowerment at the community level.[9]

Two years later, Nguyen, Chu, and others established a new organizational model that would not be over constrained by either the ideological commitments enforced by the older generation in the community or the dominant client/deficit-centered paradigm that characterized social service agencies and refugee mutual assistance associations locally and nationally.[10] Viet-AID's mission opened new conceptual and programmatic possibilities for capacity building, particularly in relation to affordable housing development and home ownership, self-sufficient economic development, child care, native language education, neighborhood safety, and, by necessity, communication and organizing within the multicultural Dorchester neighborhood across ethnicity, language, and race.[11]

While older-generation leaders praised Viet-AID for its work in the community, many were also critical of its lack of a clear, anticommunist political position. Some even withdrew from discussions regarding the proposed community center project and posted flyers around the neighborhood to raise suspicions about Viet-AID's board and staff.[12] Intergenerational conflicts remained a serious challenge for the community, retarding the establishment of a collective identity and the progress of Viet-AID's mission as a chartered community development corporation.[13] Long Nguyen, who became the first executive director of Viet-AID, reflected upon a whole range of procommunist insinuations targeting the organizers of the community center, "It's sort of like a son going to his father and getting his blessing. We didn't do that" (quoted in Sege's "A Community Finds Its Center," DI). However, pressure from the Vietnamese elders, and demands of an increasingly multiracial and multilingual community, soon made the bridge-generation community organizers critically reconsider their approach to organizing within the Vietnamese American community and throughout the Fields Corner neighborhood.

Vietnamese American Issues and Homeland Politics

Though historic and unique as an assertion of voice and space in concrete cultural and community development terms, the community center process and related creative production projects had, nevertheless, reflected the continuing power of homeland politics and identity conflicts. In the summer of 2001, a group of young people developed a mural near the corner of Adams Street and Dorchester Avenue in Fields Corner (fig. 7.1). The public art project was developed collaboratively by Viet-AID, Dorchester House, and the City of Boston Mural Program. The purpose of the mural was to

FIG. 7.1. Adams Street Mural Project, 2001. *Photo by James Bùi.*

celebrate Vietnamese culture in Fields Corner through the perspective of Vietnamese American youth. Overall, the mural received positive feedback within the Fields Corner neighborhood across many racial, ethnic, social, and age groups, including the Vietnamese community. Community leaders publicly praised the youth for trying to preserve Vietnamese heritage, and the mural was even featured on the front page of the local *Dorchester Reporter* on 30 August 2001. Despite public recognition, however, homeland politics and generational differences of vision soon took greater precedence. Some Vietnamese elders stated, for example, that the Vietnamese youth did not understand "true" Vietnamese culture; others noted that the youth could have chosen to paint other cultural symbols like countryside landscapes, rice fields, and temples. One particular elder complained bitterly that a figure in the mural "looked like a Viet Cong"; he then chastised the young adult lead artist and Dorchester resident, John Tran, for being "uneducated" and claimed that "there was no hope for the future" (unpublished Viet-AID materials, 2005).

With new generations of youth and young adults born and raised in the United States, homeland politics and identity conflicts continued to evolve in the Vietnamese American community. Many Vietnamese elders did not accept divergent views concerning politics in Vietnam, and labeled Vietnamese American youth who were not involved in homeland politics or who supported the view of gradual development and democratization of Vietnam through the U.S. engagement policy with Vietnam as communist or procommunist. They generally viewed Vietnamese youth as inexperienced, naïve, and disrespectful of their parents, culture, and tradition. Conversely, many Vietnamese youth identified more closely with influences from mainstream U.S. politics, media, and culture. In terms of political dynamics outside of their own families, some viewed the older generation stereotypically through images they acquired through U.S. media, mainstream politics, and Hollywood movies; they interpreted the political leadership of elders in the community typically as being conservative and out of touch.

While the bridge-generation organizers recognized these differing perspectives and priorities between younger and older generations regarding local and transnational political issues, they also believed that intergenerational conflicts should be minimized as much as possible. In the process, they became wrapped up in the rhetoric and iconic image of the former Republic of Viet Nam flag as a critical dimension of their sophisticated community organizing strategy. Through the vehicle of Viet-Vote, community organizers unfurled an elaborate campaign to gain recognition of the "official" flag of the Vietnamese community in the City of Boston. According to Bùi, Tang, and Kiang, the yellow flag with three red stripes embraced by Vietnamese refugees and their families was always flying at community events as well as in Vietnamese-owned houses and businesses in Dorchester, but the Viet-Vote campaign used the flag as the focal point of community mobilization to impact public policy symbolically in the city.

Success was achieved in August 2003 when — with roughly one hundred Vietnamese Americans, including many elders, cheering from the gallery — the Boston City Council voted unanimously to recognize "the Heritage and Freedom Flag as the official symbol of the Boston Vietnamese-American community" (Bùi, Tang, and Kiang 15). In response, the Vietnamese Embassy in Washington, D.C., quickly issued a formal statement of protest, asserting: "A small minority of Vietnamese-Americans who claim themselves representatives of the Vietnamese-American community living in Boston aim at sowing division, rekindling the past hatred and painful pages of the history between our two nations and among the Vietnamese themselves" (Embassy of the Socialist Republic of Vietnam). Embassy officials then personally visited City Hall to insist that the only proper flag to fly was that of the Socialist Republic of Viet Nam recognized by the U.S. government. Disregarding such claims while acknowledging the growing clout of the local Vietnamese community, one city councillor explained at a formal meeting with the embassy's deputy chief of mission, "What you feel in Washington, that is in Washington, and we here in Boston support our community here" (quoted in Abraham and Slack). Indeed, in the next city election, Maureen Feeney, the city councillor from Dorchester–Fields Corner who had sponsored the original flag resolution, was returned to office by a large majority of local voters, including many Vietnamese elders mobilized by Viet-Vote, as noted above.[14]

During this period of intense, multigenerational, local/global, diasporic, political movement, Viet-AID's bridge generation of community leaders was also expanding its own constituency beyond the Vietnamese elder population and actively cultivating broader visions and models of development. Together with an even younger generation of organizers, particularly those who had joined Viet-AID's youth development programs as staff or participants, it began to initiate new collaborations and constructions with distinct, alternative narratives and cultural representations to capture the transformations and struggles of the neighborhood. Cultural history and art projects — with intentions ranging from honoring cultural heritages and celebrating racial diversity to enabling difficult intergenerational dialogues and nurturing interracial and interethnic relationships — became the channels through which Vietnamese Americans and their neighbors expressed themselves and communicated with each other.

Younger generations of Vietnamese Americans were drawn to cultural development during the early 2000s because of Viet-AID's dynamic approach to youth and community organizing. In contrast to anticommunist, homeland-centered campaigns, Viet-AID's focus on concrete, everyday issues such as improved urban education, neighborhood safety, and affordable housing, its commitment to justice and equality, and its earnest attempts to construct a strong and diverse neighborhood, intrigued many Vietnamese American high school and college students who had their own individual or family stories to share about surviving violence and poverty within the United States. [15]

Alliances and identifications with other racial and ethnic groups, on topics about everyday life struggles, also were central for working-class Vietnamese Americans who took on creative cultural production projects in this period. The inclusion of different multilingual and multicultural programs and services within the recently completed Vietnamese American Community Center had created an environment where people of myriad nationalities and ethnicities — Cape Verdean, Jamaican, African American, Irish, or Vietnamese — could educate one another about the diverse cultures of the world connected to their neighborhood. The Center—a common place for making interracial and intergenerational connections—together with other common places like subway trains and the streets compelled some of the Vietnamese American youth to further explore new and different visions of urban cultural development to reflect the realities of the neighborhood.

Community Cultural Development Projects

Common places, new institutional practices, and daily interactions all encouraged Vietnamese American young people to develop fresh ways of interpreting and representing community politics and culture. In the summer of 2002, Viet-AID, in collaboration with the Youth Art in Action (YAIA) program of the School of the Museum of Fine Arts, completed a second mural on a neighborhood branch bank to represent the multicultural and generational diversity within the Fields Corner neighborhood (fig. 7.2).[16] Having learned from the criticism by some elders during the first mural project, the youths especially highlighted the importance of communication between older and younger generations as well as between community members across different backgrounds. Community residents, merchants, and organizations were interviewed to ensure that there was community-wide involvement and consensus in the final mural product.

Their creations also represented and were claimed by non-Vietnamese young people from many different social backgrounds. The mural visually presented a row of faces, with different ages, genders, and family origins

FIG. 7.2. Dorchester Avenue Mural Project, 2002. *Photo by Peter Kiang.*

rooted in Africa, Asia, the Caribbean, and Europe. Painted beneath the faces was a Red Line subway train on which was written "Our Community Is Strong Because We Communicate." The public transportation Red Line subway train was chosen to represent a common place of daily interaction among diverse members of the working-class neighborhood. Moreover, youth artists addressed issues of identity and culture that were of great importance to the contemporary urban environment of Boston. Inside each train car was a painted snapshot of a community meeting, arranged at different sites over a two-month period, where the diverse members discussed memories and common experiences for the mural project. Collaboration and communication through culture and art were thus recognized as actual tools for uniting people in the community.

The group's success in bringing together people from across the Fields Corner neighborhood further motivated activists and artists to continue using culture and art as a way to envision and practice community development. From 2002 to 2005, they developed three other communitywide cultural development projects that further demonstrated the central role of culture and art in documenting diversity, facilitating intergenerational dialogue, and strengthening ties between the Vietnamese community and its neighbors. Extending the themes and methods represented in the "Our Community Is Strong Because We Communicate" mural, much of the new work that appeared in the public spaces of Fields Corner combined an affirmation of the multiracial and multigenerational realities of the neighborhood, together with class (and in some cases gender) consciousness, and an appeal for community-level social transformation.

Our Voices

Specifically building on the "Our Community Is Strong Because We Communicate" theme, but through a different medium, was the Our Voices project, an example of cultural development that employed intergenerational story-sharing as a way to promote communication and understanding. In this project, Vietnamese American young people proclaimed their Vietnamese identities and showed respect to their elders, but they also questioned their cultural roles as sons, daughters, citizens, and members of an ethnic, racial, or social group. In the summer of 2003, they were trained in oral history methods and then conducted a series of interviews with Vietnamese community elders about the Vietnam War, Vietnamese culture and history, and adjustment in the United States. Incorporating important themes from these interviews as well as their own views about cultural and generational differences, they wrote, produced, and acted out a play for a multicultural audience at the Vietnamese American Community Center. Focusing on a Vietnamese American family in the Fields Corner neighborhood, the play expressed the tension between the Vietnamese expectation of filial respect and the American inability to fulfill that expectation, highlighting not only generational and cultural differences but also the socioeconomic realities faced by many Vietnamese families in this particular neighborhood. Throughout the play, the sons and daughter deal with their father's demands while the father struggles to understand his children's experiences of growing up Asian in the United States. In a climactic scene, one son struggles with how to write an essay about Vietnamese culture for school and attempts to talk to his father about the assignment. The father, however, has to work long hours and is unable to give the son his full attention. The observation/lament/critique "My father is always very busy" then echoes dramatically and repeatedly. The play also insightfully revealed the changing responsibilities shouldered by older siblings within the family, who frequently adopt bilingual caretaking roles to assist their parents and the elders. Young women, in particular, who are older sisters — such as the play's daughter — are often the primary caretakers and bearers of both the economic and cultural burdens of their families.

Although the Vietnamese American youth and elders — especially the fathers — might not have shared the same sentiments toward homeland politics, participants of both generations did make an honest effort through the Our Voices project to communicate with each other and uncover shared points of reference within the context of their current lives in Fields Corner. To recognize the multiple voices and perspectives in the Vietnamese community, youth artists developed a creative method of community cultural development that showed appreciation for elders' stories and emphasized shared, lived experiences within Fields Corner. Our Voices began with the youth listening to, showing respect for, and documenting the elders' stories, followed by theatrical expressions of Vietnamese American youth-centered issues; communitywide dialogue concluded the project. Young people provided a powerful analysis of how economic and racial disparities exacerbated intergenerational conflicts. They offered a nonessentialist definition of Vietnamese culture through their multivocal, multifocal performance presentation as well as a video documentary of the process. Most important, they enabled a diverse neighborhood-based audience to make connections and deepen understandings despite their important generational, gender, and cultural differences.

Living on the Same Trellis

Venturing out to the broader Fields Corner neighborhood, youth artists and activists produced a particularly creative and effective process of using art to address some of the alienations and difficulties of everyday life among different people in the community. Young people provided an implicit critique of segregation and inequality in the city. They also demonstrated what was possible when seemingly opposed cultural groups work together. As early as 1999, a group of community members of diverse backgrounds in Fields Corner organized with the help of Viet-AID to begin the process of transforming a trash-strewn vacant lot into a community garden. The effort spanned several years and was interrupted by many disappointments and challenges, not the least of which was finding common languages in which to conduct meetings. The neighborhood had been under siege by street criminals and suffered from lack of investment in housing and infrastructure on the part of property owners and the city. Those residents invested in their garden project had explicit intentions of improving public safety as well as promoting multiethnic interactions among their neighbors. Young people participated actively in these organizing efforts: leafleting for meetings, researching plants familiar to immigrant gardeners that would grow successfully in the New England climate, and creating a garden newsletter to keep residents informed. Through this process, they engaged the gardeners in conversations about problems in the community and their hopes for the garden. Finally, with the support of an experienced local artist-activist-teacher and a Khmer (Cambodian) master ceramicist and teaching artist, they created a twenty-five-foot frieze of carved ceramic tiles to complement the garden's vitality, and, as a visual narrative, to tell its story (fig. 7.3).

A central theme that emerged from their cross-community, multilingual conversations is captured in these colorful tiles through a Vietnamese proverb that was translated into Spanish, Creole, Vietnamese, and English. It reads:

> Dear Pumpkin,
> Please Love the Squash,
> Because even though
> You are Different,
> You Both Live
> on the Same Trellis.

In this example, a powerful cultural development strategy—made possible by interracial and intergenerational organizing—effectively engaged com-

FIG. 7.3. Community Garden Project, 1999–2003. *Photo by James Bùi/Marge Rack.*

munity members in a deeper analysis of the geographies and histories of racialized community settlement in Dorchester–Fields Corner and moved them toward experiencing real and positive multiethnic and multigenerational interactions through concrete cultural practices. The garden project was linked to the longer-term community development goals of neighborhood revitalization; it was, moreover, an honest though subtle critique of social segregation, economic disparities, and ethnic conflicts in the city. Rather than focusing on the "problems," however, the garden project highlighted an ethical and collectivist view of shared responsibility that was generated by residents at the grassroots level. In acknowledging cultural/linguistic differences and shared experiences, the garden project also opened possibilities for continuing cross-cultural dialogue, empowerment, and unity.

All that Matters

Youth artists and activists were not just telling personal and community stories with their cultural creations; they also were calling attention to the nature of cultural creativity and contestation itself. They extended the definition of cultural creations to include innovative visual, aural, digital (hi)story

projects emerging from grassroots educational programs designed specifically to address issues of street violence and the social alienation of urban
youth. A new collaboration in 2004, for example, brought together young
people in the Cape Verdean community and the Vietnamese community to
create iMovie digital stories and participate in difficult dialogues about
growing up in Fields Corner. While the music selections and narrative approach of individual stories differed in style and flow, they presented a range
of themes that reflected young peoples' shared experiences of growing up
in immigrant families, struggling with generational gaps, fighting racism in
schools, and surviving violence in urban communities. Jessica's story, "They
Say the Good Die Young," for example, highlighted community violence in
Fields Corner that had claimed the lives of many young people in the Cape
Verdean community. Her message about peace, justice, and healing was
well received, not only by Cape Verdeans but also by Vietnamese American
youth who had similarly lost friends and family members to urban violence.
Likewise, Hoa's story summarized the relationship between many U.S.-
born or -raised young people and their immigrant/refugee parents:

> I was born in Boston, Massachusetts
> My family is originally from Vietnam
> I'm not your typical Vietnamese daughter
> I do not always obey my parents
> I'm not fluent in Vietnamese
> I do not understand all of the traditions
> But that's okay
> I have many other qualities that make me who I am and that is all that matters

Substituting "Vietnam" and "Vietnamese" with "Cape Verde" and "Cape
Verdean" or other ethnicities, many non-Vietnamese young people were
able to relate to Hoa's story at the community forum where the digital stories were publicly presented. In her digital story, Hoa explained that as she
grew older, she became more mature and wanted to build a stronger relationship with her parents. Communication, she claimed, was the key to a
strong relationship. She asked parents to encourage their children to participate in extracurricular activities and support them in those activities. She
concluded her story with this direct call to the parents: "Give them [the chil-
dren] a chance to find out who they are as a person." The theme of intergenerational (mis)communication resonated widely for audience members
from both the Vietnamese and Cape Verdean communities. In fact, Hoa's
story became the focal point of their discussion at the public forum. This

combination of digital story creation, video production, and cross-cultural dialogue modeled and facilitated by young people represented a powerful intervention for community cultural development among and between youth and their families of diverse racial and ethnic backgrounds.

Conclusion

The emerging practice of community cultural development in Boston's Fields Corner was closely linked to the rise of Vietnamese American leadership during the period between the early to mid-2000s. During that period, a younger generation of Vietnamese Americans — most of whom were raised and educated in the United States — came of age to play significant leadership roles in local community politics. These bridge-generation Vietnamese American leaders, along with second-generation and immigrant youth activists and artists, turned to grassroots cultural creations for expression, interaction, and inspiration. Their cultural productions were crucial components of development, in part because they recognized that culture and identity were integral to people's core sense of existence. In recent years, Arlene Goldbard, Don Adams, and other cultural development scholars and practitioners have noted that sustainable community development depends in large part on its recognition of cultural diversity. Development is defined here not simply in terms of economic growth, but as what UNESCO describes as "a more satisfactory intellectual, emotional, moral and spiritual existence" (Article 3), especially in the face of—as many scholars, including Francis Fukuyama and Fredric Jameson, note—globalization, Americanization, consumerism, and mass media culture. Community cultural development involves the cultivation of a holistic consciousness that breathes life and action into diverse communities. Goldbard and Adams state:

> Community cultural development practice is based on the understanding that culture is the crucible in which human resilience, creativity and autonomy are forged. . . . The root idea of community cultural development is the imperative to fully inhabit our human lives, bringing to consciousness the values and choices that animate our communities and thus equipping ourselves to act — to paraphrase Paulo Freire — as subjects in history, rather than merely its objects. (17)

As "subjects in history" who were aware of both limits and possibilities in their local and global environments, young Vietnamese Americans turned to art and culture to awaken and mobilize community members of many different groups. They created common places for people to try out new identities and imagine social relations that reached within, across, and beyond cultural, generational, racial, and national boundaries. They redefined grassroots cultural creations and influenced local community organizing agendas. They nurtured cultural productions to link long-term community development goals of political representation, economic stability, and social justice with intergenerational organizing and the collaborative cultivation of cultural practices that were grounded in both the multicultural and multilingual realities of the local neighborhood as well as the transnational, diasporic sensibilities of the population. Indeed, they contributed not only to the theory/practice of community cultural development, but also to the making of local/global history for Vietnamese Americans in Boston and their neighborhood of Dorchester–Fields Corner.

Our previous work in this community setting has highlighted local/global dynamics in the political sphere.[17] Recognizing critical issues and realities in the neighborhood, including nationalist homeland politics, economic, and social injustice, complex multiethnic relations, and changing gender and family roles, we suggest here that community cultural development — as conceived and led by a younger generation born or raised in the United States — is a generative site where emerging issues, strategies, and priorities of Vietnamese American community development can be understood. In this process, we foreground the critical role of the bridge or 1.5 generation who have enabled the imagination and construction of the cultural and political future of Vietnamese Americans in the United States. Furthermore, though not the focus of this essay, we recognize that community cultural development practice also serves as a site of intervention in addressing disengagement and underachievement of Vietnamese American and other Southeast Asian American youth in urban school systems.[18]

While showing examples of meaningful intersections between culture, politics, and development, we should also recognize that similar experiences have historically existed in other Boston neighborhoods, such as the South End and Jamaica Plain, through the interventions of African American and Latino community artists and organizers. Comparative analyses of the Fields Corner case with these previous examples and with similar cases in other cities would further clarify the rich, complex ways that culture and development are intertwined in community context, while at the same time extending Lowe's call for analyses that "make . . . connections between historically differentiated forms of disempowerment" or "make space for oppositional critiques." Lowe cautions against narratives of multiculturalism that emphasize only "identity, equivalence, or pluralism" and avoid "productive irresolution, opposition, and conflict." She asserts, "The narratives that suppress tension and opposition suggest that we have already achieved multiculturalism, that we know what it is, and that is defined simply by the coexistence and juxtaposition of greater numbers of diverse groups; these narratives allow us to ignore the profound and urgent gaps, the inequalities and conflicts, among racial, ethnic, and immigrant groups" (96). In this essay, we showed how Vietnamese American young people were able to draw creatively upon the very conflicts and contradictions they faced within their own community to seek direction for long-range community development. For future comparative analyses, we agree with Lowe that we must continue to think through the ways in which "culture may be rearticulated not in terms of identity, equivalence, or pluralism but out of contradiction, as a site for alternative histories and memories that provide the grounds to imagine subject, community, and practice in new ways" (96).

The history-making visions and practices of Vietnamese American community cultural development in Boston's Fields Corner neighborhood inform and challenge the conceptual definitions of development held both by policymakers and funders as well as social scientists whose focus of analysis stresses social/structural/political/economic dimensions of community life without adequately engaging or investing in the cultural. At the same time, cultural theory, if not grounded in real, lived experiences of people, can become unrecognizable to those whose struggles and dreams are sources of our inspiration. Grassroots cultural creations and the historical conditions from which they emerged are therefore important examples for transformative cultural and political work, however modest they may be. In recognizing the value of both, we are reminded of the framework articulated by urban studies scholar/practitioner Mel King who wrote nearly three decades ago in his groundbreaking analysis of the history of black community development in Boston:

> I would like to challenge people to think differently about strategies of shaping the future of cities. We are faced with a struggle for land and a struggle for the mind. This is the core of urban community organizing today, and I think it is crucial. It is my contention that, if we win the struggle for the mind, then we will win the struggle for the land. So we have to think about where the struggle for the mind exists (1).

We suggest that Vietnamese American cultural community development in Fields Corner is a site where such a question can be critically and creatively engaged.

NOTES

1. See Neil Scott Kleiman and the Center for an Urban Future, *The Creative Engine*; Christopher Walker, *Arts and Culture: Community Connections: Contributions from New Survey Research*; Diane Grams and Michael Warr, *Leveraging Assets: How Small Budget Arts Activities Benefit Neighborhoods*; Mark Stern and Susan Seifert, *Community Revitalization and the Arts in Philadelphia*; Arlene Goldbard, *New Creative Community: The Art of Cultural Development*; Arlene Goldbard and Don Adams, eds., *Community, Culture and Globalization* and *Creative Community: The Art of Cultural Development*.

2. Though not the focus of this essay, each of these examples deserves further study. Father Joseph Diem Nguyen was assigned by Boston's Cardinal Bernard Law to establish an ethnic Vietnamese apostolate based at St. Peter's Church in Dorchester. See Vy Vu, "Community Formation: Catholic Influence on the Building of the Vietnamese Community in Boston, 1975–2005." The Vietnamese American Studies course at the University of Massachusetts Boston is "Resources for Vietnamese American Studies," developed originally by James Điền Bùi. The national student conference was hosted by the New England Intercollegiate Vietnamese Student Associations (uNVASA), whose mission is to serve as a means for youths to organize socially and civically within the local communities; see: http://www.unavsa.org/filelist.aspx?folderPath=VideoAlbum%2fFirst+North+American+Vietnamese+Student+Associations+Conference+ (2004). In recognizing the historic significance of college student networks to community development, it is worth noting that the current and founding directors of Viet-AID—whose roles are described more fully in this essay—originally worked together when they were both local college students trying to establish a regional network of Vietnamese Student Associations in New York years earlier.

3. See Patrick Michael McGroarty, "The Lion in Fields Corner: Building a Vietnamese Community in the New Boston"; Karin Aguilar-San Juan, "Fields of Dreams: Place, Race, and Memory in Boston's Vietnamese American Community"; Irene Sege, "A Community Finds its Center: Dorchester's Vietnamese Population, Young and Old, Hopes to Find Common Ground at a New Gathering Place"; and Mai-Lan Pham, "Strangers in Fields Corner: The Formation of a Vietnamese Community in Dorchester."

4. These findings are from Viet-Vote's unpublished campaign materials.

5. See McGroarty, "The Lion in Fields Corner"; Aguilar-San Juan, "Fields of Dream"; and Sege, "A Community Finds its Center."

6. For more on this process of history making, see the Smithsonian Institution's historic Vietnamese American Heritage Project collection and "Exit Saigon, Enter Little Saigon," which opened nationally in 2007 and contains a photo documenting the 1992 city hall rally for racial justice by Vietnamese Americans in

Boston; http://www.vietam.org/m_exhibit.php. See Peter Nien-Chu Kiang and Shirley Suet-ling Tang, "Electoral Politics and the Contexts of Empowerment, Displacement, and Diaspora for Boston's Vietnamese and Cambodian American Communities"; and Bùi, Tang, and Kiang, "The Local/Global Politics of Boston's Viet-Vote."

7. See Michael Rezendes, "O'Neil is Hooted Off State at Unity Rally" and "Vietnamese Leaders Hit O'Neil Remarks."

8. On refugee poverty, see Pham, "Strangers in Fields Corner: The Formation of a Vietnamese Community in Dorchester." On the politics of the Viet-Vote, see Bùi, Tang, and Kiang, "The Local/Global Politics of Boston's Viet-Vote."

9. See McGroarty, "The Lion in Fields Corner"; Aguilar-San Juan, "Fields of Dream"; and Sege, "A Community Finds its Center."

10. See McGroarty, "The Lion in Fields Corner"; and Bùi, Tang, and Kiang, "The Local/Global Politics of Boston's Viet-Vote."

11. Viet-AID's formal mission is to build a strong Vietnamese American community and a vibrant Fields Corner neighborhood through community building and civic engagement, affordable housing and commercial development, business and job development, and high quality childcare. See www.Viet-AID.org.

12. McGroarty, "The Lion in Fields Corner"; and Sege, "A Community Finds its Center."

13. For information about Viet-Aid's institutional framework as a community development corporation (cdc), see www.macdc.org.

14. The Heritage and Freedom Flag campaign and related political engagement by elders are important local stories of complex diasporic community dynamics that have far wider reach than we can adequately describe here. In 2007, for example, local Vietnamese American community leaders and political supporters filed a legislative act in the Massachusetts State Senate (Senate No. 1868) that, if approved, would require that the "only flag depicting the country of Vietnam that may be displayed in a New York state-sponsored public function or a New York public institution of learning shall be the flag of the former Republic of Vietnam." If passed, such legislation would apply to all public schools and colleges in the state. Municipal resolutions, similar to that approved in Boston in 2003, have also been passed in other Massachusetts cities with significant Vietnamese communities, including Worcester, Springfield, Lawrence, and Malden. The successful effort in Malden also led to a parallel resolution proposed in 2004 for the town to recognize officially the "Laotian Heritage and Freedom Flag" (the national flag prior to the Lao People's Democratic Republic established by the communist-led Pathet Lao in 1975) based on the argument, "This is about representation and the Laotian American community is making a conscious choice to be represented by a flag symbol that is more meaningful to their Lao heritage" (see www.laosdemocracy.com/laotian_heritage/why_is-there_a_question.htm). Moreover, resolutions on behalf of the Vietnamese "Heritage and Freedom Flag" have also passed in more than fifty cities and towns across the United

States—from Westminster, California, to Biloxi, Mississippi, from Austin, Texas, to Minneapolis, Minnesota, from Wichita, Kansas, to Falls Church, Virginia—indicating extraordinary levels of political clarity and/or coordination that deserve much more focused study. For a listing of some of these localities, see www.fva.org/vnflag/.

15. For a profile of low-income Vietnamese Americans in Massachusetts, see Michael Liu, Thao Tran, and Paul Watanabe, *Far From the Commonwealth: A Report on Low-Income Asian Americans in Massachusetts*. For a discussion of youth delinquency among Vietnamese youth, see, for example, Thao N. Le and Judy L. Wallen, "Youth Delinquency: Self-Reported Rates and Risk Factors of Cambodian, Chinese, Lao/Mien, and Vietnamese Youth."

16. For a detailed analysis of the role of Youth Art In Action (YAIA) as an alternative learning practice for Khmer American young people, see Shirley Suet-ling Tang, "Community Cultural Development and Education with Cambodian American Youth." YAIA was itself a collaboration that partnered urban youth from local communities with the Coalition for Asian Pacific American Youth (CAPAY), a pan-Asian youth leadership network in Massachusetts affiliated with the University of Massachusetts Boston's Asian American Studies Program and college students at the School of the Museum of Fine Arts in Boston. YAIA has also played an important role in the community cultural development of Khmer American youth. It was named a recipient of the 2005 Coming Up Taller Awards, an initiative of the President's Committee on the Arts and Humanities. See http://www.cominguptaller.org/awards-2005/program15.html.

17. See Kiang and Tang, "Electoral Politics and the Contexts of Empowerment, Displacement, and Diaspora for Boston's Vietnamese and Cambodian American Communities"; and Bùi, Tang, and Kiang, "The Local/Global Politics of Boston's Viet-Vote."

18. See, for example, Angeles Reyes, *Language, Identity, and Stereotype Among Southeast Asian American Youth: The Other Asian*; Katharya Um, *A Dream Denied: Educational Experiences of Southeast Asian American Youth Issues and Recommendations*; Peter Nien-Chu Kiang, Ngoc-lan Nguyen, and Richard Lee Sheehan, "Don't Ignore It! Documenting Racial Harassment in a Fourth-Grade Vietnamese Bilingual Classroom"; and Peter Nien-Chu Kiang and Jenny Kaplan, "Where Do We Stand: Views of Racial Conflict by Vietnamese American High School Students in a Black-and-White Context."

WORKS CITED

Abraham, Yvonne, and Donovan Slack. "A Fight for Viet Flag for Immigrants; Old Banner is Rallying Point." *Boston Globe*, 13 August 2003, B1, B8.

Aguilar-San Juan, Karin. "Fields of Dreams: Place, Race, and Memory in Boston's Vietnamese American Community." *Amerasia Journal* 29, no. 1 (2003): 80–96.

Bùi, James , Shirley Suet-ling Tang, and Peter Nien-Chu Kiang. "The Local/Global Politics of Boston's Viet-Vote." *aapi nexus* 2, no. 2 (2004): 10–18.

"Economic Globalization and Culture: A Discussion With Dr. Francis Fukuyama." Merrill Lynch and Co., Inc. 2001. www.ml.com/woml/forum/global.htm.

Embassy of the Socialist Republic of Vietnam in the United States of America. "Embassy Answer to the Boston Globe in Flag Resolution." 13 August 2003. www .vietnamembassy-usa.org/news/story.php?d=20030813161859.

Goldbard, Arlene. *New Creative Community: The Art of Cultural Development*. Oakland, Calif.: New Village Press, 2006.

Goldbard, Arlene, and Don Adams, eds. *Community, Culture and Globalization*. New York: Rockefeller Foundation, 2002.

——. *Creative Community: The Art of Cultural Development*. New York: Rockefeller Foundation, 2001.

Gorman, Anna. "Cambodia Town Is Now on the Map." *Los Angeles Times*, 18 July 2007, B1.

Grams, Diane, and Michael Warr. *Leveraging Assets: How Small Budget Arts Activities Benefit Neighborhoods*. Chicago: Richard H. Driehaus Foundation, 2003.

Jameson, Frederic. *The Cultures of Globalization*. Durham, N.C.: Duke University Press, 1998.

Kiang, Peter Nien-Chu, and Jenny Kaplan. "Where Do We Stand: Views of Racial Conflict by Vietnamese American High School Students in a Black-and-White Context." *Urban Review* 26, no. 2 (1994): 95–119.

Kiang, Peter Nien-Chu, Ngoc-lan Nguyen, and Richard Lee Sheehan. "Don't Ignore It! Documenting Racial Harassment in a Fourth-Grade Vietnamese Bilingual Classroom." *Equity and Excellence in Education* 28, no. 1 (1995): 31–35.

Kiang, Peter Nien-Chu, and Shirley Suet-ling Tang. "Electoral Politics and the Contexts of Empowerment, Displacement, and Diaspora for Boston's Vietnamese and Cambodian American Communities." *Asian American Policy Review* 15 (2006): 13–29.

King, Mel. *Chain of Change: Struggles for Black Community Development*. Boston: South End, 1980.

Kleiman, Neil Scott, and Center for an Urban Future. *The Creative Engine*. New York: Center for an Urban Future, November 2002. http://www.nycfuture.org/content/reports/report_view.cfm?repkey=90and search=1.

Le, Thao N, and Judy L. Wallen. "Youth Delinquency: Self-Reported Rates and Risk Factors of Cambodian, Chinese, Lao/Mien, and Vietnamese Youth." *aapi nexus* 4, no. 2 (2006): 15–44.

Liu, Michael, Thao Tran, and Paul Watanabe. *Far From the Commonwealth: A Report on Low-Income Asian Americans in Massachusetts*. Boston: University of Massachusetts Boston Institute for Asian American Studies, 2007. http://www.iaas .umb.edu/publications/general/LowIncRep.pdf.

Lorde, Audre. *Sister Outsider*. Freedom, Calif.: Crossing Press, 1984.

Lowe, Lisa. *Immigrant Acts: On Asian American Cultural Politics*. Durham, N.C.: Duke University Press, 1996.

Machida, Margo. *Asia/America: Identities in Contemporary Asian American Art*. New York: Asia Society Galleries and New Press, 1994.

McGroarty, Patrick Michael. "The Lion in Fields Corner: Building a Vietnamese Community in Boston." Bachelor's thesis, Boston College, 2006.

Pham, Mai-Lan. "Strangers in Fields Corner: The Formation of a Vietnamese Community in Dorchester." *Boston Review* 17, no. 5 (September–October 1992): 16–19.

Reyes, Angeles. *Language, Identity, and Stereotype Among Southeast Asian American Youth: The Other Asian*. Mahwah, N.J.: Lawrence Erlbaum, 2007.

Rezendes, Michael. "O'Neil is Hooted Off Stage at Racial Unity Rally." *Boston Globe*, 16 June 1992, B30.

———. "Vietnamese Leaders Hit O'Neil Remarks." *Boston Globe*, 11 June 1992, B31.

Sege, Irene. "A Community Finds its Center: Dorchester's Vietnamese Population, Young and Old, Hopes to Find Common Ground at a New Gathering Place." *Boston Globe*, 23 January 2002, D1.

———. "Vietnamese Find their Voice after Boston Councilor's Remarks, Community Focuses on Political Power." *Boston Globe*, 26 June 1992, B1.

Smith, Adam. "Vietnamese Nonprofit Builds Homes for Dorchester Residents." *Sampan*, 16 March 2007, http://sampan.org/show_article.php?display=1031.

Stern, Mark, and Susan Seifert. *Community Revitalization and the Arts in Philadelphia*. Philadelphia: Social Impact of the Arts Project, University of Pennsylvania, 1998.

Tang, Shirley Suet-ling. "Community Cultural Development and Education with Cambodian American Youth." In *Asian Voices: Engaging, Empowering, and Enabling*, edited by Lin Zhan. New York: National League for Nursing, 2008.

Um, Katharya. *A Dream Denied: Educational Experiences of Southeast Asian American Youth Issues and Recommendations*. Washington, D.C.: Southeast Asia Resource Action Center, 2003.

UNESCO (United Nations Educational, Scientific, and Cultural Organization). "2001—UNESCO Universal Declaration on Cultural Diversity." http://www.journal.au.edu/abac_journal/2002/jan02/appendix.pdf.

Viet-Vote. Unpublished campaign materials. Boston: Viet-AID, 2003.

Vu, Vy. "Community Formation; Catholic Influence on the Building of the Vietnamese Community in Boston, 1975–2005." Bachelor's thesis, Yale University, 2006.

Walker, Alice. *In Search of Our Mothers' Gardens*. New York: Harcourt Brace, 1983.

Walker, Christopher. *Arts and Culture: Community Connections: Contributions from New Survey Research*. Washington, D.C.: Urban Institute, 2002.

Wallace, Michelle. *Invisibility Blues: From Pop to Theory*. New York: Verso, 1990.

Performative Blackness and Lao Americans
Cool in a New Hampshire School

MONICA CHIU

Hip-hop music often has been at the center of heated divides in our con-temporary moment: sometimes reviled for its encouragement of mi-sogyny and violence, sometime praised for the urgent narratives it spins about racial relations and the economic dire straits of many minority citi-zens. Furthermore, hip-hop artists have been feted for their "oppositional politics," on the one hand, while critiqued, on the other, for colluding with corporate America by trading an "underground" politics of the people for fame and fortune.[1] More recently, hip-hop served to foreshadow racial strife. The inflammatory lyrics of Ice Cube's 1991 "Black Korea" illuminated antag-onisms of African American customers who berated Korean American ven-dors for increasing vigilance against African American clients. "Don't follow me up and down your crazy little market," the persona in Ice Cube's rap sings, "or your little chop suey ass will be the target of a nationwide boycott" (87). Ice Cube uncannily captured how the 1992 Los Angeles riots unfolded in racial furor. So amid contemporary anxiety over hip-hop's perceived cul-tural influences, it seems that popular culture's fictionalized resentments be-tween racial groups are not always strictly fiction. Popular culture informs us about race relations while performing necessary cultural work: excavat-ing the antagonisms and unifications between blacks and Asian Americans. Media and academic attention to the politics of hip-hop centers popular culture as a compelling site for contemporary musings about race, identity, and being American, especially in educational institutions. Despite accusa-tions against the scholarly worth of popular culture, it steadily has gained a foothold in academia, where conferences, journals, and syllabi reflect grow-ing discussions about pedagogically sound approaches to discussing popu-lar music, YouTube clips, magazine ads, commercials, advertisements, fash-ion, and other forms of popular culture in the classroom.[2] While hip-hop now is an accepted venue for academic inquiry, its physical presence in secondary institutions of education—the adoption of hip-hop personas by high school students—and not its abstract presence in academic debates negatively impacts teachers' assessments of students' academic performance. Minority students attach their own identity politics to hip-hop, but often to the detriment of their perceived academic abilities.

This analysis traces how Lao American boys in a small New Hampshire town used media-inspired hip-hop in the early years of 2000 for entertainment, as a fashion guide, and as an influence on daily speech and gesture.[3] Because of hip-hop's potential for incendiary lyrics, the musical venue allowed them to vent their frustrations as a minority group in a predominantly white state and provided them access to Americanization. Stereotypes of "bad" media-inspired African Americans—wherein "bad" translates as "cool"—offered them an alternative to the "good" but emasculating and staid stereotypes of Asian Americans as the model minority, a type not amenable to the peer affirmation they were seeking. However, the link that teachers and administrators crafted between the boys' performance of blackness and the boys' academic potential tells a cautionary tale about hip-hop's cultural currency in this particular academic venue. My work focuses on popular culture's impact on race relations. I use an ethnographic study as a template to investigate how media-inspired hip-hop is used by Lao American youth, tracing the cultural work of popular culture. As a potential social compass, popular culture sheds its designation as pure entertainment and provides a site for productive inquiry.

Becoming American, Becoming Black

Stacey Lee expresses in her aptly titled *Up Against Whiteness: Race, School, and Immigrant Youth* that identity politics are thoroughly entangled with academic issues: "Messages about race are central to what the children of immigrants learn in our schools. . . . Lessons about race—what is said as well as what is not said—saturate school policies, curricula, and interactions with peers and teachers" (2). When acculturation is pivotal to peer approval, perceptions of racial belonging vastly influence student behavior. This study relies on an eclectic variety of materials—studies on the immigrant second generation; cultural criticism that investigates popular culture; and notions of blackness and "yellow face"—to interrogate the Lao American boys' accommodation of media-inspired blackness. While this blackness assists them in achieving social acceptance among their non–Lao American peers, it unfortunately profoundly impacts views that institutional authority casts on the boys' academic potential. In this section, I first will review literature on immigrant acculturation, racial identification, and educational achievement. I then will discuss model minority subjects and performative blackness.

Former ethnographic and academic models of assimilation suggest that immigrants and their children must shed racial and ethnic affiliations in order to act white or, in passing, become whitened. However, passing is impossible for some immigrants whose racial visibility prohibits this assimilative possibility. New evidence of selective acculturation among immigrant families trumps these former models of a perceived necessary assimilation.[4] Acculturation can be as bare-bones as learning English proficiently, but this proficiency does not guarantee student motivation and high grades, nor does it guarantee smooth assimilation among peers.[5] Excelling academically is certainly one avenue by which the children of immigrants can assimilate.[6] But often parents who demand academic excellence and respect for authority simultaneously discourage Americanization by blocking their children's liaisons with Anglo students.[7] Research also shows that children of immigrants who are less acculturated to America in general (not necessarily by any deliberative parental gestures) can be successful academically.

Asian immigrants and their children face barriers created by the myth of the model minority, an explanation that generalizes Asian immigrant and Asian American academic successes. Educational achievement models based on model minority parenting anticipate and structure particular reactions to Asian and Asian American academic achievement (as superior to that of other immigrant groups as well as to other national minorities, such as African Americans), much to the students' disadvantage. Furthermore, this model pits minorities against each other, conveniently allowing the socially constructed problem to become a strictly minority-versus-minority issue. Contrary to this accepted view, Khatharya Um finds that Southeast Asian Americans held the fewest higher degrees, in 2003, out of the many Southeast Asian ethnic groups in the United States, including Vietnamese, Vietnamese-Chinese, Cambodian, Lao, and Hmong.[8] Furthermore, institutional hindrances to higher education (specifically colleges and universities) for many minority students are often masked by institutional practices where "acceptable GPAs" are gleaned from English as a Second or Other Languages (ESOL), or sheltered courses, as recorded by Mongkol Tungmala—all of which obfuscate reasons for their inability to enter college when they have been receiving "good" grades all along (45–46). In his ethnographic work with Vietnamese students in San Diego, Kenji Ima often finds that the students "do not see how their future is related to schooling and work[,] . . . are disconnected from the wider community and can only find companionship with other youths who share their situation" (200–1). Finally, contrary to the goals of most secondary institutions, some immigrant parents of Southeast Asian American students encourage employment in manual labor as soon as their children graduate from high school (high school representing a tool for learning English, not for preparing children for higher education). That is, the quantitative benefits of education for some immigrant families pertain to future employment and monetary gain as opposed to how many nonimmigrant parents view education as possessing qualitative aspects.[9] Students inherit these messages about academic worth and achievement, which dispel the myth of the model minority at the same time that institutions uphold them, as will become evident in this chapter.

The construction of Asian Americans has been dichotomized between threat and passive citizen, between the alien (and later threatening yellow peril) and the model minority.[10] Being Asian or Asian American, therefore, is a negotiated factor in one's ability to be "progressively" whitened (invoking acceptance, assimilability, tractability) and the dangers of being blackened (conjuring up negativity, resistance, incorrigibility). But Asian Americans who are "neither black nor white," borrowing from Gary Okihiro, have remained "perpetual foreigners or honorary Whites," according to Mia Tuan, and their eventual designation as model minorities represents a burden, a misconception, and a political wedge pitting so-called successful Asian Americans against so-called regressive, resistant African Americans.[11] Is being a model minority a form of inclusion or exclusion? By whose standards and whose definitions are students Americanized? The words of a Korean immigrant sum up the inextricability of racialization and Americanization by emphasizing the incongruity that lies in acting "American" but looking Asian: "I identify with Americans, but Americans do not identify with me" (quoted in Portes and Rumbaut 191).

Asian American students in my study whose peers do not accept their gestures toward becoming white and who find the model minority myth unaccommodating turn to hip-hop's cultural currency and its association with blackness. Hip-hop can provide an associative link between cool music and a cool listener; more important, media-inspired hip-hop blackness is coupled with agency, masculinity, and acceptance by mainstream culture. "Styling Blackness," according to Patricia Williams, represents a desire "to fit in with the White kids" (n.p.). It also can offer models of resistance. Media-inspired hip-hop cool is a way of "acting black" by listening to rap, mimicking rap's distinctive language of violence and sexual predation, creating rap music and lyrics, and dressing in clothing exhibited by gangsta rappers. Blackness is aligned, on the one hand, with a facet of popular culture that signifies difference, and, on the other, with sameness in its ability to Americanize (or homogenize) nonwhite subjects. Meanwhile, whiteness is rendered invisible in relation to these so-called visible markers of otherness. As a case in point, Ellis Cose examines how the cultural currency of blackness in the media is both envied and reproduced at the same time that African Americans possess little economic and social power.

Unfortunately, blackness is too often equated by the dominant population with stupidity, intractability, poverty, violence, and a threatening sexual masculinity. "Acting black" is a complicated notion that, according to Lee, contributes to her Hmong American subjects (who attend a Wisconsin high school) to become "Blacken[ed] in the dominant imagination," even to their "criminalization," thus negatively influencing others' views of their academic potential (65, 66). Similarly, Um finds that once the Southeast Asian students of her study, who attend schools in the University of California system, felt labeled as "gangsters" or "at risk, or simply as possessing limited capability" because of their clothes, music tastes, or speech, the students felt that teachers did "not deem it worthwhile to invest any time or resources in cultivating their potential," resulting in a "systemic neglect" (8). Furthermore, Lao youth who speak "coarse and inappropriate" "youth street" English, states KaYing Yang, exacerbate the impression that they are not academically capable, thereby disempowering them at the same time that association with "cool" signifies their desire to be empowered (10).

Nonwhite immigrant youth negotiate their identities "within a racial hierarchy where Whites are positioned at the top," says Lee (2). They shed their racial and ethnic affiliations in order to Americanize. They learn to act white or, in passing, become whitened. However, passing may be impossible for some immigrants whose visible, physical markers of race prohibit this route toward assimilation. Furthermore, the visibility of minorities' physical difference is always compared and contrasted to the perceived invisibility of a hierarchically superior whiteness to which many immigrant students aspire (an impossible goal given their visible differentiation) and toward which our culture and our institutions subtly guide them as indications of success and acceptance by peers, teachers, and other institutional members.

If becoming American has resulted in styling a type of blackness — and if this blackness is regarded warily by teachers and administrators — then looking different (Asian or black or Latino) continues to suggest that minority students accord themselves with white, mainstream America in order to be accepted. There exists no smooth cultural integration, and seamless institutional belonging, of nonwhite students.

On this vexed, historical matter of the incorporation of racial subjects into national belonging, Leslie Bow wonders how Jim Crow laws accommodated Asians, "a supposed 'third' race," one that did not fit "a cultural and legal system predicated on the binary distinction between colored and white" (3): for example, where would Asians sit on the segregated buses of the Jim Crow South? Her argument about the interstitiality of the Chinese in the Deep South helps to illuminate the in-between state of contemporary Lao American students. While the Chinese of Bow's study willfully recreated themselves as white by identifying away from blackness to climb a social-class ladder through racial formation, the Lao American boys of my study at Millshore voluntarily identify through blackness, not in order to become black, but in order to become white. At the same time, both the Chinese of Bow's study and the boys of mine understand the impossibility of physically becoming white.

Despite a common acknowledgment that there exists no such thing as race, two race-related arguments operate against each other: performing as a racial subject (against one's bodily markers; that is, Asian Americans who perform blackness) and, subsequently, being denied that performance (based on one's biological indices). For example, while Asian American boys can "become black" in clothing, language, and gestures, they are prohibited from forgetting that they inhabit a "biologically" Asian body. I call this performance a type of yellow black facing (see Sylvia Chong), which cleverly incorporates the performative gestures of both yellow facing and black facing in order for a subject to "be" another race (black) at the same time that these performances prohibit an underlying (Asian) physical body to escape its social inscriptions. Yellow facing, a practice that borrows from vaudeville black facing, describes a procedure by which white actors could visually represent Asian characters on stage or in the movies by yellowing their skin, blackening their hair, and pulling back the outer corners of their eyes with face tape. A white actor temporarily may become Asian, but the reversion back to whiteness is a simple feat. In naming the current gestures of the Lao American Millshore students' performances as yellow black facing, I can illuminate the boys' inability to escape their visibly raced bodies so simply in performing blackness — the inability to racially pass as anything but Asian American. They are read back into their "place" as model minorities (a place regarded as a biological imperative), simultaneously cementing culturally constructed negative notions of blackness and problematic positive notions of the model minority. The discussion of constructions of race as a necessary portal to understanding its effects is thus curiously removed from some academic contexts while it continues to dominate discourses of self- and national construction in others.[12]

The Vietnam War, Lao Refugees, and the Racialization of Millshore

Discussions of race are central to understanding Millshore's place in the lives of Lao refugees whose children attend Millshore schools. I will begin with the implications of the United States' Secret Wars during the Vietnam War and then move to mapping the lives of Lao refugee families in the predominantly white town of Millshore.

The Secret Wars in Laos, 1964–1973, fueled and funded by the CIA but not congressionally approved, devastated the nation economically, politically, and ecologically, explains Robert Proudfoot (32). In its politics of containment, says Martin Stuart-Fox, the United States, in conjunction with the Royal Lao Army, recruited both highland Lao and mountain-dwelling Hmong, training the latter as guerilla fighters, to stabilize a strategically important region known as the Plain of Jars (a region infiltrated by North Vietnamese) and to staunch the flow of supplies and men from North Vietnam to the South on the Lao portion of the Ho Chi Minh trail (138–39). Despite an estimated two million tons of bombs devastating the Lao countryside by 1973 (an estimated three million by 1977, according to Proudfoot [33]) and destroying nearly 3,500 villages under Communist Pathet Lao control, the bombings never successfully curtailed movement on the trail. When the defeated United States withdrew between 1975 and 1979, leaving Laos under the leadership of Pathet Lao forces (who renamed the nation the Lao People's Democratic Republic, a socialist government" [Proudfoot 30]), "[A]s many as three-quarters of a million people, and a quarter of the entire population, had been driven from their homes to become refugees in their own country" (Stuart-Fox 144). Routed by starvation, disease, an unstable new government, a collapsing economy (a result of American intervention and a weak Lao economy), and fear (those Lao who assisted the United States were sent to harsh re-education camps or killed), thousands of Lao citizens and former Royal Lao military police and officials left Laos for Thai refugee camps, which were already overburdened by South Vietnamese and Cambodian refugees (Proudfoot 33–34). Some languished in camps for more than three years before finally being sent to European nations or to the United States.

Nationally, 135,000 Lao currently live in the United States, mostly in San

Diego and the San Francisco Bay areas, according to the Southeast Asia Resource Action Center. More locally, the 2000 U.S. Census reports that of the 241 Asians in Millshore's total population of 8,027, only 145 residents are Lao or Lao American. In the early 1980s, this predominantly French and Polish working-class town experienced the arrival of a few ethnic Lao refugee families sponsored by a local Catholic church. The ethnic Lao Lum (or Lowland Lao) were attracted to the region's abundant factory labor, its quiet community for raising families, and its cheap rental and home markets (which have unfortunately skyrocketed in price since then). Also, Millshore is not far from more substantial Lao communities in Lowell and Boston, assisting Lao Millshore residents in retaining close contact with relatives and friends living in those Massachusetts locations. That the area was considered by Lao residents in the late 1980s as a safe, quiet place to raise children spurred an influx of Lao families to the region until 1991. The introduction of a handful of ethnic Laos to such a small town has demanded the community's self-revisioning. Tom Schram reports that while the existing community was "not antagonistic" to the changes wrought by the refugee influx, it was also "less than receptive" ("Laotian Refugees" 127). In fact, two recent Millshore arrivals (both non-Lao), mentioned to me the difficulty of living as "non-natives" in such a tightly knit community.

In 2001, a racist crime propelled the existence of this nearly unknown Lao American population into local and even national mainstream discussions. According to one white informant, the healing activities following the tragedy provided a unification through grief more substantial than the unity that the community offered through two annual hometown cultural events. Hostilities against racial groups often promote a thickening of ethnic identity (a desire to promote and not downplay their socially constituted differences) and encourage political mobilization by those ethnic subjects who are at the center of racial conflict.[13] No studies exist about ethnic solidarity in Millshore before and after the crime: What demands, if any, were made by Laos and Lao Americans, and were they met or rejected? How did they impact Millshore's public schools? One discouraging answer might be found in a total absence of the availability of in-town Millshore adult English language courses before and after the incident.

The town hosts an annual heritage festival featuring local crafts and homegrown pride, including traditional Lao dance performances. While many non-Lao residents enjoy the dances and happily purchase food cooked by Lao women, as rising attendance results in overwhelming food demand, the women are becoming increasingly less inclined to prepare food. Millshore residents are thus no different from the rest of the nation in satisfying their curiosity and their stomachs on the "exotic" fare produced by immigrants and their descendents, often neglecting to delve any deeper into the culture than through this alimentary layer. In rendering the ethnic Laos cultural ambassadors who bring expertise about "there" (Laos) to the culturally ignorant people "here" in Millshore, the community conveniently avoids discussing how "there" and "here" are inextricable in both attractive and problematic ways. This attitude was reflected again when several Millshore teachers lamented the decline in grades and the evidence of belligerent behavior among some of the Lao American boys. Their concerns suggested that something was awry within Lao American families or Lao American communities that were affecting the boys' behavior and academic achievement; while they hoped to glean insights about "them," they stopped short of inquiring into racial assumptions they themselves and the wider academic institution possessed that might be influencing social attitudes, personal pedagogy, and Lao Americans' self-identity and academic success. Culture as a detriment when divorced from ethnic festivals highlights just the inextricability between racialization and institutionalization that this study sets forth.

A Black New England

Statistically, New Hampshire is the whitest state in the nation. Except for the racially diverse city of Manchester, state elementary and secondary schools enroll predominantly white students. Attracting and retaining African American students at the state's flagship university are perennial issues. The arrival of a handful of immigrant Lao families to Millshore in the early 1990s (in the midst of a second migration from Boston and its surrounding suburbs), many of whom did not speak English well, posed challenges to Millshore. However, a mere eight to ten years later, second-generation Lao American students (born in the United States), continued to push pedagogical initiatives surrounding students who spoke English at school and Lao at home, initiatives revolving around the school's role in Lao American students' self-assessment about their sense of belonging. Two literary pieces exemplify this point: below are the poetry and lyrics of two youths who attended Millshore Junior and Senior High School at different times. The first, rather sentimental poem was written in 1995 by Tran, an introverted and often embarrassed first-generation Lao youth in a "remedial" classroom. The second poem (really, song lyrics) was created in 2003 by Steven, an academically struggling Lao American eighth grader. [14]

I love-U-Mom

I didn't mean to tell you
I didn't mean to go far away from you
So U have to understand, Mom, I love you
The word Mom, It's still always in my mind
Mom isn't just a word
Mom can be good or bad
but always in my mind
Mom, it's very important to me
Mom, can be a teacher to her child
Mom, can be a good wife to her husband
Mom, can be a housewife who cares for a family
Mom, can be everything for a female
So, Goodbye, Mom, Mom
Please pray for me
When I see the sun rise up in the morning
I think of your face
When I was young, every time I was down
You built me right up and taught me right
from wrong
Even though, I was the Black sheep of the family
You still care about me
Mom, mom I would missing U
And I always love you, Mom!
— Tran, a first generation Lao eleventh grader at Millshore
    Junior and Senior High School from Fu (1995)

do it cuz we gotta
picture me ridin on my enemies
smoke a blunt, and sippin on hennessy
with my eyes half way shut, bust my glock sideways
niggah what, niggah what, niggah what
you aint got shit on me
frontline souljah on a killin spree
picture a g [gook] like me
blastin a glock in your mouth,
like tha hoe [*sic*] you are
rhymes like these can leave your momma scarred [*sic*]
and leave your bitch ass scared of me

and that Nuc Lao Souljah Family
see I got it all planed [*sic*] out
step one: we boutta run up in your crib
step two: blow off you mommas wig
step three: we gonna hunt you down
step four: blast rounds of pounds
catch your ass slippin
and then throw you in tha corner
pistol whip your ass, and put you in a coma
wake your ass up, put tha glock in your mouth
Make you say your prayers
And blow your brains out
[Chorus not included here]
— Steven, a second-generation Lao eighth grader at Millshore
    Junior and Senior High School, fall 2003

While the former poem focuses on an appreciation of the maternal, the lat-ter hones in on violent revenge against an unnamed affront. What has oc-curred in the short space between Tran's tenure at Millshore, when he wrote affectionate poems about his mother, and Steven's tenure, when he posted on the Web violent song lyrics about somebody else's mother? Is the dras-tic contrast between the poem and song lyrics suggesting an equally drastic social and academic climate change in the eight years separating the boys' experiences in Millshore? The urgency of the lyrics, despite their ugliness, points to how performative blackness — exemplified in the hip-hop nature of the song — invites the Lao American boys to refashion themselves out of earlier cultural constructions that cast them as quiet, meek, amenable, or as the model minority (specifically exemplified by Tran). Their actions do not signal a desire to "become" black, as outlined earlier, but rather to be ac-cepted by their white peers; in essence, becoming cool by becoming black allows them to whiten. The Lao Americans' growing pride in their own cul-ture, manifested in this ability to assert and refashion themselves, albeit in non-Lao ways, marks a positive move. But despite a sharp rise in ethnic pride by the second-generation youth over the first, this Americanization comes at the price of some of the youths' academic success.

In their adoption of this black styling, coupled with renewed pride in their Lao American heritage, the boys both understand and to some degree contest race as a visible marker of identity. When the boys attempt to whiten (to assimilate) through blackness, their poor academic work prohibits them from this venue at the same time that their model minority status suggests academic supremacy. While such yellow black facing offers the students a type of social currency (they are accepted by other non-Lao peers as cool), unfortunately, their underlying "yellow" bodies iterate the problem in such racial performances between looking and being. That is, the teachers then pinpoint where the boys have gone awry (in acting black) without interrogating where the institution itself reduces the political complexity among the social construction of race, being raced, and seeing race. The political practices of all such "race-ing" curb the boys from self-envisioning beyond bodily markers, erupting, so I surmise, in the anger and frustration of Steven's lyrics above.

Those Lao Americans in sartorial hip-hop style (baggy pants from which boxer shorts peek out from waistbands, oversized jackets and sweatshirts, do-rags, and sunglasses) perform what Tricia Rose calls an "appropriative critique": "Early 1990s trends — oversized pants and urban warrior outer apparel, as in 'hoodies,' 'snooties,' 'tims,' and 'triple fat goose-down coats' — make clear the severity of the urban storms to be weathered" (436). According to Rose, hip-hop artists "traverse contemporary crossroads of lack and desire in urban Afro-diasporic communities" and foster "both resistance to and preparation for a hostile world that denies and denigrates young people of color" (434). The Lao American students I worked with express their marginalization not through an affinity for blackness (they do not want to be black) nor through an African American politics of resistance, but rather through a radical sartorial and linguistic division to advertise how they view themselves as savvy and hip. Steven, for example, uses the term "niggah" in various contexts: against blacks as well as to show Asian solidarity by using the term to signal himself and, on occasion, other Lao Americans. This free application indicates little awareness over the fraught debates surrounding the political uses of the term "niggah" by African Americans themselves. When asked to self-describe, he replies, "juvenile delinquent," "adolescent," and "nice." Thus, the adoption of hip-hop walk, talk, and wear indicates a desire for acceptance by his peers and not necessarily a connection to the struggles or social justice goals of other ethnic minorities. As a case in point, Rose finds that many "rappers have nicknames that suggest street smarts, coolness, power, and supremacy: L.L. Cool J (Ladies Love Cool James), Kool Moe Dee, Queen Latifah, Dougie Fresh (and the Get Fresh Crew) . . . Ice-T, Ice Cube, etc." (435).

The boys' collective adversity, defiance, and disobedience suggest their unarticulated feelings of disempowerment despite the school's, the teachers', the students', and even the larger community's denial, in most cases, of any blatant racism. But all of the boys quickly reject any affinity with African Americans; they implicitly understand gradations of racial acceptance in being Anglo or African American. They prefer recognition of their difference through their ethnicity as Lao Americans and not through a correspondence to blackness: they can dress in the style of media-inspired hip-hop gangstas, but deflect any confusion over their possible racial affiliation. If the Lao American youths *are* the minority in Millshore, then in some ways they both react to and dictate the terms of this minority status.

As much as the Lao American boys take pride in and defend their ethnic affiliation by categorizing themselves pan-ethnically as Asian American or as ethnically Lao, they do so in ways that suggest a symbolic racial identity. (None of the boys identified themselves strictly as American, choosing instead Lao, Lao American, Asian American; some conflated identity with nationality by calling themselves Laos.) They may self-identify as Asians in situations where they feel confident, even cocky, as when Andrew proudly (and wrongly) stated that teachers would not prevent him from walking the hallways sans hall pass because it was his Asian right. Kimpon, on the other hand, wants to be considered "just Laos," to "go with my folk culture." Among the many tattoos covering his body, "Laos," in two-inch-high letters, was inked prominently down his left arm, contributing to the cool appeal that his sunglasses, ripped T-shirt, do-rag, Honda Accord, and bad-boy attitude exuded.

In many ways, it is cool to be Asian as long as one possesses such material accoutrements. Would Tran, the author of the first poem who identified strongly with his "folk culture," be deemed equally cool and acceptable by Kimpon? Or, more important, how does one's exhibition of "culture" render one cool? What types of exhibition are considered unacceptable and which embarrassing? Andrew, for example, considers himself Asian American; he'd rather not be called Lao or Lao American for he deems Laos a "Third World nation." His self-identification exemplifies how immigrants adopt majority (usually negative) views about themselves and their homelands. If so, then Kimpon's Asianness is not what renders him cool: Asian American men have historically been feminized, and this stereotype persists. "Articulations of national subjectivity," states David L. Eng, "depend intimately on racializing, gendering, and sexualizing strategies" (3). Kimpon's adoption of stereotypical hip-hop–inspired gang symbols offers him masculinity, peer acceptability, and therefore an acceptable American identity. Thus, even though Steven, obsessed with popular-culture gangsterism, defines a "thug" as "a person who doesn't care about what others think of them," we know he is keenly affected by peer approval. Lao American students supplement their Asian American identities (regarded by the majority as feminized, nerdy, weak, and backward) with gang symbols to compensate for their lack of self-esteem, not their possession of it, and to accommodate to U.S. gender norms. The students adhere to the notion that to be male in America is to be strong, the antithesis of how Asian American manhood has been defined and perceived both culturally and politically.[15]

Feelings of inadequacy arise and notions of coolness quickly dissipate in the classroom when discussions turn to school, academics, and the students' futures. When two immigrants from China join this school's ESOL classroom in the fall of 2003, some of the Lao American boys compare their own academic shortcomings — their self-described lack of intelligence — to one of the new student's successes. But in subsequent interviews and in casual conversation, the notion of intelligence as an indicator of success is less prominent than that of self-motivation as a prime factor in being academically successful. Many of the Lao American boys and girls describe themselves as lazy. Patrick, according to a casual conversation I had with his mother, spends all of his free time in his room playing games, watching TV, or surfing the Web. Indeed, 95 percent of my subjects claim to have finished their homework in class or to have no homework at all; half of them are academically at risk or are earning low grades in non–college preparatory classes. They admit that they should study harder, but are not inclined.[16]

Lao American pride among the juniors and seniors of my study contrasts sharply with that of Lao students of three earlier studies undertaken in Millshore: in Tom Schram's 1993 and 1994 essay-length studies and in Danling Fu's 1995 book *My Trouble Is My English: Asian Students and the American Dream*. Students in the latter studies were deeply conscious of and subsequently embarrassed by their Asianness, pointing to differing modes of assimilation among immigrants past and present. Lao and Lao American students may have once attempted to minimize "the more conspicuous aspects of their ethnicity," according to Schram ("Laotian Refugees" 128), but current students announce their Lao affiliation proudly, suggesting a thickening or strengthening of the youths' Lao identity. One can conclude that Lao American students at Millshore have certainly been mainstreamed from their status as minority "players along the margins" (to borrow the title of one of Schram's articles), but with academic consequences. While the disruptive, disrespectful students in Schram's work are Anglo students — and Lao Americans are simultaneously appalled by and in awe of such delinquency and misbehavior — disrespectful students in the current ESOL classroom are Lao Americans, practicing attitudes that will least aid their academic prospects. According to both Fu and Schram, the "lower track" classrooms of the mid-1990s became disorganized study sessions where

American students pepper their sentences with foul language and are visibly displeased to be paired with Lao students for academic exercises (in the belief that the latter will deter them academically with their faulty English and inability to understand the directions for class exercises). According to Schram, even though Lao students initially resisted the negative influences of their peers—who often sat in the back of the class, chatting and intimidating others—this "contributed little to their overall academic standing" because their good behavior was "obscured by teachers' low expectations for their academic achievement and persistent cultural and communicative difficulties with them" ("Laotian Refugees" 128, "Players Along the Margin" 74). Teachers adopted the philosophy of "getting them [the Lao students] through high school" by "facilitating the students' social fit rather than their academic aspirations" ("Laotian Refugees" 128). These lowered expectations reveal the cultural work of marginalization within the educational institution. Because the school's administration emphasizes social integration, often through the promotion of vocational professions for students in this lower academic track as opposed to a more academic program, both groups of students (Lao and non-Lao) regard themselves as less intelligent and capable than peers in the college preparatory track.

The students I observed were taking predominantly B-level (below average) classes and most of them used foul language regularly, played around on the ESOL computers rather than doing homework, skipped classes, or arrived at school and classes tardy. Furthermore, Lao American students' visible difference in Millshore is exacerbated by their presence in remedial (ESOL) classrooms, which are racially stigmatizing spaces, according to Schram, and a clear institutional demarcation from the rest of the student body ("Laotian Refugees" 130). (The classroom itself, approximately 22 feet by 12 feet—a hallway of sorts—was once a storage room, and later served as a student lounge until it was needed as an ESOL room, typical of how ESOL classrooms evolve with a growing student body and limited building space.)[17]

Because both first- and second-generation students, as Lee writes, are "up against Whiteness," their differing degrees of racial pride and their behaviors are not necessarily mere generational differences, an explanation that too conveniently divorces their actions and behaviors from the larger social institutions in which the students circulate. In each case—past and present—their self-selected behavior (model minority geek or hip-hop cool) elicits attention, both positive and negative, from non-Lao peers. Even though Lao American students in Millshore now control the parameters of inclusion and exclusion within their ethnic group, their Americanization in touting ethnic pride invites a critical re-examination of the kinds of questions we currently pose. Rather than ask, "How do we 'fix' them so that they fit?" we should ask, "What institutional barriers might be encouraging this behavior, and how do we work through them?"

More important, we could ask to what extent might the school practice a "culture of avoidance," as Lorraine Delia Kenney calls it, in which exist "sanctioned ignorances" (118, 123). A 2004 racist incident that should have constructively destabilized the school's image of racial harmony was, instead, effectively managed in order to keep the peace, thus bypassing the critical examination of what school officials, according to my interviews, understood as a "qualified racial peace." In a ninth-grade history class discussion about immigrants, a non-Lao student stated angrily that new refugees were stealing jobs from nonimmigrant adults, receiving handouts from the government (giving examples of free cars and expensive designer clothing), and were exempt from paying taxes. Enraged, he threatened to beat with a baseball bat the first Asian person he encountered in the school's hallway. While I doubt he had any knowledge of the 1982 murder of Vincent Chin by baseball bat, committed by two Detroit autoworkers enraged by the success of Japanese auto sales in the United States, his words conjure up that brutal past. They echo the brutality of Steven's song lyrics. His immediate, and I assume necessary, removal to the school's behaviorist also conveniently excised his offensive comments from necessary class examination, either with or without his presence. This incident points to the necessity of exposing false and stereotypical positions on immigration in order to counter them. One cannot address racism without addressing race. The incident also illustrates a covert resentment against Millshore's immigrants by vocal representatives of the non-Lao student body (who are most likely parroting parental comments), a resentment that is not so easily glossed over. The silence over the event devalues the Lao American students, who must have possessed some opinion about the stereotypes evoked in the classroom (although I understand that, at a later date, the incident was discussed in the class). Avoiding such difficult conversations contributes to the potential recurrence of unexpected, racist eruptions, when teachers must address the threat of violence over the pedagogically useful content of such a moment. "Conflict avoidance is thus a component of White talk," a type of "race evasion," a reliance on silence to keep a fragile, racial peace, says Jonathan W. Warren (147, 146).

In another, albeit quieter, racial incident, a staff person in Millshore's front office confessed to the newly hired ESOL teacher Ms. Reese that the development of a successful ESOL program at Millshore would, unfortunately, attract more of "them," or more Lao Americans. Her comment exposes racist sentiments uttered by front-office staff who, one assumes, guide and care for all students. When Millshore's principal read a near-final draft of my study, she was appalled that any of her staff would voice such sentiments amid her publicly proclaimed goal to create a school that "loves all of its students equally." Her incredulity at the comment and her insistence that such utterances were impossible at Millshore exacerbate rather than dismantle the problem. She did, however, express frustration that Ms. Reese had not reported the event so that she could have addressed the staff person appropriately. Individual attitudes that run counter to institutional philosophies of inclusive care and inclusive education — or perhaps what is now called "institutional excellence" — are thus allowed to evade the radar of everyday interaction and to cripple its best intentions. Thus programs slated particularly for children of immigrants (and for minorities) are undermined and rendered substandard for insidious purposes, especially when attitudes about attracting too many of "them" translates into decreased monetary allocation to "our" (the right) white students.

Addressing the Vietnam War is one important way of discussing, in class, the intricacies of Southeast Asian refugees' daily life in the United States. The war is only briefly covered in Millshore's history courses, which focus heavily on material limited to events through the conclusion of World War II. (The Vietnam War is covered more fully in a modern U.S. history course at level 5, a college preparatory course in which few Lao American students enroll.) Rather, the Vietnam War is discussed in geography courses, suggesting the importance of charting territory and the relevance of imperialism over addressing the devastating personal consequences of the politics of war. Additionally, Millshore's former school superintendent berated my use of the term "Vietnam War," naming it the "Vietnam Conflict," thereby erasing the trauma of a *war* experienced by many of the parents whose children now attend the school. (Ironically, many Southeast Asians dub it the "American War.") Millshore's Lao American students themselves knew little about the reasons for their parents' immigration to the United States: "war and stuff," responded one student; "one of my relatives was the king," said another. Such responses beg for curriculum on the Vietnam War to inform both Lao American youths and other students who are ignorant of the reasons for the presence of refugee and Lao second and third generations in Millshore. Perhaps such a curriculum could help to abolish the violent racism exemplified earlier by an enraged white student, by a staff member, and in the aforementioned racist murder of a Lao resident.

Other well-intentioned actions on the school's part may have been more damaging than advantageous. According to Ms. Reese, an expert on Southeast Asians from the U.S. State Department was invited to Millshore Junior and Senior High when it first grappled with an influx of Lao students. (Why the school had not worked more closely with the elementary school long before the children's transition to higher grades is baffling.) This expert offered a disturbing narrative of differing Southeast Asian work ethics to Millshore teachers, who were eager to understand their new pupils. The expert commenced his presentation thus: if presented with a fruit tree, how would the Vietnamese, the Cambodian, and the Lao access the fruit? The Vietnamese would climb the tree to pluck the fruit, he replied; the Cambodians would chop down the tree for easier access (but with the unfortunate consequence of destroying its future harvesting potential); and the Lao would sit beneath the branches, waiting for the fruit to fall. Of those teachers at Millshore who remember this lecture, to what degree does it still influence their assessment of Lao and Lao American students' academic potential?

Growing negative perception of the Millshore Lao American boys, who are no longer attractive models in the model minority paradigm, is a symptom of a larger challenge involving finding support and recognition for Lao students in places that intersect with, and do not diverge from, those places where non-Lao students often seek support. The Lao American subjects are caught in an interstitial space, but a fruitful one nevertheless; according to Homi K. Bhabha, what is "alien" or "oblique" to the center of enigmatic authority is also the most richly pertinent to understanding that center (xi).

Conclusions

This study announces that popular culture can be a powerful political motivator, prompting unexpected actions by underrepresented minority groups. Min Song finds cultural expressions profoundly useful in plumbing the depths of what he sees as an absence of more positive cultural and artistic expressions nationwide before the Los Angeles riots. The event itself eventually promoted "imaginative and critical works of profound pessimism" (2). According to Song, creative works by Korean Americans about the riots (documentary films, plays, and novels) help us to make sense of the political climate: the strange, the depressing, and the inflammatory. Thus, the creative works by Tran and Stephen, quoted in full earlier, are powerful tools by which educators can read their students. Popular culture informs us about race relations while performing necessary cultural work: excavating racially embedded antagonisms and unifications.

Furthermore, this study illuminates Lowe's understanding of the "*racial formation* that is produced in the negotiations between the state's regulation of racial groups and those groups' active contestation and construction of racial meaning" (65). The Lao American subjects participate in what Lowe calls "Asian American cultural practices" that create identities in flux, always negotiated in relation to history, materialism, and culture (64). If all cultures are in process, then so, too, is that of the so-called invisible (white) culture into which Lao American students fit or from which they are rejected. As a case in point, in Evelyn Nien-ming Ch'ien's study of "weird English," a fascinating and productive language unbound by grammar rules and logical usage, she appreciates how nonstandard English (of the type often used by immigrants and refugees) can be discussed as clever "deviance" in some cases, not necessarily embarrassing mistakes. She continues: "vernaculars and pidgin speech were once dismissed as an undignified representation or parody of ethnic groups, [but] now the use of accented English has aesthetic capital" (19). Clearly, the Lao American subjects recognize this aesthetic capital, among peers, of hip-hop–inspired English while teachers and administrators perceive it as a problem of incorporating Lao American students into parameters of institutional culture and hegemonizing their English and their institutional actions. The youths are marked as malleable, therefore, and the institution is perceived as static. The desire to "fix" what has "gone wrong" by focusing solely on the Lao Americans' performative blackness and academic record conveniently overlooks that race, as one identity among others, operates in concert with as well as beyond the academic realm, an identity in flux.

The institution understands some levels of racialization, but savvy students engage in racial work in very complicated ways. To perform a type of yellow blackface as resistance to social and academic repudiation is a clear indication of the boys' comprehension of the complexities of race: that one can "be" one race and perform another. In speaking of Asian Americans as interstitial — or "aberrant" groups that can highlight how race is continuously read "along a black-white continuum" (25) — Bow states, "The space between the social enactment of an identity and its idealization reveals the structures that consolidate social power in its multiple manifestations" (26). Hence, the demand is not to reculturize the students (nor to transform them back into the model minority); rather, it is to pay careful attention to the institutions and cultural arenas in which we and our students circulate.

Attending to popular culture and its racial formations advance how we can make political sense of self-representation.[18]

NOTES

1. These terms are used in "Got Next: A Roundtable on Identity and Aesthetics after Multiculturalism." Greg Tate mentions the "oppositional Left of [hip-hop's] progressive politics" (35), and Mark Anthony Neal mentions Tricia Rose's discussion of "the underground of hip-hop and the underground of actual people" (35).

2. For example, two recent, academic collections examine representations of Asian Americans in popular culture: Mimi Thi Nguyen and Thuy Linh Nguyen, eds, *Alien Encounters: Popular Culture in Asian America*; and Shilpa Davé, LeiLane Nishime, and Tani Oren, eds., *East Main Street: Asian American Popular Culture*.

3. My work is based on a ten-month ethnographic study in Millshore Junior and Senior High (a pseudonym) in its English as a Second or Other Language (ESOL) classroom, including observations in one Millshore summer school session. I gleaned additional data from Karen Elizabeth Hayden's master's thesis focusing on Lao Americans in this Millshore school and Andrea Minnis's master's thesis (she interviewed the same students I did). Three other studies focusing on the school's Lao American students include two essays by Tom Schram and a monograph by Danling Fu, all cited throughout this chapter. The study's methods are interpretive, drawing on interviews with nine Lao American students (six boys and three girls), all of whom attended obligatory ESOL study sessions. Because I was most intrigued by and concerned with most of the boys' styling of a media-inspired cool and its implications of "blackness" and their poor classroom behavior, and because the Lao American women I interviewed and observed expressed no interest in modeling this paradigm, my study focuses on the boys, who are mentioned by pseudonyms in the study: Steven (an eighth grader whom I initially met in the summer school program and whose song lyrics appear later in this chapter), Kimpon (a graduating senior obligated to attend summer school in order to make up for class absences), Andrew (a junior), Neil (a sophomore), Jonathan (a sophomore), and Patrick (a sophomore). A study focusing on the girls, their more prevalent academic successes and reasons for them, is an important study for another researcher.

4. See Alejandro Portes and Rubén G. Rumbaut's *Legacies: The Story of the Immigrant Second Generation*.

5. See Portes and Rumbaut's *Legacies*.

6. See Alejandro Portes's *Immigrant America: A Portrait*.

7. See Margaret Gibson's *Accommodation Without Assimilation: Sikh Immigrants in an American High School*.

8. For more on Southeast Asians and their academic degrees, see Portes and Rumbaut's *Legacies* as well as Mongkol Tungmala's "An Exploration of Familial and Social Influences on the Superior Educational Achievement of Laotian High School Students in Jordan School District."

9. See Tom Schram's "Laotian Refugees in a Small-Town School: Contexts and Encounters."

10. See Gary Okihiro's *Margins and Mainstreams: Asians in American History and Culture*; Ronald Takaki's *Strangers from a Different Shore: A History of Asian Americans*; Takaki's *Iron Cages: Race and Culture in 19th-Century America*; and Robert G. Lee's *Orientals: Asian Americans in Popular Culture*.

11. See Mia Tuan's *Forever Foreigners or Honorary Whites? The Asian Ethnic Experience Today* and Lisa Lowe's *Immigrant Acts: On Asian American Cultural Politics*.

12. See Michael Omi and Howard Winant's *Racial Formation* and Ronald Takaki's *Strangers From a Different Shore*.

13. See Portes and Rumbaut's *Legacies*.

14. The 2003–4 Millshore student body total was 621, which included 37 Lao American students: 14 of them in junior high, 23 of them in senior high. The six Lao American boys of my study represented approximately 16 percent of the school's total Lao population.

15. For an astute argument about Orientalism, homophobia, and literary politics in the works of African American and Asian American writers, see Daniel Y. Kim's *Writing Manhood in Black and White*.

16. At the time of the study, two Millshore Lao American senior girls and one senior boy were applying to four-year colleges; most of the others aspired to four-year colleges but tempered these dreams with expectations of attending two-year technical colleges and joining the manual labor force. Millshore's Lao American ESOL students often unquestioningly accept recommendations (voiced or assumed) by authority figures about their lack of potential for academic success, a kind of institutional hindrance to their higher education in universities and colleges.

17. See Tonda Liggett's Ph.D. dissertation "Multicultural Education in Multilingual Classrooms: The Role of Race and Culture in the Teaching and Pedagogy of New ESOL Teachers." In her memoir about being a Hmong refugee to Minnesota, Kao Kalia Yang says this about her ESOL classroom: "I had been taken out of the Hmong classroom and placed into a regular classroom, except for reading hour when I had to go to an English as a Second Language closet (because it was small and there were no windows, it really must have been a closet)" (160).

18. I received the following updates in the summer of 2008 about a few students in my study: Patrick, the boy least invested in performing blackness, joined the Marines and was deployed to Iraq twice; Steven and Andrew both dropped out of high school; Kimpon graduated after summer school; Neil graduated. As far as I know, none of them attend college.

WORKS CITED

Bhabha, Homi K. "Preface to the Routledge Classics Edition." In *The Location of Culture*. 1994. New York: Routledge, 2007.

Bow, Leslie. "Racial Interstitiality and the Anxieties of the 'Partly Colored.'" In *Journal of Asian American Studies* 10, no. 1 (February 2007): 1–30.

Chang, Jeff. "Race, Class, Conflict, and Empowerment: On Ice Cube's 'Black Korea.'" *Amerasia Journal* 19, no. 2 (1993): 87–107.

Ch'ien, Evelyn Nien-ming. *Weird English*. Cambridge, Mass.: Harvard University Press, 2004.

Chong, Sylvia. "Yellowface of a Different Color: Performing the Japanese Enemy in American World War II Films." Paper presented at the Association for Asian American Studies annual conference, Atlanta, Georgia, 2006.

Cose, Ellis. *The Envy of the World: On Being a Black Man in America*. New York: Washington Square Press, 2003.

Davé, Shilpa, LeiLane Nishime, and Tani Oren, eds. *East Main Street: Asian American Popular Culture*. New York: New York University Press, 2005.

Eng, David L. *Racial Castration: Managing Masculinity in America*. Durham, N.C.: Duke University Press, 2001.

Fu, Danling. *My Trouble Is My English: Asian Students and the American Dream*. Portsmouth, N.H.: Boynton/Cook Heinemann, 1995.

Gibson, Margaret A. *Accommodation Without Assimilation: Sikh Immigrants in an American High School*. Ithaca, N.Y.: Cornell University Press, 1989.

Hayden, Karen Elizabeth. "Between Two Worlds: Laotian High School Students in a Small New England Town." Master's thesis, University of New Hampshire, 1991.

Ima, Kenji. "Testing the American Dream: Case Studies of At-risk Southeast Asian Refugee Students in Secondary Schools." In *California's Immigrant Children: Theory, Research, and Implications for Educational Policy*, edited by Rubén G. Rumbaut and Wayne A. Cornelius, 191–208. San Diego, Calif.: Center for U.S.-Mexican Studies, 1995.

Kenny, Lorraine Delia. "Doing My Homework: The Autoethnography of a White Teenage Girl." In *Racing Research, Researching Race: Methodological Dilemmas in Critical Race Studies*, edited by Frances W. Twine and Jonathan W. Warren, 111–133. New York: New York University Press, 2000.

Kim, Daniel Y. *Writing Manhood in Black and Yellow: Ralph Ellison, Frank Chin, and the Literary Politics of Identity*. Stanford: Stanford University Press, 2005.

Lee, Robert G. *Orientals: Asian Americans in Popular Culture*. Philadelphia: Temple University Press, 1999.

Lee, Stacey. *Up Against Whiteness: Race, School, and Immigrant Youth*. New York: Teachers College Press, 2005.

Liggett, Tonda. "Multicultural Education in Multilingual Classrooms: The Role of

Race and Culture in the Teaching and Pedagogy of New ESOL Teachers." Ph.D. diss., University of New Hampshire, 2005.

Lowe, Lisa. *Immigrant Acts: On Asian American Cultural Politics*. Durham, N.C.: Duke University Press, 1996.

Minnis, Andrea L. "Leveling the Playing Field: A Look a the Role of Adult-Child Relationships in the Lives of Lao American Students in a Rural, New England Community." Master's thesis, University of New Hampshire, 2004.

Nguyen, Mimi Thi, and Thuy Linh Nguyen Tu, eds. *Alien Encounters: Popular Culture in Asian America*. Durham, N.C.: Duke University Press, 2007.

Okihiro, Gary. *Margins and Mainstreams: Asians in American History and Culture*. Seattle: University of Washington Press, 1994.

Omi, Michael, and Howard Winant. *Racial Formation in the United States: From the 1960s to the 1990s*. 2nd ed. New York: Routledge, 1994.

Proudfoot, Robert. *Even the Birds Don't Sound the Same Here: The Laotian Refugees' Search for Heart in American Culture*. New York: Peter Lang, 1990.

Portes, Alejandro, and Rubén Rumbaut. *Legacies: The Story of the Immigrant Second Generation*. Berkeley and Los Angeles: University of California Press, 2001.

Portes, Alejandro. *Immigrant America: A Portrait*. 2nd ed. Berkeley and Los Angeles: University of California Press, 1996.

Rose, Tricia. "A Style Nobody Can Deal With: Politics, Style, and the Postindustrial City in Hip-hop." In *Mapping Multiculturalism*, edited by Avery F. Gordon and Christopher Newfield, 424–44. Minneapolis: University of Minnesota Press, 1996.

Schram, Tom. "Laotian Refugees in a Small-Town School: Contexts and Encounters." *Journal of Research in Rural Education* 9, no. 3 (1993): 125–36.

———. "Players along the Margin: Diversity and Adaptation in a Lower Track Classroom." In *Pathways to Cultural Awareness: Cultural Therapy with Teachers and Students*, edited by George D. Spindler and Louise S. Spindler, 61–91. Thousand Oaks, Calif.: Corwin Press, 1994.

Song, Min Hyoung. *Strange Future: Pessimism and the 1992 Los Angeles Riots*. Durham, N.C.: Duke University Press, 2005.

Southeast Asia Resource Action Center. "Laotian and Hmong Refugees." http://www.searac.org/laoref.html. Retrieved 2 February 2004.

Stuart-Fox, Martin. *A History of Laos*. Cambridge: Cambridge University Press, 1997.

Sue, Stanley, and Sumie Okazaki. "Asian American Educational Achievements: A Phenomenon in Search of an Explanation." In *The Asian American Educational Experience: A Source Book for Teachers and Students*, edited by Don T. Nakanishi and Tina Yamano Nishida, 133–45. New York: Routledge, 1995.

Takaki, Ronald. *Iron Cages: Race and Culture in 19th-Century America*. New York: Oxford University Press, 2000.

———. *Strangers from a Different Shore: A History of Asian Americans*. New York: Penguin, 1989.

Tate, Greg, Vijay Prashad, Mark Anthony Neal, and Brian Cross. "Got Next: A Roundtable on Identity and Aesthetics after Multiculturalism." In *Chaos: The Art and Aesthetics of Hip-Hop*, edited by Jeff Chang, 33–51. New York: Basic Civitas, 2006.

Tuan, Mia. *Forever Foreigners or Honorary Whites? The Asian Ethnic Experience Today*. New Brunswick, N.J.: Rutgers University Press, 1998.

Tungmala, Mongkol. "An Exploration of Familial and Social Influences on the Superior Educational Achievement of Laotian High School Students in Jordan School District." Ph.D. diss. Brigham Young University, 1998.

Um, Khatharya. "A Dream Denied: Educational Experiences of Southeast Asian American Youth: Issues and Recommendations." Southeast Asia Resource Action Center. http://www.searac.org/pryd-3_11_03.html. Retrieved 21 November 2003.

Warren, Jonathan W. "Masters in the Field: White Talk, White Privilege, White Biases." In *Racing Research, Researching Race: Methodological Dilemmas in Critical Race Studies*, edited by Frances W. Twine and Jonathan W. Warren, 135–64. New York: New York University Press, 2000.

Williams, Patricia. J. "Compelling Interests that Shape Race and Education in America." Keynote address at the Association of American Universities and Colleges' biennial conference, Nashville, Tennessee, October 2004.

Yang, Kao Kalia. *The Latehomecomer: A Hmong Family Memoir*. Minneapolis, Minn.: Coffee House Press, 2008.

Yang, KaYing. "Southeast Asian Americans and Higher Education." Southeast Asia Resource Action Center. www.searac.org. Retrieved 19 November 2003.

9

On the Edges of Indigenous

A Personal Narrative of a Cambodian Sociologist Researching Cambodian Refugees in Massachusetts

LEAKHENA NOU

According to census statistics reported by the Institute for Asian American Studies at the University of Massachusetts Boston, Asian Americans represent the fastest-growing racial group in Massachusetts, having grown by nearly 68 percent since 1990. Like Cambodians elsewhere in the United States today, many of the Cambodians in New England arrived under the auspices of the 1980 Refugee Act and subsequent resettlement program. During that period, approximately 157,500 Cambodians entered the United States under three categories: refugees, immigrants, and humanitarian and public-interest parolees.[1]

The Cambodian refugees in Massachusetts have experienced numerous far-reaching and pervasive pre-migration stressors prior to resettlement, especially in relation to the traumatic challenges (such as near-death starvation and torture) they encountered during life under the Khmer Rouge regime (1975–79). Whether post-migration stressors — such as linguistic and cultural barriers — also play a role in refugees' ability to adjust to life in New England and the larger context of the United States remains largely unexplored. Based on my previous research, my hypothesis is that the adjustment difficulties experienced by the vast majority of Cambodian refugees may stem from a relationship between exposure to stressors, use of ineffective coping strategies, and lack of access to quality social support; these three factors, when combined, appear to affect psychological well-being and quality of life.[2]

There is a serious shortage of scholarly research on this topic. The shortage is made worse by the lack of Cambodian scholars doing ethnographic and empirical research on their own community, research that can contribute to the unique storytelling of Cambodian adjustment from an indigenous perspective. This situation quickly becomes a self-perpetuating three-step cycle: first, insufficient numbers of qualified indigenous scholars create a "research vacuum" that is quickly filled by nonindigenous (generally non-native) researchers; second, Cambodians, who have learned to be agreeable to outsiders and authority figures raise few, if any, objections to whatever the researchers conclude; third, the research—flaws and all—gets published and becomes accepted as "truth" by Cambodian and non-Cambodian communities alike, in spite of the fact that the findings are fundamentally incompatible with indigenous communities.

As a native scholar, I am in many ways compatible with my ethnic Cambodian research populations. We share a cultural and historical context, while at the same time I am able to draw on my academic training from the dominant Western culture. Even so, my research in three Cambodian communities in New England offered challenges both anticipated and unexpected. From my gender and age, to a pervasive lack of trust throughout the community, to a cultural tendency to avoid "impolite" negative statements, the research process was surprisingly challenging as well as extremely rewarding to me as a Cambodian medical sociologist.

Although nonindigenous interpretations from diverse academic fields contribute greatly to the development of knowledge about the Cambodian experience, conclusions drawn by non-native scholars cannot take the place of the culturally precise realities of Cambodians or dominate the social construction of their indigeneity. Native Maori researcher Linda Tuhiwai Smith, whose work focuses on the deep connection between colonialism and research on indigenous peoples, agrees, pointing out that research as a concept now has negative connotations in the community and often discourages participation.

In this era of globalization, development scholars call for the promotion of indigenous paradigms and professionalization focused on indigenous issues influenced by social and human capital, multiculturalism, and development. Nina Laurie, Robert Andolina, and Sarah Radcliffe point out that interculturalism views "the indigenous subject as an actor involved in the construction of a dialogue based on the location of indigenous people in discrete cultural spaces of mutual respect" (477).

Laurie, Andolina, and Radcliffe's concerns are echoed by numerous researchers in psychology who cite an emerging need for indigenous theories or psychologies that move beyond the realms of Western individualistic cultures to Eastern collective or interdependent cultures.[3] Uichol Kim and Young-Shin Park assert that "cultural differences exist due to the diverse goals that cultures pursue; the methods people use to attain the goals, and the differential use of natural and human resources" (75). Several Asian scholars echo a similar sentiment, calling attention to the need for indigenization and the development of indigenous psychologies.[4] According to Azuma, "when a psychologist looks at a non-Western culture through Western glasses, he may fail to notice important aspects of the non-Western culture since the schemata for recognizing them are not provided by his science" (quoted in Kim and Park 49). Likewise, Uichol Kim and John W. Berry argue that, when considering indigenous psychologies, each culture should be understood from its own frame of reference; and Kuo-Shu Yang stresses the need for the development of indigenous psychologies "as an evolving system of psychological knowledge based on scientific research that is sufficiently compatible with the studied phenomena and their ecologic, economic, social, cultural, and historical context" (quoted in Kim and Park 245).

The dearth of Cambodian scholars doing research within their own communities has meant that the actual impact of social policies on the Cambodian American population has scarcely been investigated. These social policies were largely generated by non-Cambodian scholars using a Eurocentric model and largely failed to integrate indigenous knowledge. Even in an exemplary clinic such as the Metta Health Center in Lowell, Massachusetts, where highly trained, well-intentioned, non-Cambodian practitioners work passionately to improve the health of their clients, it is not clear whether the programs, practices, and social policies based on this accepted body of nonindigenous research has the desired impact (as indicated by the results of indigenous quantitative research such as my own).

As a Cambodian scholar, I was motivated to do whatever I could to fill this vacuum and confront the insider-versus-outsider research issue head-on. In particular, I wanted to ensure that indigenous voices were heard in the storytelling of Cambodians in the diaspora, and that the role of homeland politics would be considered as an influence on their psychosocial well-being.[5]

I knew that I needed to develop a theoretical perspective that would speak directly to the lives of Cambodians. This approach is similar to the concept of critical personal narrative employed by Myriam Torres in her work on discrimination and typecasting of Hispanic-Latinos (and Latinas) in the United States. Like Torres, I needed to challenge existing research, assumptions, and interpretations by mainstream scholars (who may have inadvertently studied the Cambodian phenomena only through Western lenses), while doing my best to avoid the pitfall Patricia M. Greenfield identified as the "colonized mind," wherein knowledge about human behavior is circulated mainly through the transmission of Western ideas.[6]

With the goal of using the results of indigenous research to generate improved social policies and thereby influence social change, I set out to research Cambodian communities in Massachusetts and unravel mysteries linked to their psychosocial adjustment challenges as well as to their cultural strengths.[7] My research approach is similar to what Paul Jackson refers to as "indigenous theorizing," which he describes as "the study of phenomena within a culture through the application of theoretical frameworks (ways of thinking and seeing) and methodologies that are appropriate to and derived from within that culture" (52). Earlier, John G. Adair offered a more specific definition of this process as "constructing local knowledge in a local context and [providing] a fundamental challenge to the assumption within Europe and North America" (quoted in Jackson 52).

I had an overarching personal mission to seek out the truth behind the significant rates of psychological stress and lack of well-being among Cambodian refugees in the United States, while contributing to the currently limited body of academic research on this topic. My role as an ethnic Cambodian sociologist (and a young female one, at that) also made this project a unique contribution to the scholarly dialogue. Research done on Cambodians often focuses on input from anthropology, education, political science, law, social work, and psychology, with few critical considerations from a sociological perspective. I wanted to take this opportunity to tell the Cambodian story by using sociological techniques that would reveal indigenous data (on the micro and macro levels) affecting the adjustment of Cambodian refugees in Lowell, Lynn, and Revere, Massachusetts.

The Cambodian population in Massachusetts is in many ways similar to Cambodian populations elsewhere in the diaspora; the scars from the Khmer Rouge genocide found in our study echoed the results of earlier and contemporary studies of mental health on Cambodians in the United States and other resettlement host countries (Australia, France, and New Zealand, to name a few). High levels of distress are still widespread among Cambodians more than three decades after resettlement. However, the individuals who participated in my study are unique because of their keen ability and willingness to face the horrors of the past and the adjustment stressors of the present simultaneously and with remarkable resiliency.

In this essay, I will discuss the cultural and linguistic issues I encountered during my fieldwork and methodological obstacles my research team and I faced while conducting the study. I will highlight issues that arose during the project, especially issues of insider-versus-outsider research and ethnic community-based resistance to research. By describing research difficulties and sharing personal accounts from my fieldwork with Cambodian Americans in Massachusetts, I hope to assist present and future researchers conducting similar studies.

I will also offer readers a firsthand account of the complications, rarely explored in Asian American studies, associated with ethno-empirical research as experienced by a Cambodian female scholar. I will outline the research process in general terms to provide insight into conducting empirical and qualitative investigations on Cambodians and will then examine the lessons I learned (sometimes the hard way). Finally, I will make recommendations and note the limitations of the study in order to help other researchers avoid the same pitfalls.

The process of establishing oneself to conduct indigenous research within Cambodian communities in Massachusetts required several main steps. The first step was to secure institutional support, even before the research itself began. Although a detailed discussion of this process is beyond the scope of this chapter, there were two critical preresearch tasks that required an understanding not only of the academic research process, but also of the Cambodian community itself. The first of these tasks was to secure the approval of the Institutional Review Board (IRB) at the University of Massachusetts Boston. This approval process can take six months or longer. In addition to protecting our subjects, the IRB's approval of the project further legitimated it and gave my participants another reason to see me as a "real" scientist, regardless of my age or gender.

The second preresearch challenge was finding qualified Cambodian research assistants trained in empirical sociobehavioral areas, an extremely difficult task. Because of the scarcity of trained Cambodian research assistants, I found local Cambodian professionals willing to undergo basic training in social research and serve as research assistants. Three such individuals joined my research team at the recommendation of community leaders and academic institutional affiliations: Stephen Thong, who is resourceful among the Cambodian communities in Lynn, Revere, and Lowell, served as a primary community liaison to build public awareness for the project; Bou Lim and Kirirath Saing, both experienced, professional translators, came onboard to translate and ensure the accuracy of all research materials. Kirirath also held a key responsibility as the community liaison to Cambodian communities in Lynn and Revere.

As research began, our third major step was to gain access to the three Cambodian communities in New England. The preliminary phase of the project—reaching out to potential respondents—required that we contact relevant and well-known local individuals who had established strong relationships with Cambodian communities in Lowell, Lynn, and Revere. Social networks with Asian American professors within the University of Massachusetts Boston system led to referral contacts. With assistance from an active community leader in Lowell, we held an informal dinner meeting where ten or more young Cambodian professionals and community advocates met to discuss social issues in Lowell's Cambodian community and learn more about the proposed project. The intimate atmosphere provided everyone with the opportunity to get to know one another personally and to assist attendees in trusting me as a researcher, which would lend tremendous support for the research project. A few weeks later, our community liaison introduced me to several community health/mental health providers and elder members at a meeting in Lynn. At this meeting, we explored the health providers' perceptions of the need for the study, as well as their willingness to support it.

Within a month, with support from the Institute for Asian American Studies, we convened a larger public forum at the University of Massachusetts Lowell to introduce the study and gain support in recruiting participants from community leaders in the audience. After the forum, the mental health director from the North Suffolk Mental Health Association in Revere, Massachusetts, asked if the sample could include the Cambodian population living in Revere. We welcomed this opportunity to expand our sampling pool.

After reaching out to our three communities to gain access, our fourth major step was to establish rapport with our study participants, which we aimed to accomplish by first establishing rapport with community leaders. This process requires effective insider-community interaction, and is especially difficult in a community that has long-standing issues regarding trust. The insider's approach has the advantage of allowing the researcher to relate more directly and connect more personally with research respondents. A critical question to be considered is what the recipients of the research will gain from participation in the study. "Selling" participation in sociobehavioral research (especially unpaid research) to Cambodians is difficult due to their limited experience with and understanding of social research. I knew that I needed to begin by explaining the project and its goals and how those goals would benefit the target populations. I would do this by using the insider's interactive approach, in which participants' experiences and opinions would help me define cultural beliefs and indigenous perceptions about stressors and responses to those stressors and to define and evaluate indicators of life satisfaction among first-generation Cambodian adults. Although it was not always apparent to respondents why I used this approach, many appreciated the opportunity to be heard and have their comments documented.

A critical step in creating an effective insider-community interaction is earning the trust of influential members of the community, individuals who would, in turn, recruit other participants. One strategy I used was to build a sense of familial or social connectedness with participants by referring to myself as a niece or sister when engaging with respondents; such use of fictive-kin terminology is common in Cambodian culture. I also always remained aware of my own use of the Khmer language in relation to the age, gender, and status of the respondent with whom I was interacting. This proper linguistic behavior, which I understood intuitively as a native of Cambodia, is a sign of respect toward others in the culture.

Although being an indigenous researcher makes establishing trust easier, it must be noted that Cambodian survivors of the genocide often simply prefer to let go of previous horrific life memories and tragic experiences in order to avoid reliving them. They also fear revealing personal and family vulnerabilities to the public, wary of airing their dirty laundry to outsiders. These reasons, along with a desire to "save face" for themselves and their families, discouraged many people from participating in the study.

The process of recruiting participants and gaining their trust was also hampered by internal politics within certain social groups at the research sites. For example, one respondent cited as stressors the "lack of trust among Cambodians, [lack of] communication, respect, and the ability to reach out to each other, which by extension contributes to lying and manipulation in the Khmer community"; another mentioned "the shame of being the focus of community gossip"; and another noted "the existence of social injustice and corruption in Cambodian society." These comments, stated by respondents to our team, explained the intensity of a lack of trust within the community. In his speech at the Northern California Indochinese Assistance Programs Conference in San Francisco in 1980, David Ratnavale of the National Institute of Mental Health reiterated how trust works among Cambodians: "the Khmer tend to share inner feelings only with a person's own adult family members; anyone outside a person's individual kinship system network wanting to know how he feels about life or his job may succeed only in heightening a sense of suspicion or vigilance."

This almost instinctive distrust meant that I found myself a stranger in my own ethnic community, always under a cloud of suspicion for my research motivations. There were many times when I did not feel a sense of belonging and feared negative repercussions from Cambodians as a result of my seeming intrusion into people's lives. People were not prepared to share tragic stories of the past, and they hesitated to be part of the study because of their deep-seated fear that any information they shared would be used against them or, at best, have no positive impact on their socio-personal welfare. Survivors of the Khmer Rouge period cannot be blamed for this attitude; during the genocide, revealing personal information almost certainly led to execution.[8]

After establishing a basic level of trust with community leaders and participants, I faced the unexpectedly complicated challenge of gaining their respect as a scholar. When first introduced to a community leader, I was often bombarded with questions about when I left Cambodia and the professional backgrounds of my parents before the Khmer Rouge. Some individuals assumed I could not understand the hardships they endured because my family escaped Cambodia just prior to the tragedies of the Khmer Rouge.[9]

My academic qualifications were also probed with much curiosity and apparent skepticism. One respondent claimed that, as a postdoctoral researcher, I was still in training to earn a Ph.D. and not "officially" a doctor. I suspect this resistance was partially due to the fact that many Cambodians have never seen a Cambodian scholar serve as the principal investigator (PI) on any large-scale research project in their community or anywhere else. This scrutiny and skepticism would have been less troubling had it been applied across the board to all researchers. Non-Cambodian researchers, however, are accepted as authorities almost automatically; this type of social inquiry and interrogation on the personal and academic backgrounds of non-Cambodian scholars rarely happens, even though some of those same researchers have published inaccurate research results that have negatively impacted the Cambodian community. This tendency to automatically grant credibility to and regard Westerners with reverence worked against me as a Cambodian researcher. More important, it continues to work against the Cambodian community itself.

Another challenge in gaining respect as a legitimate researcher was my status as a young woman leading an all-male research team. This presented a significant psychological hurdle for the three Cambodian communities in which I was conducting research. Distinct features of Cambodian culture dictate that being female and being young are two reasons not to be taken seriously, regardless of educational or professional achievement.

Finally, although there were many supporters for the research project, some individuals remained skeptical about how sociological research might benefit the community and wary of anyone affiliated with a major public institution. In general, according to our community liaison team, initial informal contacts made with potential respondents indicated resistance, heightened levels of suspicion, and a lack of understanding of empirical social research. Because of this, we decided to turn to local Cambodian media outlets in order to reach out to the study's populations, give them objective information about the project, allay their fears and suspicions, and increase the effectiveness of our recruitment efforts.

Cambodian radio and television announcers were asked to make a brief informational announcement explaining my background and qualifications, the project's methods and aims, and our target participants (male and female Cambodian survivors of the Khmer Rouge genocide, thirty to sixty-nine years old, in Lowell, Lynn, and Revere). As I will discuss later in this chapter, the results of this approach were not what I had anticipated but, in the end, we recruited eighty participants.

Our last major task before launching the research phase included finalizing the translations of all research materials and the survey package, which totaled thirty-eight pages. This finalizing was accomplished through group consensus translation, applying the individual and group review processes. This procedure took into account American and Khmer conceptual views and equivalency as they pertain to technical criteria and semantic content. The team developed a set of nine criteria to inform their work and serve as guiding principles in the translation review process.[10] These criteria reflect Yang's definition of indigenously compatible research: "a way of doing research in which the researcher's theory, methods, tools and results sufficiently or adequately represent, reflect or reveal the natural elements, pattern, structure, mechanism and process of the studied psychological or behavioral phenomenon embedded in its ecological, economic, social or cultural context" (quoted in Jackson 279).

Using our nine criteria, the research assistants independently translated the different scales and research materials; at the end of the exercise, they exchanged their work for review before meeting with me to discuss specific concerns regarding linguistic and cultural equivalency of items, directions in filling out the survey package, confidential information sheets, and media announcements. The entire survey package and all related materials were then successfully pretested prior to their use with the respondents.[11]

At last, after scheduling focus groups and survey sessions and securing appropriate sites within each of our three communities, we were ready to conduct the research itself. At each focus group and survey session, respondents were given verbal instructions about the purpose of the study, asked to read the research information sheet (in Khmer or English, depending on their preference) before agreeing to participate, and provided with the option of withdrawing from the study at any time if they felt uncomfortable.

The research information sheets were also given to respondents. Every effort was made to ensure respondents understood that their participation was voluntary and that all information collected would be protected. Once this was understood, I guided respondents in lengthy (three- to four-hour), semistructured focus group discussions to explore indigenous conceptions of relevant concepts under study (such as social support, negative life events, and daily hassles), and walked respondents through the series of instructions in the survey package to ensure accuracy. On average, respondents spent between forty-five minutes and four hours to complete the survey package; respondents who took more than an hour to complete the survey tended to be more cautious participants, asking many questions to be sure they fully understood each survey point.

In addition to our actual data collection, we conducted a series of informal outreach events and held discussions with members in the Cambodian communities on social stress. We came across several enthusiastic participants who wanted to share their views about social stress in the Cambodian community at greater length. The views offered by these participants reflect personal observations and experiences with sources of stressors in the community and do not necessarily reflect the opinions of the Cambodian population as a whole.[12]

One elderly Khmer man shared his concerns about negative influences on the Cambodian population in Lowell. In this man's view, major problems include a widespread breakdown in family social structure, a cultural clash between rural versus urban lifestyles, racial discrimination by the Lowell police department, Cambodians' difficulty understanding legal and immigration policies affecting them, and the pervasiveness of gambling and alcohol. These observations are supported by Asian American scholars studying Cambodians in the United States, such as Sucheng Chan, who has written at length on the problems of family disharmony, gambling, alcohol and substance abuse among Cambodians; and Jeremy Hein, whose research concluded that most Cambodian refugees in the United States had experienced "severe antagonism" and "perceive extensive prejudice and discrimination" (153).[13] The elderly Khmer man was also troubled by his belief that community leaders, at times, put profits before the long-term well-being of the community and that young Cambodians lack good role models.

Other views were shared by a second Khmer man, this one in his late fifties and self-identified as a former community leader. According to him, social stress in the Cambodian community is linked to loss of trust in one another, loss of identity resulting from homeland politics dating back to early Cambodian history, and Buddhism's lack of moral education. He suggested behavioral solutions, such as meditation to strengthen one's identity. These comments are grounded in Cambodia's cultural and political history: the fact that the Cambodian genocide was inflicted by Cambodians on their own people created barriers in sustaining trusting relationships. To survive or receive food during the Khmer Rouge, people were forced to betray family and friends, often resulting in their torture or death. The views shared by this participant are common, as documented in research by David Chandler and other Cambodian historians.

These research participants were not the only people to express such surprising views. Unexpected comments were also shared by several Cambodian mental healthcare providers, who expressed feelings of being exploited and belittled, treated unjustly, and even humiliated by Western scholars and practitioners. They were concerned that little, if any, action had been taken to rectify this alleged mistreatment. These sources felt as if they had little value as contributors to various mental health research projects in the Cambodian community conducted by non-Khmer researchers, in spite of their extensive training and background in mental health practices. The practitioners went on to note that mental health treatment and programming suggestions made by Cambodian service providers were rarely taken seriously in the data-collection process, and furthermore that Cambodian service providers were not always credited in publications for their contributions to research projects. These comments are isolated, but they warrant further investigation.

The personal testimonies offered by these Cambodians offer unique community, cultural, and historical insights that empower them and offer them an ability to defend themselves from outsiders intentionally or unintentionally imposing Western values and perspectives on the Cambodian experience. Research models proposed by nonindigenous social scientists are often designed to satisfy government and funding agencies and rarely offer Cambodians, or other indigenous peoples, the opportunity to critically examine their own life encounters. Echoing this observation, Aihwa Ong describes the use of the Western biomedical intervention as a process of control with coexisting good intentions and a desire to manage "diseased" and "deviant" populations, restricted by the availability of limited resources. In time, according to Ong, this process led to the oversimplified but politically useful notion that being Cambodian essentially meant being medically depressed; this new "fact" made it easier for state and local health clinics to obtain much-needed funding from the federal government.

Studying the psychosocial adjustment of Cambodian refugees requires that researchers and practitioners understand concepts of health, well-being, and illness from the patients' subjective and personal standpoints, free from judgment or Western perceptions and perspectives. Significant findings on the mental health status of Cambodians and serious deficiencies in the Western healthcare system serving the Cambodians have revealed the need for Cambodians to be a proactive part of the solution. Marshall and colleagues reported that many Cambodians still bear traumatic scars from the Khmer Rouge, and, in fact, that Cambodians experience rates of mental illness six to seventeen times higher than the national average for adults. They also noted that cases of post-traumatic stress disorder (PTSD) and depression often overlapped, with 42 percent of respondents reporting both. The more trauma respondents endured, the worse their symptoms were.[14]

My work offers indigenous Cambodian communities the opportunity to identify barriers hindering their access to appropriate health/mental healthcare services; it also offers strategies for improving Cambodians' mental and physical well-being.[15] In many ways, my research also compliments the work of Joan M. Anderson, who finds that "the tensions and ethical dilemmas of postmodern, postcolonial, and neocolonial events . . . have far-reaching implications for health, well-being, and human suffering" (238).

By the end of spring 2005, our study was complete, and we began to compile our data in preparation for sharing our results with the three communities. A forum for this purpose was held on 8 June 2005 at the library auditorium at the University of Massachusetts Lowell, drawing a wide range of audience participants, from community leaders to housewives to academics. Respondents were especially encouraged to attend the forum so that they could see firsthand how the data they provided was analyzed to tell the story of their collective experiences scientifically. The audience also saw a presentation on the rigors of the translation process. In short, we made ourselves and our project fully transparent to the community we studied. Several community leaders approached us after the forum to express their happiness and satisfaction with it, noting that previous non-Cambodian researchers did not make public presentations on their research findings, an oversight that only perpetuates Cambodians' general lack of understanding about the impact of their participation in research. The forum showed audience members that, with their participation, scientific data could inform policy development and benefit their community.

The challenges we faced while conducting this research might also be instructional to other researchers working in Cambodian communities. These challenges ranged from the fundamental to the logistical, as can be seen in the following points. Our first challenge included the lack of experience with, appreciation for, and knowledge about empirical sociobehavioral research among Cambodians. This lack makes it extremely difficult to encourage Cambodians' participation in such projects, even when the research is conducted by native Cambodians. Our team also found that individuals were unlikely to volunteer for the study with no financial incentives (we had no budget for such incentives), which could explain the low number of respondents in our research sessions. On average, we had from two to ten respondents per data-collection session, and unexpected participants were welcome because they increased our sample size. According to the U.S. Department of Health and Human Services, the Cambodian refugee population in the United States is the most economically disadvantaged group among all Asian Americans.[16] In Chan's study of Cambodians in Los Angeles County, research results indicated that Cambodians on average fall far below the poverty line and rank *lower than all other ethnic groups* on nearly every economic and social adjustment indicator.[17]

Recruitment became still more difficult when we did not receive full support from one or two community gatekeepers who thought the study to be invasive or feared that the process might trigger people's PTSD symptoms. Despite our explanations, these individuals did not understand either the IRB approval process or the fact that the survey had already been used (without incident) among college students in Cambodia. Given these misunderstandings, we could not rely on these gatekeepers to share information about the project in a timely and open way. For example, there were potential and eager respondents who reported never having heard about our scheduled data-collection sessions despite the fact that we had informed community gatekeepers who had agreed to pass along this information.

A frequent challenge included respondents who failed to keep scheduled appointments, or provided us with a series of excuses when, in fact, they simply did not wish to participate in the study. While on the surface and in person many individuals, service providers, and community leaders expressed support and enthusiasm for the study, on further follow-up, some were not interested after all. This tendency to respond politely and save face is culturally predictable: among Cambodians, avoidance is a much more culturally appropriate response than outright rejection. Of course, this demurral makes life much more difficult for the researchers, as we try to second-guess an individual's true inclination. It is particularly discouraging and frustrating to discover this lack of interest after scheduling meetings and activities around such individuals' schedules.

Occasionally, we faced challenges that could not be foreseen even with the most meticulous planning. For example, one respondent flatly rejected the term "Khmer Rouge" in the question that asked respondents whether they were in Cambodia during the Khmer Rouge regime. This respondent insisted the Khmer Rouge did not exist during 1975–79, and by extension, the genocide did not occur in Cambodia. Attempts were made to clarify this point by asking if the respondent was in Cambodia between 1975 and 1979 rather than to engage in a political debate about the Khmer Rouge's presence, especially when our objective was only to get a "yes" or "no" response. After much questioning about this individual's background, we discovered that he was reported to be a former Khmer Rouge soldier prior to resettling in the United States.

Finally, we were perplexed as to why people did not respond to our media advertisements for the study as we had expected them to. Upon reflection, I believe that this poor response can be explained by Cambodian culture itself: ours is a culture that relies heavily on personal connections, so use of the media to reach people may not have projected a message that was personal or inviting enough to motivate individuals to get involved. My impression is that people want to feel personally invited and that achieving this connection requires reaching out to them as individuals, either by personal phone calls or visits by the PI. Despite exhaustive efforts to recruit respondents through the media, very few individuals called to request information about the study as a result of these announcements, and I would not recommend using them in this way again.

Having learned from both the challenges and successes of this study, my assistants and I are able to recommend approaches and actions to other social researchers doing this type of work within their own community and for non-native researchers exploring underlying cross-cultural factors unique to ethnic populations affected by war and devastation. The following suggestions will help anyone attempting similar research in the Cambodian community or in other settings bearing a resemblance to the ones we studied.

1. *Identify reputable community liaisons to work full-time on outreach efforts for the project.* In order to recruit participants successfully, you need liaisons with good characters and uncontroversial pasts. For example, a few respondents informed me that the divorced and part-time professional status of one of my liaisons interfered with people's ability to trust our team and take the study seriously. For successful recruitment, liaisons must also have good interpersonal relationships with known leaders and institutions within the community. I suggest building a research team of an older woman and a younger man to give the research project the kind of respect it deserves without too much cultural baggage and controversy.

2. *Always seek reputable social mediators or institutional gatekeepers within*

the communities to act on behalf of the PI to solicit support for the study. In our case, these included Buddhist monks and indigenous healthcare or social service providers. This approach removes the impression that the PI is conducting research for his or her own purposes at the community's expense. Include mediators and gatekeepers in visible, public positions at every phase of the research process. Invite them to your academic institution and introduce them to operational personnel such as research assistants and the IRB. The more these gatekeepers and mediators experience of the research process, the deeper their understanding of it will be, and the better they will be able to communicate this understanding to their community. These actions demonstrate the lengths to which even an indigenous researcher must go in order to dismantle the wall of distrust that exists in Cambodian populations.

3. *Allow enough time to build rapport with social and institutional actors within the communities, including potential respondents.* A cross-sectional study for one year does not allow sufficient time to collect data and establish interpersonal ties with research subjects. The implementation of a longitudinal study may yield more opportunities for a researcher to gain trust and become familiar in a community, which could then result in greater participation rates and a more diverse sampling frame. Scheduling extensive time for the project also allows researchers to avoid collecting data during bad weather or stormy conditions. Our research efforts began in earnest in the dead of a cold New England winter. Severe snowstorms in January and February wreaked havoc with carefully scheduled appointments with respondents. Respondents are far more likely to participate in research activities when the weather conditions are pleasant. Lack of time and continuing family obligations are two additional reasons frequently cited for lack of interest or inability to attend appointments. Nevertheless, there were several exceptional incidents in which respondents brought their young children to the survey sessions or came despite heavy snowstorms. One participant was determined to attend the survey session regardless of environmental obstacles and made a cross-town journey to the session by bus, in a snowstorm, with her children in tow. This sort of commitment to the project was heartening, to say the least.

4. *Participate actively in discussions with community leaders and practitioners on using the research as a product beneficial to the community itself.* To avoid feelings of exploitation in the communities participating in the study, share your research results in a series of educational forums and workshops that include discussions of how the data can be used to in-

form policy. Also, keep accurate translations of all pertinent research findings on file and available as a community resource. For example, this study's report is available from the Institute for Asian American Studies to all academic and community agencies serving Asian communities.[18] A series of separate academic publications on this study are also accessible online as a resource for Cambodian health and mental health scholars (and other interested parties). Once these documents are circulated within the community and their mystique is removed, people can begin to see the connections between research and practical solutions for community development.

5. *Connect with the social system that traditionally provides the individual with a sense of belonging.* In Cambodian culture, the family plays a central role as a source of social support. Obtaining the active participation of heads of families would contribute to greater participation by other members of the family and throughout the community. Ratnavale aptly echoed this point in his speech at the Northern California Indochinese Assistance Programs Conference: "We need to recognize the therapeutic value of certain social institutions. . . . At all costs we must support the family, or what's left of it, and other mental health promoting institutions, remembering that patients separated from their families are further endangered."

6. *Maintain social and professional relations with institutional affiliations or individuals involved in the project, even after completing the study.* Keep in contact through updates on your personal and professional development and publications. By doing so, scientists will be in a better position to solicit support for future research projects. More important, they are helping individuals in the community develop new attitudes toward research and researchers in their communities and in the world at large.

The current, ongoing Cambodian trauma is the result of the horrific and terrifying events confronting the Cambodian people during the Khmer Rouge genocide. The trauma affected both the individual and collective psyches of the people, permanently damaging their memories and altering their present and future identities in irreparable ways. My fieldwork with Cambodians in Massachusetts has shown that a general and profound lack of trust throughout Cambodian communities underlies the trauma they feel even as refugees. This distrust is the most significant and fundamental challenge I faced as an indigenous researcher; it would have been virtually insurmountable to an outsider.

Conducting indigenous research in any culture poses unique challenges. In the Cambodian case, these hurdles include traditional values and social stigmas related to mental health and related research; religious beliefs that encourage people to accept whatever comes their way; a cultural disinclination toward open displays of emotion and exposing personal weakness; and a political legacy that gave individuals every reason in the world not to trust anyone or divulge personal information for fear of extreme personal injury or death. These challenges are tenacious and pervasive even today.

Nonindigenous research has left many long-standing questions unanswered, perpetuating an imbalance of power and a lack of trust between participants and researchers. Meticulously planned and executed indigenous research that is applied to benefit the participants and their communities is a promising option. My role in the research project as an indigenous scholar permitted me to collect culturally relevant data on the lives of Cambodians through intimate focus group discussions and surveys. Our participants' honesty and insight resulted in impressively rich data, as all eighty courageous respondents who participated in this study were comfortable enough with our Cambodian research team to share their personal and painful experiences. It is reasonable to assume that these individuals reflect the views of more hesitant members of their community. We learned that, when given the opportunity to share their thoughts on living as refugees in the United States, Cambodians are extremely insightful regarding their situation.[19]

This indigenous research adds an important layer to our understanding of the persistent psychological effects of the Khmer Rouge genocide among Cambodian victims and survivors. A number of other studies also speak directly to the ongoing negative impact of surviving trauma such as genocide.[20] In my work, I aimed to create a new, more practical and ethical paradigm for doing research with Cambodians around the world. It is my sincere hope and conviction that, over time and through positive research experiences, Cambodians will become increasingly more willing and able to trust judiciously. Indigenous researchers are in a uniquely influential position, one that comes with challenges, but one that also represents our single best hope for helping the Cambodian community heal the wounds of its past, by using approaches and treatments that support their unique social, cultural, historical, and psychological contexts.

ACKNOWLEDGMENTS

I am greatly indebted to the eighty research participants, without whom this study would not have been possible. This study was conducted with financial and logistical support from the Institute for Asian American Studies at the University of Massachusetts, Boston. I especially thank Dr. Paul Watanabe for giving me the resources and intellectual freedom to conduct the study. Special thanks are due to my core research team, who devoted extensive time and commitment to the project: Bou Lim, Kirirath Saing, and Stephen Thong; I extend my deepest appreciation to Bou and Kirirath for their unique individual translation expertise. We also thank leaders and volunteers within the Cambodian community, including Dorcas C. Grigg-Saito, Sonith Peou, Samkhann Khoeun, and Chan Touch at the Metta Health Center in Lowell, Suzy Mom Doss at Neighborhood Legal Services in Lynn, and countless other individuals and community organizations that offered unconditional support for the study.

NOTES

1. See "From Immigrants to Refugees' Redefinition" by Norman L. Zucker and Naomi F. Zucker.
2. See Leakhena Nou's "A Sociological Analysis of the Psychosocial Adaptations of Khmer Refugees in Massachusetts"; her "Exploring the Psychosocial Adjustment of Khmer Refugees in Massachusetts from an Insider's Perspective"; and her "A Qualitative Examination of the Psychosocial Adjustment of Khmer Refugees in Three Massachusetts Communities."
3. For further readings on this subject, see Paul Jackson; Uichol Kim and Young-Shin Park; and Gregory Smith, Nichea Spillane, and Agnes Annus.
4. See *Indigenous Psychologies: Research and Experience in Cultural Context* by Uichol Kim and John W. Berry, cited in Uichol Kim and Young-Shin Park.
5. See Nou's "A Qualitative Examination."
6. Cited in Paul Jackson's "Indigenous Theorizing in a Complex World" (51–64).
7. Respondents were refugees from Cambodia living in Lowell, Lynn, or Revere, Massachusetts. All respondents ($N = 80$; 60 percent males and 40 percent females; 55 percent between the ages of 30 and 39 and 45 percent between the ages of 40 and 69) were survivors of the Khmer Rouge genocide (1975–79). They were selected through a quota nonclinical sample based on convenience and recruited through grassroots contact in the Cambodian communities. Data collection took place from late January 2004 until early April 2005.
8. Stephen Thong discovered similar reasons for people's concerns about participating in the study, which he shared in an e-mail dated 12 May 2005: "I learned that Cambodian people, both educated and uneducated ones, were not thinking critically. In other words, they lacked confidence and trust. During the period of data collection, the community showed some reluctance to fill out the surveys. They seemed to lose interest when they were required to provide their personal background. I felt that perhaps they didn't want to reveal their identities, status or they simply felt they didn't benefit anything from this study. . . . The Cambodian community may realize that the research about them was important but they

felt there's no direct benefit to them individually. . . . Had [they] been compensated, I think, there would be more participation from respondents. Most people worried more about their economic situation rather than a study about their clinical or psychological symptoms. . . . In conclusion, it is not easy to work with the Cambodian population. First, because [of their] level of education, they may lack understanding about the importance of accurate and honest information. Second, they didn't really care. Worse than that, because of their insecurities, they blamed others for the cause of their insecurities."

9. As a government employee and high-ranking military officer in 1972, my father received news that Cambodia was unstable, and he was able to move to Bangkok, Thailand. He was stationed there for three years, during which time he sent for my mother, my two siblings, and me. We joined my father in Bangkok before we all moved to the United States in 1975. We first resettled in Camp Pendleton, and then we were sponsored by a Christian family in Long Beach, California, where we began to set down new roots.

10. The nine criteria were the following:

Does the Khmer translation of survey items accurately reflect the original meaning as written in English (including the tone and level of emphasis in expression)?

Is the Khmer version of survey items concise and readily understood by respondents of various reading abilities?

Is there a need to provide additional explanations or examples in survey items to clarify or simplify certain terms in Khmer that may be technically correct, but are jargon, too formal, or unfamiliar vocabularies?

In providing clarifications, does the Khmer version diverge from the English in terms of scope of meaning, length, and format for each survey item?

Is each survey item culturally appropriate when translated into Khmer? If not, what is an equivalent way of asking or expressing the question asked (to avoid offensive questioning or social taboos)?

Does each of the survey items make sense to Cambodian readers in terms of a Khmer worldview?

Is the language sufficiently polite and proper in Khmer while adhering to the original intent of the English version of survey items?

Is the style used in the Khmer language consistent across the survey items in the same scale and across different scales?

Are editorial issues considered in the translation of each survey item (e.g., accuracy and consistency in spelling and professional presentation of scale in the survey package)?

11. We pretested the survey package before administering the research materials to the larger sampling frame; this procedure enabled us to identify items that might be perceived in a negative light or seen as errors by individuals with a different frame of reference regarding symptoms of health and mental health. This step is essential in any cross-cultural research project. Two respondents volunteered to

pretest the survey to give their thoughts on the relevancy of survey items as they related to Khmer thinking and understanding of concepts. These individuals were selected for two main reasons: (1) they were enthusiastic about being part of the study; and (2) they demonstrated an ability to explain their experiences verbally in detail and offer constructive criticism of the survey package.

12. See Nou's "A Qualitative Examination" and her "Exploring" for in-depth analyses and reports by respondents on their experiences with social stress in their communities.

13. See also Nou's "A Sociological Analysis."

14. See Marshall, Schell et al.

15. For more extensive discussions on cultural and institutional barriers and policy recommendations, see Nou's "A Qualitative Examination," her "Exploring," and her "A Sociological Analysis."

16. This is according to the U.S. Department of Health and Human Services.

17. Chan cited in Tamara C. Daley.

18. See Nou's" "Exploring."

19. See Nou's "A Qualitative Examination" for a lengthier discussion of the level of honesty and deep insights by the Cambodian respondents on their situation. Non-Cambodian scholars and policymakers often assume that Cambodians do not have deep reflections on their contextual situations.

20. Rita Chi-Ying Chung and Fred Bemak; Tamara C. Daley; Marshall, Berthold et al. (2006); Marshall, Schell et al. (2005); and Catherine Nicholl and Andrew Thompson.

WORKS CITED

Anderson, Joan M. "Lessons from a Postcolonial-Feminist Perspective: Suffering and a Path to Healing." *Nursing Inquiry* 11, no. 4 (2004): 238–46.

Chan, Sucheng. *Survivors: Cambodian Refugees in the United States*. Urbana: University of Illinois Press, 2004.

Chandler, David. *Voices from S-21: Terror and History in Pol Pot's Secret Prison*. Berkeley and Los Angeles: University of California Press, 1999.

Chung, Rita Chi-Ying, and Fred Bemak. "Revisiting the California Southeast Asian Mental Health Needs Assessment Data: An Assessment of Refugee Ethnic and Gender Differences." *Journal of Counseling and Development* 80 (2002): 111–19.

Daley, Tamara C. "Beliefs about Treatment of Mental Health Problems among Cambodian American Children and Parents." *Social Science and Medicine* 61 (2005): 2384–95.

Etcheson, Craig. *After the Killing Fields: Lessons from the Cambodian Genocide*. Lubbock: Texas Tech University Press, 2005.

Hein, Jeremy. *From Vietnam, Laos, and Cambodia: A Refugee Experience in the United States*. New York: Simon and Schuster, 1995.

Institute for Asian American Studies. "Asian Americans in Massachusetts." *Community Profiles in Massachusetts*. Boston: University of Massachusetts, June 2004.

Jackson, Paul R. "Indigenous Theorizing in a Complex World." *Asian Journal of Social Psychology* 8 (2005): 51–64.

Kim, Uichol, and John W. Berry. *Indigenous Psychologies: Research and Experience in Cultural Context*. Thousand Oaks, Calif.: Sage Publications, 1993.

Kim, Uichol, and Young-Shin Park. "Integrated Analysis of Indigenous Psychologies: Comments and Extensions of Ideas Presented by Shams, Jackson, Hwang and Kashima." *Asian Journal of Social Psychology* 8 (2005): 75–79.

Laurie, Nina, Robert Andolina, and Sarah Radcliffe. "Indigenous Professionalization: Transnational Social Reproduction in the Andes." *Antipode* 35, no. 3 (2003): 464–91.

Marshall, Grant N., S. Megan Berthold, Terry L. Schell, Marc N. Elliott, Chi-Ah Chun, and Katrin Hambarsoomians. "Rates and Correlates of Seeking Mental Health Services among Cambodian Refugees." *American Journal of Public Health* 96, no. 10 (2006): 1829–35.

Marshall, Grant N., Terry L. Schell, S. Megan Berthold, and Chi-Ah Chun. "Mental Health of Cambodian Refugees Two Decades after Resettlement in the United States." *Journal of the American Medical Association* 294, no. 5 (2005): 571–79.

Nicholl, Catherine, and Andrew Thompson. "The Psychological Treatment of Post-Traumatic Stress Disorder (PTSD) in Adult Refugees: A Review of the Current State of Psychological Therapies." *Journal of Mental Health* 13, no. 4 (2004): 351–62.

Nou, Leakhena. "Exploring the Psychosocial Adjustment of Khmer Refugees in Massachusetts from an Insider's Perspective." In *Southeast Asian Refugees and Immigrants in the Mill City: Changing Families, Communities, Institutions—Thirty Years Afterward*, edited by T. L Pho, J. N. Gerson, and S. Cowan. Hanover, N.H.: University of New England Press/University of Vermont Press, 2007.

——. "A Qualitative Examination of the Psychosocial Adjustment of Khmer Refugees in Three Massachusetts Communities." Occasional papers. Boston: University of Massachusetts, Institute for Asian American Studies, 2006. http://www.iaas.umb.edu/. Also at *Journal for Southeast Asian American Education and Advancement*, http://jsaaea.coehd.utsa.edu/index.php/JSAAEA.

——. "A Sociological Analysis of the Psychosocial Adaptation of Khmer Refugees in Massachusetts." In *Strengths and Challenges of New Immigrant Families: Implications for Research, Theory, Education, and Service*, edited by R. L. Dalla, J. DeFrain, J. Johnson, and D. A. Abbott. Lanham, Md: Lexington Books, 2008.

Ong, Aihwa. *Buddha Is Hiding: Refugees, Citizenship, the New America*. Berkeley and Los Angeles: University of California Press, 2003.

Ratnavale, David. "Mental Health Problems, Cambodian Refugees and Persons Involved with Their Relief, Rehabilitation, and Resettlement." Northern California Indochinese Assistance Programs Conference, San Francisco, California, 1980.

Smith, Gregory T., Nichea S. Spillane, and Agnes M. Annus. "Implications of an

Emerging Integration of Universal and Culturally Specific Psychologies." *Perspectives on Psychological Science* 1, no. 3 (2006): 211–33.

Smith, Linda Tuhiwai. *Decolonizing Methodologies: Research and Indigenous Peoples.* New York: St. Martin's, 1999.

Torres, Myriam N. "To the Margins and Back: The High Cost of Being Latina in America." *Journal of Latinos and Education* 3, no. 2 (2004): 123–41.

U.S. Committee for Refugees and Immigrants. "Refugee Reports" (titled "Indochinese Refugee Reports" through 1980). May 1979–Dec.1995, vols. 1–16.

U.S. Department of Health and Human Services. *Mental Health: Culture, Race, and Ethnicity* (supplement to *Mental Health: A Report of the Surgeon General*). Rockville, Md.: Substance Abuse and Mental Health Services Administration, Center for Mental Health Service, 2001.

Yang, Kuo-Shu. "Monocultural and Cross-Cultural Indigenous Approaches: The Royal Road to the Development of a Balanced Global Psychology." *Asian Journal of Social Psychology* 3, no. 3 (2002): 241–63.

Zucker, Norman L., and Naomi F. Zucker. "From Immigrants to Refugees' Redefinition: A History of Refugee and Asylum Policy in the United States." In *Refugees and the Asylum Dilemma in the West*, edited by E. G. Loescher, 54–70. University Park: Pennsylvania State University Press, 1992.

Contributors

Amy Bangerter received an associate of arts degree in Russian from Ricks College in 1994. She received bachelor's and master's degrees in English from Brigham Young University in 1995 and 1998, respectively. During this time, she spent a year and a half in Taiwan studying Chinese. She graduated from the George Washington University with a Ph.D. in American literature in 2005. Most recently, she has taught and researched at the American University in Dubai. She is currently on hiatus from pursuing her academic interests in order to "pursue" her four boys. She lives with her children and husband in Arlington, Virginia.

James Điền Bùi currently serves as regional director of the National Association of Vietnamese American Service Agencies (NAVASA), a national nonprofit organization aimed at building local institutional capacity to develop long-term development projects, including housing, microbusiness initiatives, and policy research. He has worked with other community development agencies in Boston and Los Angeles on linking affordable housing and community organizing, and he has worked in South Vietnam and northern India on microcredit economic development projects. He holds an adjunct faculty position at the University of Massachusetts Boston in the Asian American Studies department. He received his graduate certificates in real estate and economic development in 2001 from MIT–Tufts University and a Master of Social Work degree in community organizing from the University of Michigan that same year. He graduated from the University of Illinois at Urbana-Champaign in 1998.

Lucy Mae San Pablo Burns is an assistant professor in the Department of Asian American Studies at the University of California, Los Angeles, where she teaches courses on Filipino American Studies, feminist performance and race, and race and gender in performance. She is a coeditor, with Roberta Uno, of *The Color of Theater* (Continuum, 2005). From 1994 to 2000, Burns worked at the New WORLD Theater in Amherst, Massachusetts, as the education and access coordinator and the literary manager. Her writings have appeared in various academic and art journals. She is currently working on a manuscript on the Filipino performing body.

Constance J. S. Chen is an assistant professor of history at Loyola Marymount University. Her work has appeared in the *Journal of Asian American Studies*, *Amerasia Journal*, and various anthologies. She is currently completing a book that examines the ways in which cross-cultural encounters shaped the development of ethnic identities, aesthetic definitions, and nationalist discourses for Asian Americans, white Americans, and East Asians in the nineteenth and twentieth centuries.

Monica Chiu, associate professor of English, teaches Asian American Studies and American literature at the University of New Hampshire. She is the author of *Filthy Fictions: Asian American Literature by Women* (Alta-Mira Press, 2004), and her essays have appeared in *Mosaic*; *MELUS*; *LIT: Literature, Interpretation, Theory*; *Hmong Studies Journal*; and the *Journal of American Studies*. She is working on a book addressing contemporary Asian American literature and detection.

Krystyn R. Moon is an assistant professor at the University of Mary Washington in Fredericksburg, Virginia, where she teaches in the history and American studies departments. She is the author of *Yellowface: Creating the Chinese in American Popular Music and Performance, 1880s–1920s* (Rutgers University Press, 2005) and is currently working on the history of temporary immigrant statuses in the United States.

Anjana Narayan is an assistant professor of sociology at California State Polytechnic University, Pomona. She recently completed her dissertation "Ethnic Organizations and Ethnic Identities: The Use of Websites for Creating Transnational Gendered Identities" (University of Connecticut). The study specifically examines how selected religio-nationalist organizations are creating public representations of women and men, including "their" ethnic community through their Web sites, and analyzes what elements are used to create gender distinctions. She has currently coedited (with Bandana Purkayastha) the book *Living Our Religions: Hindu and Muslim South*

Asian American Women Narrate Their Experiences (Stylus, 2008). She is a recipient of several universitywide awards, including the 100 Years of Women's Scholarship Award. She also received a citation from Connecticut Governor Jodi Rell for her scholarship, activism, and commitment to women's issues. She holds a postgraduate degree in social work from the Tata Institute of Social Sciences (TISS), Mumbai. She was associated with a range of innovative initiatives in the field of women and development in India.

Leakhena Nou is an assistant professor of sociology at California State University, Long Beach. She was formerly dean of the University of Cambodia's College of Social Sciences and a postdoctoral fellow at the University of Massachusetts Boston. She has shared her research on mental and physical health among Cambodians — particularly among survivors of the Khmer Rouge genocide (1975–79) and their children — with community organizations, think tanks, representatives of the United Nations, and at diverse professional and academic conferences.

Bandana Purkayastha, associate professor of sociology and Asian American studies at the University of Connecticut, was educated in India (Presidency College) and the United States. She has published more than twenty-five peer-reviewed journal articles and chapters over the last six years. These appeared in the United States, the United Kingdom, Germany, and India and focus on issues of race, gender, class, and human rights. Her recent books are *The Power of Women's Informal Networks: Lessons in Social Change in South Asia and West Africa* (coedited with Mangala Subramaniam; Lexington Books, 2004) and a research monograph, *Negotiating Ethnicity: Second-Generation South Asian Americans Traverse a Transnational World*, on the children of highly educated immigrants (Rutgers University Press, 2005). Three other books are forthcoming: *Living Our Religions: Hindu and Muslim South Asian American Women Narrate Their Experiences* (with Anjana Narayan); *Asymmetric Warfare and Peace* (coedited with Giuseppe Caforio and Gerhard Kuemmel); and *Invisible in the Mirror: Canadian Americans and Transnationalism* (with Susan Lucas). She is the deputy editor of *Gender & Society*.

Karen Sánchez-Eppler is professor of English and American studies at Amherst College. The author of *Dependent States: The Child's Part in Nineteenth-Century American Culture* (University of Chicago Press, 2006) and of *Touching Liberty: Abolition, Feminism, and the Politics of the Body* (University of California Press, 1993), she is currently working on a book tentatively titled "The Unpublished Republic: Manuscript Cultures of the Mid-Nineteenth-Century United States." She is one of the founding editors of the new *Journal of the History of Childhood and Youth*.

Shirley Suet-ling Tang is assistant professor in the Asian American Studies Program and American studies department at the University of Massachusetts Boston. Her work examines race, (im)migration, development, and the social consequences of war. Her research/teaching interests include comparative urban cultural history; Southeast Asian American community studies; and creative expressions at local and transnational levels. She is currently writing a book on the development and displacement of the Khmer (Cambodian) American community in Revere, Massachusetts.

Index